Following In His Steps

Following
IN HIS STEPS
A Biography of Charles M. Sheldon

Timothy Miller

Timothy Miller

gift 1988

THE UNIVERSITY OF TENNESSEE PRESS / KNOXVILLE

A version of chapter 3 appeared as an article in *Kansas History* 9,
no. 3 (Autumn 1986), 125–37. It is reprinted by permission.

The paper in this book meets the minimum requirements of the
American National Standard for Permanence of Paper for Printed
Library Materials.

The binding materials have been chosen for strength and
durability.

Library of Congress Cataloging in Publication Data

Miller, Timothy, 1944–
    Following in his steps.

    Bibliography: p.
    Includes index.
    1. Sheldon, Charles Monroe, 1857–1946.
2. Congregational churches—United States—Clergy—
Biography. I. Title.
BX7260.S5M55 1987   285.8′32′0924 [B] 87-5871
ISBN 0-87049-537-2 (alk. paper)

For my parents,
Paul A. Miller and
Margaret Jean Thompson Miller

Kansans
Congregationalists
Tireless workers for social justice

Contents

Illustrations

Introduction

Charles M. Sheldon is most frequently remembered as the author of the all-time best-selling inspirational novel *In His Steps*. But to place him in such a pigeonhole does him a serious disservice because in his eighty-nine years Sheldon was many things to millions of persons.

An author, yes—not only of a single best seller, but of some fifty books and hundreds of articles for religious and secular periodicals, as well as poems, hymns, plays, and sundry other creations. Sheldon first wrote for pay as a teenager in Dakota Territory, and his writing continued throughout his life, the last articles being published posthumously. But he ranked other of his roles as more important than his writing. He was a minister of the gospel, a tireless shepherd of souls in his home parish in Topeka, and a loving pastor to those the world around who admired him.

He was a reformer. Ever the idealist, he believed in the social gospel goal of the establishment of the kingdom of God on earth and worked throughout his life for better human conditions. Long before it was fashionable (if it ever was) Sheldon argued and fought for basic rights for blacks, women, Jews, and all other minorities. He also worked strenuously for religious reform and for the transcendent cause of world peace. And his reformist zeal made a real impact on his community, especially, and on the world.

He was a believer. He espoused a thoroughgoing faith in God and in the teachings of Jesus. His simple faith shines from nearly every sentence of his writings, and he never departed from a childhood practice of frequent prayer and daily Bible reading.

He was a popularizer, in the best sense of that term. His appeal was never to society's elite nor to the great intellectuals of the day, but he had an overpowering faith in the wisdom of the common people, and his writing was for them. He eschewed theological adornments, focusing on Jesus, the one unifying center of all Christianity.

And he was a supremely gentle and warm man. His loving nature is nearly always the first thing mentioned about him by those still living who knew him, because for all of his vigor in denouncing evil in the world, he had only love for individual human beings.

Although descriptive statements like these may be made confidently, Sheldon is not entirely contained within them. Despite the simplicity of what he preached, the straightforwardness of his social thought, Sheldon was also an enigmatic and ambiguous figure. Although his thinking tended toward reductionism—questions generally were resolved by applying the aphorism that one should try to do in life what Jesus would do were he in one's shoes—his mind was capable of complexity and subtlety.

He was, for example, simultaneously mild-mannered and strident. In person he was almost shy and eager to give no offense. He was a man beloved for his kind, retiring nature. Yet his writing was not nearly so mild. His villains—the class included more than a few very real people—were denounced with utmost vigor. Woe be to the tenement owner, the selfish capitalist, the racist—unless Sheldon came face to face with the offender. Then everything changed. Everyone, up close, was a candidate for sainthood, or at least redeemable.

Sheldon had firm ethical convictions, yet was a situationist. His ethical ideal of imitation of Jesus yielded many specific and incontrovertible positions for him: the true disciple would not drink, or work on Sunday, or exploit others. But clear principles do not necessarily produce invariable courses of action, and Sheldon was strangely prone to bless all kinds of behavior so long as it was conscientious. His Jesus was a pacifist, for example, but Sheldon recognized that some would-be disciples read things differently, and if they went off to war to fight for the Savior, he didn't object.

Sheldon had a true passion for people, but remained personally so distant that it is quite difficult today to get much of a feeling for him as a person. He urged people to bare their souls for the Master, but his own remained shrouded.

Sheldon's most complex ambiguity is over the question of his relative liberalism or conservatism. Today his audience—and it's still a big one—is overwhelmingly conservative. Liberals, when they think of him at all, tend to dismiss him as a sappy sentimentalist or a popularizer, and they don't read him. But conservatives do, and their publishing houses keep Sheldon's magnum opus *In His Steps* in print in many editions, selling tens of thousands of them a year. Yet Sheldon was no conservative; he was, for example, capable of jettisoning parts of the Bible he found less than useful. He hinted at skepticism of doctrines many conservatives would find essential— the virgin birth, to name one—and readily accepted higher criticism of the Bible. Yet his appeal was and is to evangelicals, who find his work inspiring and confirming.

Theologically, there is no way to classify Sheldon other than as a liberal. Some have skirted the problem by coining a neologism, making Sheldon an "evangelical liberal" or some such. Such a characterization is a bit off the mark, however: "Pious liberal" might be better. At any rate, Sheldon managed to stay out of the bruising fray between liberals and conservatives throughout his lifetime. At the peak of the battle, in the 1920s, the prolific pen of Sheldon was silent on the issue. Nowhere in his writings is there to be found a comment on the Scopes trial, for example, or on Harry Emerson Fosdick's polemics, although he believed in evolution and was not far from Fosdick on many issues. Sheldon was doing plenty of topical writing in those days; in the early twenties he was a major contributor to the *Christian Herald*; and, although he could easily have made himself heard, he didn't. Was he trying to stay in the good graces of his largely conservative audience? Was he trying to give no offense to anyone? Did he really not have important convictions about anything except personal piety? No answer is readily apparent.

One other seeming paradox about Sheldon, however, is much more easily explainable. Sheldon was not a startlingly brilliant or original thinker; how, then, could he be so convincing to so many readers, many of whom were no dummies? The answer is that Sheldon's appeal was based not in intellect but in passion. Sheldon had few new or blinding insights, but the urgent conviction he possessed permeated every page he wrote. His readers must have sensed as they read Sheldon's books that they were not dealing with someone who would preach virtue and live a private life of dissolution, or whose literary success would corrupt him, but rather with someone who strove with every ounce of his being to live the pure life he advocated in virtually everything he ever wrote. No more heartfelt passion ever came from a portable Corona.

This is a book about the passionate Sheldon's life and ideas. It is not an intellectual biography; it would make little sense to try to depict Sheldon as a great thinker. He was a person of tender heart and sensitive feelings—and one who wanted nothing less than to save the world. Moreover, he was always convinced that he and other like-minded souls would get the job done before long.

This book represents an effort to provide a fair and detached picture of Sheldon, warts and all. But, although Sheldon's ideas may be open to criticism, his personal life, even on close inspection, seems to have had few warts. He got somewhat testy in his latter years, but on the whole he seems to have lived what he preached. A prohibitionist, he never drank; a pacifist, he never engaged in violence; an advocate of family life, he never strayed, even though his own domestic life must have been sometimes unsatisfying. If any personal muck existed, it escaped notice, including that of many journalists seeking any scrap—especially any detrimental one—they could find about the great cleric. Sheldon's shortcomings were concentrated in his great piety, which overwhelmed his intellect, and in his naive faith and trust in the perfectibility of people, which sometimes set him up to be victimized.

Sheldon was an important figure in the social gospel movement, especially for his role in bringing contemporary social concerns to the person in the pew. This biography attempts no systematic analysis of his role in the movement; it is, rather, deliberately confined to supplying as much information as possible about Sheldon's life and ideas. The author hopes that this basic information—most of it never previously collected—will be useful to those who will one day interpret the relationship of Sheldon and the many other persons who made up the social gospel.[1]

The Sources

Sheldon left a legacy of millions of words, including a book-length autobiography and several shorter autobiographical sketches. His contemporaries wrote of him extensively, adding millions of words more. Therefore it would seem that more than enough material for a comprehensive biography would be readily available.

But such is not the case. There are, in fact, serious source problems for such a project. In the first place, the bulk of Sheldon's writing is not very useful to the biographer. Nearly all of it is thoroughly exhortative in nature; it is designed either to inspire the reader or to assist in a reform crusade. And even the relatively small amount of useful autobiographical material must be approached with care, because most of it—especially the book—was written late in Sheldon's life and entirely out of an imperfect memory. John W. Ripley, the eminent Topeka historian, says that one crucial section of the book contains "an average of one error per page."[2] Similarly Sheldon's pamphlet on the history of *In His Steps*, which has often been cited by scholars, was written when Sheldon was eighty-one and is loaded with mistakes. It is not hard for one who peruses the printed record to get a good grasp of Sheldon's ideas—but details of his life are another matter.

The secondary sources, many though they be, also have limitations, chiefly those imposed by Sheldon's avoidance of publicity. Over and over he refused interviews, and in some instances his inaccessibility may have led reporters to embroider their accounts in order to have something to send back to the home office. One frustrated correspondent wrote in 1900 that Sheldon "shrinks from a newspaper interview as he would from a blow." But Sheldon did take long enough to tell why he declined the attention: "The message is in my books—let people read it there. If they cannot discover my motive by reading the books I have written, of what use are they, and why waste time talking about myself?"[3]

The problems with sources notwithstanding, much Sheldoniana has been preserved. Members of Central Congregational Church of Topeka have preserved the best Sheldon archive, including most of his books and thousands of clippings and other artifacts. The Kansas State Historical Society has the next best collection and the one in the best state of preservation. Many items by and about Sheldon exist in standard journals. In addition, I have collected one other Sheldon resource: in the summer of 1981 I interviewed some three dozen persons who knew Sheldon. Although the interview project would have yielded much more fruit had it been undertaken a decade or two or three earlier, it did serve to fill in some gaps in the record.

Acknowledgments

This project could not have been completed without the help of dozens of individuals. Most essential was the help from the staffers of "Sheldon's Church," as Central Congregational was once widely known: Ed Soule, the church business administrator; Gerald Eslinger and Lesslie Anbari, Central's ministers at the time of my research; Martha Pettit, Mike Branaman, and Lauren Myer, who also provided practical help and moral support.

John Ripley deserves far more thanks than can be conveyed in a paragraph. As Topeka's premier local historian he has amassed a wealth of knowledge on Sheldon and has shared his resources freely. He provided continual encouragement and stimulation throughout the project, and was a delight to work with. He knew Sheldon well and has been instrumental in preserving this important part of Topeka's history.

Special thanks go to the Topekans—mostly Central Church members—who consented to be interviewed on their memories of Sheldon. They gave the history a personal flavor that could not otherwise have been captured. Several of the interviewees, incidentally, were members of the Altruist Club, a women's group founded by Sheldon to give him special assistance in his work. The Altruists today are the chief group preserving his memory, especially by maintaining and regularly opening to the public Sheldon's little private study, a building which once sat in his back yard and now reposes in a Topeka park. Altruist Miriam Franklin was especially helpful and arranged interviews with several of her colleagues. Caroline Walbridge made available special materials in the Topeka archives of the United Church of Christ.

The Kansas Committee for the Humanities provided a timely grant which enabled the work to begin; that funding for early research and interviews is deeply appreciated. Later the work was further supported by the Kansas School of Religion, and that support was also important to the progress of the project.

My colleagues at the department of religious studies at the University of Kansas were supportive throughout. Deserving special mention are James Woelfel, who suggested the project to me years before I actually undertook it, and Robert Shelton, who provided many support services. Three loyal and diligent student typists—April Harris, Lynda Zeis, and Ann Heinrich—provided service beyond the call of duty in transcribing the often garbled interview tapes. Their supervisor Montie Rosencrantz helped steadily as well. A colleague in another university office, Larry Hoyle, provided invaluable aid as I struggled to figure out how to do word processing.

Help has also come from several Sheldon scholars whose works are cited in footnotes in this volume. In addition, good assistance was provided by Sheldon scholar Ralph Woodworth, by Larry Jochims, a research historian at the Kansas State Historical Society, by David Sterling of Winona, Minnesota, by G.W. Ayers of Waterbury, Vermont, by Robert Bader of Lawrence, by Barney Bloom of the Vermont State Historical Society, and by Eva Kurtz of Topeka.

A special thank you is in order for the librarians at the Kansas State Historical Society, the Topeka Public Library, and the University of Kansas. They very patiently and efficiently filled my requests and generally made the project much more pleasant than it might have been. May their budgets increase.

Tamara, Jesse, and Abraham have sacrificed for several years in seeing the project through to completion. Their patience and endless supportiveness were invaluable and incredible.

Following In His Steps

1. The Early Years

C harles Monroe Sheldon entered the world on February 26, 1857, at Wellsville, New York. He was preceded by a brother and followed by three sisters, which made quite a handful for a family living on a poor Congregational preacher's budget. Wellsville was only one of many stops for the Rev. Stewart Sheldon and his wife, Sarah Ward Sheldon: By the time young Charles was twelve years old they had moved from Wellsville to Central Falls, Rhode Island, to Chillicothe, Missouri, to LeRoy, New York, to Lansing, Michigan, and then to Yankton in Dakota Territory, where they finally caught their breath for a few years.

The family was of Puritan stock and has been traced back to one William Ward who, under persecution, moved from Scotland to Northern Ireland, and then to Massachusetts not long after its colonization. Sheldon's parents, who were second cousins, were in the sixth American-born generation.[1] They were related to, among other luminaries, Ethan Allen and General Artemus Ward—although neither was a direct ancestor.

Sarah Ward Sheldon's childhood was not an easy one. When she was eight her mother developed an aneurism of the aorta and was bedridden for years. Her father died while Sarah and her three brothers were still children; they went to live with other relatives in LeRoy and Cuba, New York. Before his early death, Jabez Ward, Sarah's father, was a physician and surgeon (and dentist, for that matter, although Sarah later wrote, "I think the latter was limited to the extracting of teeth") at Perry Center, New York.[2] But before the breakup of the family, Sarah Ward had been a schoolmate of Stewart Sheldon's.

Sarah Ward Sheldon, mother of Charles M. Sheldon, ca. early twentieth century. Kansas State Historical Society.

Stewart Sheldon saw a bit of adventure before marriage and ministry set in. After graduating from Hamilton College in 1848, he took a trip to Labrador and then succumbed to gold fever and took a boat around Cape Horn. Along the way he stopped for a year to teach in an English school in Valparaiso, Chile; finally, in 1849, he made it to California and spent two years working a placer mine.

Stewart Sheldon, father of Charles M. Sheldon, ca. early twentieth century. Central Congregational Church (UCC), Topeka.

Although he didn't exactly prosper, he did make enough money to go home—this time by way of Vera Cruz, Mexico. Apparently his return home was a shock; years later Charles wrote that the rest of the family had given him up for dead.[3]

Settling down, Stewart Sheldon entered Auburn Theological Seminary and after graduating took up the Presbyterian ministry.

But within two years he had switched to the Congregational denomination, and he received Congregational ordination in August 1854. Two years earlier, in July 1852, the world traveler had married, at Cuba, New York, his childhood playmate who had never been out of the state of New York.[4] Pastorates in the New York villages of York Center and Silver Creek preceded the one in Wellsville where the couple's second child was born.[5] Life was hardly luxurious for the Sheldons; Stewart's journal at the beginning of the York Center pastorate recorded:

> Made our home with a good family, paying $4 a week for board and room. Salary $500, from which board bill deducted, there was left for other expenses of living, the snug sum of $292. . . . The people called on Mrs. Sheldon and myself at our boarding house and left a donation. A very liberal sum of 20 dollars, fifteen all in cash.[6]

Next came Wellsville, birthplace of Charles, and subsequently more moves from parish to parish. The next stop after Wellsville was Central Falls, Rhode Island, where the Sheldons remained for six years, mostly during the Civil War. It was there that young Charles acquired his first memories of church life. He wrote many years later that by the time he was six years old he would count the number of manuscript pages turned as his father preached, knowing that when forty of the small pages had been turned, the sermon was about to give way to "the big pan of beans that was our invariable Sunday dinner." And he began to notice his father's pulpit manner, which he would later imitate: "He used few gestures, seldom raised his voice, did not walk up and down, but . . . held his hearers' attention."[7] Life was filled not only with Sunday worship services, but with prayer meetings, missionary meetings, temperance meetings, revival meetings, conferences, and the like. "Going to church," Sheldon later wrote, "was as much a matter of course as going to bed, and sometimes the result would be the same."[8]

Three pastorates after Central Falls the growing Sheldon family was in Lansing, and Stewart developed health problems of a serious nature; his physician told him that only by going West could he keep on living, and then only for a year or two. Sarah Sheldon's brother Joseph Ward, who had lived with the Sheldons in Central

Following In His Steps: *A Biography of Charles M. Sheldon*

Falls while he was attending Brown University, had in the meantime become the minister of First Congregational Church of Yankton, the first Congregational church in Dakota Territory, meaning that his parish was the whole territory. He urged the Sheldons to join him there.

Thus Stewart Sheldon became the first home missionary superintendent in Dakota territory, founding a hundred churches in ten years. Soon after arriving in Yankton, which Sheldon later remembered as "a garrison town made up of cowboys, Indians, saloons, and a red-light district,"[9] the family homesteaded "160 acres of rolling prairie, every foot of it tillable."[10] Stewart Sheldon also bought a woodlot eight miles away on the Missouri, and there he and his sons cut enough ten-inch cottonwoods to build a 32-by-16-foot cabin on their claim. The cabin was the essence of simplicity, with two rooms—one up, one down. Cloth hung from the rafters which divided the "rooms" upstairs, where the whole family slept. It was a big family, with Ward, Charley, Alice, Agnes, and Sarah, plus Edith, who died in early childhood.[11]

Throughout his life Charles Sheldon referred often, and glowingly, to life on the prairie, which he always regarded as the best and most useful part of his life. Certainly there was romance in prairie life as Sheldon met American Indians and the U.S. soldiers who fought them. One group of Indians, Sheldon related, lived in tepees near the Sheldon family claim. The men came over and sat on the ground in front of the Sheldon house. Charles would serve them refreshments and came to befriend them. He may have been exaggerating when he wrote, some sixty years later, that "I was brought up among the Sioux and Dakotas" and that he and Uncle Joseph Ward "hunted with the Dakotas, fished with them, slept with them on the open prairie, and learned some of their language,"[12] but certainly that contact had much to do with his long-standing conviction that racial prejudice was wrong, with his staunch advocacy of human community. In 1922, long before concerns about white treatment of Native Americans had become very prevalent in America, he wrote of his regrets for the "wrongs inflicted on their people for years by brutal Indian agencies and land grabbers."[13]

At least once Sheldon saw the forces of the other side as well. In March 1876, the family watched George Armstrong Custer and his troops arrive to prepare for their advance into Sioux territory. When blasts of prairie wind blew down the soldiers' tents, they found shelter in homes, including the Sheldons'. In May, Sheldon watched Custer's regiment leave Yankton on its way to its last stand.[14]

Sheldon was a voracious reader on the farm. He found a man in Yankton who had a collection of Scott's Waverly novels, and he borrowed them, a volume at a time, carrying them home wrapped in a piece of oilcloth to protect them from the weather. He also read all of Shakespeare, and much of Dickens, Thackeray, Bulwer-Lytton, George Eliot, and many others. Although his formal education in Yankton was thin, he clearly acquired a remarkable familiarity with some excellent literature.

Sheldon had plenty of adventures on the prairie, several of which he recorded in his autobiography. He once was riding his pony home from Yankton, borrowed book under his coat, when a violent thunderstorm hit:

> The pony headed about and we started towards the farm again, but after going a quarter of a mile we came to a swale which was roaring full of water, a wide turbulent muddy torrent, at least sixty feet wide, and from my recollection of it as a familiar part of the rolling prairie, all of ten feet deep. It was getting dark and while I knew that if I waited a while the water would go down, since it was not a regular stream, I did not relish the night rides over the trackless prairie and the pony seemed to feel the same way, for after a moment of trembling hesitation when I pushed him towards the swale he plunged in. I thought just in time of my book, and slipping off the pony's back, remembering how the cowboys managed their crossing of the Big Muddy when they drove their Texas cattle over, I pulled the book out and held it up as high as I could reach, holding on to the pony's tail with the other hand. He was a good swimmer; while we were carried some distance down the stream we made a safe landing, and reached home rejoicing, wet and hungry, and happy to find on unwrapping the oil cloth that the book was dry. . . ."[15]

There was at least one other narrow escape, when a contrary cow gored Sheldon and opened one of his arteries while he was trying to collar her. His ever-resourceful father first stopped the bleeding with a tourniquet and then closed the wound with five stitches using a harness needle. Blue mud applied to the wound completed the treatment, but Charles was an invalid for weeks afterwards. And then of course there were the usual prairie hazards—getting lost and nearly freezing to death in blizzards, narrowly avoiding rattlesnakes, and the like.[16]

There was always plenty of work to do, since the family was forced by economic necessity to be nearly self-sufficient. They made their own household goods, such as candles; they trapped coyotes and timber wolves for coats; they shot prairie chickens, wild geese, and ducks for food. "I do not think we ever bought any regular commodity except sugar and coffee," Sheldon wrote of the period on the prairie.[17] Sometimes the family fare was simple; for years breakfast consisted solely of boiled wheat with cream and sugar.[18] Sometimes they were probably lucky to have even wheat, since crops were harvested only three times during the five years spent on the homestead (one year everything was lost to grasshoppers; another year, to hail).[19] Some jobs were arduous—digging, by hand, a well some sixty feet deep, or breaking the sod with a mule team—and sometimes Charles didn't like the tasks. But ever after he believed that the hard work of the homestead was a critical lesson in his life: "I have never ceased to wonder over the stupidity of those who regard physical toil as something to be avoided as a burden and even a disgrace. If there was anything that Dakota farm taught us all for life it was the dignity and joy of work with our hands."[20]

No matter how urgent the farm work, nothing was more important in the Sheldon family than regular prayer and worship. The most memorable part of the daily routine included reading a chapter from the Bible. Each morning the family would sit together in the "parlor" of the log cabin and read aloud, each member of the family old enough to participate taking two verses in turn. The whole Bible was read "word for word, without the omission of a syllable," even including the genealogies.[21] Thus Sheldon heard the whole Bible read out loud five or six times, a heritage he later treasured, although at the time, like most normal boys, he thought the reading excessive and his father's prayers too long.[22] Prayer accompanied the daily Bible reading and was employed in all sorts of special situations; when Stewart Sheldon was nearly killed digging the homestead well, for example, the family immediately joined in offering a prayer of thanks for his deliverance. As a result, Charles was a devout believer in daily prayer all his life. And, of course, every Sunday the family would go to church, usually at Uncle Joe Ward's church in Yankton.

It was at the Yankton church that Charles Sheldon had his conversion experience, a quiet and unemotional one. One night close to midnight, when he was in his late teens, he and his father were riding from Yankton back to the homestead in their carriage, and his father asked him, "Charley, don't you think you ought to make a confession of your Christian faith?" He stewed about his father's suggestion and couldn't sleep that night. At the next service, with Joseph Ward leading, after teetering for a time, he finally resolved to make the leap and stood up in the meeting. What he told the congregation was not recorded, but he later remembered that he began "to feel strangely happy. It [seemed] to me that a great burden [had] rolled off my back." When they arrived at home that night, Stewart told Sarah, "Charley stood up tonight." Then "Mother [reached] out and [clasped] me in her arms. . . . I was deeply moved at seeing tears rain down Mother's cheeks."[23]

But all was not hard work and spirituality in Sheldon's early life. There was often time for recreation. Although some vulgar entertainments, such as card-playing, the theater, and the circus, were taboo in the Sheldon household, chess and checkers and backgammon were not, and so those games filled many long evenings. In good weather young Charles often studied prairie flowers and geological specimens, initiating a life-long interest in rocks. At one point he learned some magic tricks and became fairly proficient at them, enough so that when he went away to school he was able to perform tricks to try to pep up attendance at his glee club's concerts.[24] And family members also entertained themselves by playing tricks on each other, especially on April Fool's Day. Sheldon recalled once spending the greater part of half a day making, out of long potatoes, imitation candles that looked like home-dipped ones, and then watching with glee as his father tried to light them.[25]

It was during the long winter nights that Charles began to write. At about the age of twelve, moved by Scott's Waverly novels, he took to settling down in the evening, after the chores had been finished, and composing stories. Fairly soon an item was accepted—without payment—by the Yankton paper, and thus encouraged, Charles began to send articles off to editors of more prominent publications. Then, after many rejections, he suddenly sold an article for seven dollars to a small Boston paper, and was so gratified that he stepped up his literary output—only to receive more rejections.[26]

Thus began the career of the author of two score or so books and hundreds of published articles—not to mention more than a few items rejected by editors. It was in Sheldon's college years that his writing became fairly serious; by then he was writing for the *Youth's Companion* magazine, a Boston young people's weekly, fairly regularly.[27] His early work was mainly light fiction, verse, and personality sketches.

Sheldon's parents were his principal spiritual models. His father taught clean living, a love of the Bible, and faith in the power of prayer. His mother gave each child a Bible as he or she became old enough to read, and occasionally read aloud from such works as *Pilgrim's Progress* on Sunday afternoons. Sheldon remembered her as utterly unselfish, frequently depriving herself for the benefit of the children.[28]

Uncle Joe Ward was also a great hero to the growing boy. In some cases Ward was a crusader, particularly against alcohol, and Sheldon surely followed in his uncle's footsteps in that regard. But Ward, like Sheldon, never lost sight of human beings. He was fearless in his attack on the liquor trade, as manifested by saloons in Yankton, but when a barkeeper's family was in need, he was the first to come to their assistance.[29] The most touching interchange between Charley and Uncle Joe occurred one day when Ward was tired and busy and Charley was bothering him, leading Ward to speak sharply and tell the boy to go home. Late that night, long after Charles had gone to bed, Ward went to the Sheldon home and said,

"Charlie, I spoke harshly this afternoon, and I have come to ask your pardon. I cannot sleep until I have it." Charles, then about nine years old, never forgot the great man's journey of apology.[30] In his own life, after he had achieved international fame Sheldon never neglected the less successful people he encountered.

After five years on the prairie, Stewart Sheldon's health was again robust, despite the predictions of the physicians who had told him that he was going to Dakota to die, and he was appointed home missionary superintendent for the territory. At that point he sold the farm, moved the family into Yankton, and threw himself into the work, founding hundreds of churches and Sunday schools.[31] During the 1876–77 school year, Charles and Ward Sheldon attended the Yankton Academy, yet another Joseph Ward project. Charles found himself the only boy in a classroom full of girls; boys, after all, were needed for farm work. But he survived the year, his last in Yankton.

Thus closed the prairie chapter of Sheldon's life, a chapter he always treasured for its having taught him hard work and a love of nature. What did he get from living on the frontier homestead which would help point up the future direction of his life? He picked up some of the frontier virtues—self-reliance, mechanical and agricultural knowledge, independence, the ability to make do with little. But although he did live for some years in a log cabin, his experience there was not as primitive as the image that term conjures up. Life wasn't luxurious for the Sheldons in a material sense, but the elder Sheldons were well educated, and their life was much more civilized than one might have expected, given the setting. Most Dakota boys had very little schooling; they stayed at home and worked. Sheldon went to school every year, and when he had exhausted the local educational resources, his parents stood ready to see him off to higher learning experiences.

Certainly Sheldon's enduring love of books and learning became apparent during the prairie years. He came to realize just how precious the printed word could be and went to great lengths to read good literature. He also was propelled toward his life-long commitment to clean living, perhaps because of the isolation of the prairie, although his parents certainly taught that course through example as well. And, of course, he received rigorous training in religious living. The daily family Bible reading and discipline of prayer made a profound impact that was to remain with him throughout his life.

Stewart and Sarah Sheldon were determined that their sons receive good educations, and so in 1877 both boys headed east, Charles to the Phillips Academy in Andover, Massachusetts, and Ward to Brown University—both of them schools their uncle Joseph had attended. Charles was three or four years older than most of his classmates and felt awkward. He had hoped to study natural science, but found that it wasn't a part of the rather rigid program, and thus spent his two years studying such subjects as Greek, Latin, mathematics, French, history, and English.[32] Although his parents helped him out, their means were limited, and Sheldon found it necessary to work. He seems to have done so cheerfully enough, locating a job as a janitor in which he swept the academy building, replaced broken windowpanes, pumped water, blacked the shoes of faculty members, and did various chores. After all, he had learned a lot about manual labor in Dakota.

Surviving details of Sheldon's campus life in prep school are few, but apparently he learned some important lessons in human relations. In his autobiography he wrote, for example, of having had some minor disagreement with a roommate which culminated in the refusal of both to build a fire in the heating stove in the room—this in the middle of winter. As Sheldon recalled, "For a whole week we sat around bundled up in heavy overcoats or took refuge in the other fellows' rooms to get warm. One night while I was trying to write a letter home the ink froze on my pen and the water in the bedroom wash basin was a chunk of ice." Finally the principal of the academy intervened to end the all-around obstinacy.[33]

Shortly before his death Sheldon told a story to Glenn Clark that well illustrated his love of books and learning during his years at Phillips. Late one Saturday afternoon at the beginning of Christmas vacation Sheldon was in a second-hand bookstore in Boston and saw an attractively-bound copy of *Les Misérables*. The price: one dollar. Sheldon had $1.17 in his pocket; the train ticket back to Andover cost 63 cents. As Clark related it,

There ensued a deep inner debate, then he laid the dollar down and with the book protected beneath his warm overcoat from the cold drizzle that immediately set in he started on his twenty-one miles hike up the railroad track. He reached his quarters at two o'clock in the morning, lighted his German student lamp, threw more fuel in his stove, and did not stop reading until he had finished Book One, "Fantine." Then as the world was waking up he threw himself upon his bed in the deep contentment of one who had found what he had long been seeking for.[34]

Reading was not the only old passion Sheldon indulged at Phillips. He was still interested in writing, and joined the staff of the *Phillipian*, the student newspaper. During his final year at the Academy he was made editor-in-chief.[35]

In 1879, after two years at Phillips, Sheldon was ready for college, and following in the footsteps of Joseph Ward again he enrolled at Brown University in Providence. The first thing Sheldon did upon arriving in Providence was to join the Round Top Congregational Church, where he quickly was enlisted as a Sunday school teacher and as a bass in the choir. Thereupon followed his first important piece of religious leadership. Early in his freshman year he made a point of getting to know Lee Wong, his Chinese laundryman, and learned that there were fifteen Chinese in Providence who had little contact with the larger culture. Sheldon volunteered to start a Sunday school class for them if the church would provide a place to meet and help secure teachers; thus Sheldon founded what he proclaimed "the first Sunday School for Chinese laundrymen in America." All fifteen of the Chinese men attended the class at 4 P.M. each Sunday, probably at least as much out of a desire to learn English as to receive a Christian religious education. Learn English they did, using the Bible as a text. Sheldon reported that after three years, most of them had a good command of the language.[36] Apparently his church life as a whole was productive in Providence, because in his junior year at Brown Sheldon made his final decision to enter the ministry.[37]

He continued to work at a wide variety of jobs to support himself, but he also earned a good bit of his keep—perhaps as much as half of it in his last college years—as a writer. Early in his college career he joined Delta Upsilon, a literary fraternity that gathered for original readings and criticism every Friday night. From this gathering emerged a group of Brown students who called themselves the "Penwipers" who wrote stories and sent them off to magazines, especially the *Youth's Companion*. Although far more of his articles were rejected than accepted at the magazine, enough were purchased for two dollars each that Sheldon fairly prospered.[38] He learned one trick many another writer has practiced: he would often sit on rejected articles for some time, then rewrite and resubmit them and often have them accepted.[39]

Providing most of his own financial support naturally entailed Sheldon's taking summer jobs, and his taste in them seemed to run to work in resorts. One summer he worked as a waiter at the Pavilion Hotel on Lake Winnepesaukee in New Hampshire, and another he worked "slinging clams" at a resort on Narragansett Bay in Rhode Island. His knowledge of the classics secured him a tip worth nearly a month's pay at the former job; one day an elderly diner complained about an underdone piece of beef, and Sheldon quickly responded with a line from Homer in which the poet referred to "the good 'red' oxen." The hotel guest turned out to be a Greek scholar who knew the line; at the end of his stay he left his erudite waiter a ten dollar tip, not a bad increment for a twelve-dollar-a-month job.[40]

Sheldon's academic record was mixed. He was indeed a whiz at the classical languages (the companion with whom he most often polished his Greek and Latin translations was Charles Evans Hughes, later secretary of state and Supreme Court justice),[41] but the lack of provision for electives in the Brown curriculum meant that he could take virtually no natural science, the subject he most wanted to study, and compelled him to take several mathematics courses, which he detested.

By the fall of 1883 Sheldon's sights were clearly set on the Congregational ministry, and he chose to attend Andover Theological Seminary, which was just down the road from his old prep school in Andover, Massachusetts. He took the standard course of study, including theology, church history, homiletics, elocution, and Hebrew.

As always, his financial resources were meager and he worked his way through school in much the same way he had earlier done at Phillips and Brown—reading out loud for and giving massages to a seminary professor, tutoring a few Phillips students, offering pulpit supply to small churches, and writing for the *Youth's Companion*.

At Andover Sheldon became more prolific a writer than ever. His *Youth's Companion* contributions became more frequent and began to constitute an important part of his financial self-support. He learned the art of churning out reams of material, sometimes writing a story a day for weeks on end.[42]

As it happened, Andover Seminary was experiencing great changes and controversies during the years Sheldon studied there. The school had been founded early in the nineteenth century as a bastion of Congregational and Calvinist orthodoxy, a counterweight to the Unitarian tendencies which had so much infected other Congregational seminaries, especially Harvard. Champions of orthodoxy thus strove earnestly to keep Andover from sliding into liberalism. But that turned out to be easier said than done. By the 1880s some slippage was taking place, and with the appointment of five new professors in 1883 there was a major infusion of the "new theology," which involved such innovative features as accepting modern biblical criticism, adopting a relatively optimistic appraisal of human nature, and seeing God as immanent in human affairs. A new periodical, the *Andover Review*, became the vehicle for "Progressive Orthodoxy," as the new ideas eventually came to be called. The controversy between the old-line Calvinists and the new moderates peaked in 1886, Sheldon's graduation year, when heresy charges were brought against five members of the editorial board of the *Review*. The Board of Visitors of the seminary held a trial, singling out Professor Egbert C. Smyth and condemning him for, among other things, allegedly believing in the fallibility of the Bible and maintaining that there "will be probation after death for those who do not decisively reject Christ during the earthly life."[43]

Although the Andover Heresy was multifaceted, it was this theory of a "Second Probation"—that those who did not get to hear the message of Jesus in their earthly lifetimes would get a chance to hear it and accept it in the afterlife—that was the most controversial, even though it was not at all new. (Such thinking goes back at least as far as Martin Luther, who, as Martin Marty has noted, "had trouble believing that his favorite secular humanist Cicero might not be found in paradise." Luther, sounding quite Andover heretical, wrote, "I do hope God will help Cicero and such men as he to the remission of sins—and if he must remain out of grace, then he will at least be some levels higher than our cardinals, and the bishop of Mainz.")[44]

Sheldon has left us relatively few clues about his theological thinking at this point in his life. When writing about it many years later he liked to belittle the notion that he received any theological orientation at all at Andover, since he was by then pushing what he came to call "untheological Christianity." Action, he said, was all, and theorizing was a rather useless and thus objectionable—what with all the reform the world stood in need of—waste of valuable time. Nevertheless, no social action program makes sense without some kind of philosophical underpinning, and Sheldon must have received more of those underpinnings than he ever wanted to admit while he was at the seminary. His theological outlook must have been shaped, at least subtly and probably substantially, by the emerging Christocentric liberalism at Andover. It is hard to imagine that Sheldon, who for decades proclaimed the solemn Christian duty of centering one's life on Jesus, was not influenced by such a professor as Egbert Smyth, who taught that "A theology which is not Christocentric is like a Ptolemaic astronomy, —it is out of true relation to the earth and the heavens, to God and the universe."[45] And Smyth was hardly alone in propounding such thought at Andover. Indeed, Sheldon kept among his mementoes until his death a pamphlet stoutly defending the whole theory of future probation.[46] The impact of the emerging, dynamic liberalism of Andover Seminary must have been substantial; Sheldon was nothing if not Christocentric, and he never flinched at being considered a heretic.

The first job offer Sheldon got upon graduation was from Lyman Abbott, the editor of the independent New York religion and social concerns journal *The Outlook*, who asked him to join the editorial staff of that periodical. Abbott, apparently, had taken note of Sheldon's voluminous writings for the *Youth's Companion*. But Sheldon, although tempted by the offer, wanted to preach. Finally a pastoral call did arrive, from the Congregational church in Waterbury, Vermont. But the new pastor wasn't needed until October, so Sheldon borrowed two hundred dollars from a friend of his father's and sailed for England. He had the time of his life on his first trip abroad, listening to the great preachers and occasionally selling stories to local popular magazines.

Sheldon began his Waterbury sojourn by being ordained on November 16, 1886, and initiated his active pastorate the following Sunday, November 21.[47] The church was a New England classic, with about 175 members and a white frame building. He boarded in the local hotel and apparently prospered on his nine-hundred-dollar annual salary. He was able to cover the extensive rural portions of his parish using a feeble pony and buggy, which he inherited from his ministerial predecessor, S. H. Wheeler, whose eleven-year stint there had been a popular one.[48]

From the beginning Sheldon was willing to work hard, both in the pastorate and in other ways. He threw himself into his preaching, writing his sermons out, reading them aloud, and revising them repeatedly. He soon was also busy initiating social reforms. He preached sermons advocating a wide range of social projects and services, including a public reading room and library, a public gymnasium, an organization to promote neat and attractive housing, assistance to small businesses, a good local newspaper, big Bible study groups, and other such things.[49]

Several of his proposed innovations were implemented. For example, Sheldon found dancing, the main local youth amusement, not very uplifting. So he organized a reading club for the youth of the two local churches and ended up with nearly a hundred participants. They read *A Tale of Two Cities* aloud the first winter, and interest in the club ran so high that Sheldon launched a successful drive to create a town library.[50] When he discovered that the town had no hearse (and when the dignified townspeople were once embarrassed when the coffin fell out of an inferior borrowed hearse) he passed the hat, and within a few days the hearse had been purchased.[51]

One winter, over two dozen citizens, mostly young men, died of typhoid. The good church members were willing to call it Providence, but Sheldon, working with a young physician, demonstrated to the skeptical multitude—who were maddeningly slow to accept it—that the real problem was that the drinking water wells were too close to the pigpens. In time he saw clean water supplies installed, and the typhoid epidemic cease.[52]

Perhaps Sheldon's most ingenious project was the abatement of street dust. Waterbury was built along a wide, unpaved main street, and the wagon traffic stirred up thick clouds of dust, to the great chagrin of housewives who wanted to keep their homes spotless. Sheldon, on an earlier walk of exploration around the village, had discovered a spring on a hillside above the town and cleverly rigged up a pipe which took the water to a tank—the remains of a cider press—in the hayloft of a barn near the main street. Then he secured another cider tank, had it mounted on a lumber wagon, and hired an elderly man to drive it around. Up and down Main Street went the sprinkler all summer, and the dust vanished. Sheldon was the man of the hour for the fastidious housekeepers.[53]

In addition to his social reforms and civic improvement projects in Waterbury, Sheldon was interested in innovations in church life. Some of his ecclesiastical innovations were modest enough; for example, he sometimes used a blackboard to write out the biblical text and main points of his sermon to make it easier to follow, and sometimes he illustrated his sermons by taking little artifacts—flowers, leaves, stones—into the pulpit. But others were more substantial and clearly made quite an impression on Sheldon's parishioners.[54]

His "boarding around" was the most talked-about new idea. Very soon after arriving in Waterbury Sheldon decided that he had to get to know his parishioners as well as possible, and asked to live with each family for a week. And so he did. Starting on Sunday he would go home with a family, eat dinner with them and spend most of the afternoon with them; and then after the evening church service he would return and visit until bedtime. Although he slept in his hotel room, throughout the following week he would eat lunch and dinner with the family and then stay for the evening, perhaps helping the children with their homework or amusing them with magic tricks. In all he "boarded around" with forty or forty-five families in his first year, and indeed got to know them well.[55]

Perhaps even more successful was Sheldon's idea of having a sermon a month printed for general distribution. In 1887, after a few months in Waterbury, Sheldon discovered that several of his parishioners were partially deaf. So he went to Montpelier and made arrangements to have his sermons printed, and the next Sunday printed copies of that very day's sermon were distributed to the surprised churchgoers, who could thus read along with the minister. The idea caught on quickly; soon Sheldon was distributing his sermons not only in his own church but at the local post office and in village stores. At the beginning of 1888, after the experiment had been under way for several months, Sheldon's press run had grown from seventy-five to over three hundred, and even that printing ran out.[56] He also took to the printing press to drum up business: sometimes he would distribute an outline of his sermon for the following Sunday, urging his parishioners to use it as an aid for following the sermon and as a reminder for any questions they might have about the sermon, questions he would attempt to answer at the Sunday evening service.[57]

When summer arrived, Sheldon had yet another idea for the church. The edifice sat on a good-sized lot, and Sheldon decided to dig part of it up for a garden. Although many of his parishioners again thought him odd, he bought seeds, borrowed a spade, and raised enough vegetables to sell to the local hotel and people in the town. And Sheldon, ever the great evangelist, even managed to persuade a few unchurched green thumbs to start attending his services.[58]

But all was not reformed at Waterbury. Sheldon had a notable failure in trying to change what he later called Waterbury's "pagan" funeral practices. Sheldon always considered death the beginning of a wonderful new life, but, he wrote, "When I ventured to preach a 'cheerful' funeral sermon, I found the family and audience were shocked and offended and thought I was frivolous and lacking in spiritual understanding of the Christian life."[59] The local tradition, he discovered, was that "The minister who could provoke the greatest mourning and put the whole audience to tears and sobs was the greatest preacher in the community."[60] Moreover, after a long sermon "extolling the virtues of the deceased even if, as I would afterwards discover, he had very few," Sheldon was expected to conduct a graveside service with another long sermon. None of it sat well with him. The final coup came on a twenty-below-zero day when he asked the pallbearers to keep their hats on during the long graveside service, and the family members were deeply offended.[61] With twenty-one funerals his first winter, most of them resulting from the typhoid epidemic, Sheldon had plenty of opportunities to be dismayed by local customs.[62]

The most important thing that happened to Sheldon in Waterbury occurred in the summer of 1888: he met the young woman who would later become his wife. Mary Merriam's family moved from Vermont to Kansas that year, when her father's health failed and he sought a healthier climate. Shortly before the move young "May" went to Waterbury to stay with her grandmother for a month. When her grandmother told her that a new minister had come to town, May was disappointed, because she had fond childhood memories of riding in the former minister's buggy.[63] When Sheldon came by the home in the course of his parish calling, May wasn't interested in meeting him. But meet him she did, and soon afterwards he asked the young woman, seven years his junior, to take a buggy ride with him, a remarkable overture for the minister who had scrupulously avoided dating any local woman. She accepted the ride, thus becoming the talk of the town, but declined a second invitation and told her grandmother that she would never marry a minister. Back at home, she told her parents the same thing.[64] But the firmest intentions. . . .

Sheldon was happy in many ways at Waterbury; of his parishioners there he later wrote that "they loved the Bible and read it every morning and evening and had family prayers after breakfast. They came to church through blinding snow storms and put money in the plate for foreign missions and lived a daily devout and spiritual life."[65] But it was also clear that a young minister who was anxious to try a myriad of new ideas would eventually tire of battling conservative New Englanders whose ideas about church life were, in the main, firmly fixed. There must have been several minor skirmishes with the old guard; one that is known involved the game of tennis. Sheldon, a good player, was reprimanded for being on the court. A deacon told him that such conduct was unbecoming for a minister.[66] He eventually was ready to move on, and hoped he could find a new church which had not previously had a minister, so he would be free to pursue his own programs.

By the time he was finished with Waterbury Sheldon was thirty-one, and some contours of his personality and outlook were becoming fairly clear. He was well established as a lover of words whose reading and writing were as dear to him as anything in life. Certainly he had established his genius for human relations at the personal level; the people of Waterbury were fond of their minister and by and large were not intolerant of his whimsy. When he resigned in November 1888, the church council recorded in its minutes that it could see no reason why "the pastorate should be dissolved; but rather, strong reasons why he should continue."[67]

Still, the fit of pastor and congregation was imperfect. Sheldon was still young, and he yearned for a place to live and work where tradition had not yet bound up the whole town. More importantly, perhaps, reform was in the air. The social gospel movement was becoming ever more influential; the progressive era was at hand. For someone who felt called to change the world, Waterbury wasn't the place to be. The man of action was ready to go, and part of that going meant leading a lively, young church.

2. A Young Man Goes West

Topeka in the late 1880s was a vibrant city that, despite the recent deflation of a big land boom, was sprawling and growing with the young state of Kansas. Since 1854, when Kansas Territory was opened to settlement and the first cabins erected at what would become Topeka, the town had come to be measured in miles, not blocks, and thus many of the settlers came to believe that new institutions were needed to keep up with the growth.

The First Congregational Church had been founded in late 1855 and was operating by 1856 as the "Free Congregational Church," the original name reflecting the burning antislavery sentiments of the New England emigrants who saw to it that their native denomination was planted in the frontier soil.[1] But by the eighties those living in the rapidly expanding western reaches of the city—and especially those in the vicinity of Washburn College, whose campus lay well away from downtown—found it difficult to get downtown regularly for religious services. There was a mule-drawn streetcar line from downtown out to the college, but during muddy times it was wholly unreliable—the conductor and passengers would often have to get out and poke the mud out from between the wheels and body of the car, one rider recalled. And it took an hour to travel from the college to downtown even under ideal conditions.[2]

A committee was appointed at First Church to look into the practicability of establishing an extension Sunday school somewhere near the college. The Sunday school was duly set up in a room over a new grocery store in 1887, and at the end of the next year it had become Central Congregational Church, so named because it lay between downtown and the Washburn campus.

View of rapidly growing Topeka, looking northwest from statehouse, 1888. Kansas State Historical Society.

Following In His Steps: *A Biography of Charles M. Sheldon*

The first topic quickly became the hiring of a pastor. Everet B. Merriam, Sheldon's future father-in-law, who had just moved to Kansas from Vermont, had heard the young minister preach at Waterbury, and suggested he be considered for the position. Sheldon was ready to leave Waterbury and in short order came to Kansas to preach a trial sermon at First Church. The sermon was well received, and he was called by a unanimous vote of members of the new church. Sheldon closed out his work in Waterbury and showed up in Topeka in time to begin work there on the first Sunday of the new year, January 6, 1889.[3]

The fledgling pastor was offered a salary of one thousand dollars per year, a skimpy sum even in 1889. At the end of a year it was raised to twelve hundred, where it stayed for many years. Raising money was hard for the little church. Sheldon, however, was glad to be there. He found a temporary home with the Everet Merriam family, staying there until his parents moved to Topeka a few months later, and he joined the congregation in its austere meeting hall, a room so sparsely furnished that it contained neither pulpit nor communion table, but only some chairs, benches, and an organ. Sheldon used the corner of the organ as his pulpit.[4]

The church over the grocery store was an immediate success; the upper room was often packed. Fortunately, however, the First Church missionaries had not expected the new church to live thus forever and, even before Sheldon arrived, had begun construction of a permanent edifice, an ample stone structure. The congregation began to worship in the new building on June 23, 1889, and that day Sheldon announced his credo—that this would be a church open to all, a church preaching

> a Christ for the common people. A Christ who belongs to the rich and poor, the ignorant and learned, the old and young, the good and the bad. A Christ who knows no sect or age, whose religion does not consist alone in cushioned seats, and comfortable surroundings, or culture, or fine singing or respectable orders of Sunday services, but a Christ who bids us all recognize the Brotherhood of the race, who bids throw open this room to all. . . . I cannot help feeling that God has, through the power of his dear Son, great things in store for us.[5]

Stirrings of Activism:
The Christian Sociologist

The spirit of the social gospel, of the churches' duty to try to right the ills of society, was much in the air when Sheldon went to Topeka, and he lost little time in surveying the social environment there with an eye toward improving it. He was systematic in his gathering of information on social problems, but he was emphatic that such data-gathering had to have a social end. Decrying many sociologists (for such he considered himself) for producing excessively abstract work, Sheldon announced that "the end of sociology is not theories or statistics but advice, work and help of the individual with the masses. The investigation of conditions is not sociology unless such investigation helps the man."[6]

His first excursion into "practical sociology" in Topeka came just about a year after his arrival, in January 1890, when there was a depression on. An unusually severe winter was causing grave hardships for the many unemployed. The problem struck home, according to a Central Church historian, when a man walked up to Sheldon's home and asked for work, which Sheldon could not provide. He could only watch helplessly as the man walked away, discouraged.[7]

Sheldon quickly decided that he needed to know more about the condition of the unemployed, and so he undertook to explore their world. Putting on his oldest clothes, he spent a week searching the city of Topeka for work, with little luck.[8] He tried stores and factories, coal yards and flour mills, with nary a nibble. He walked into every store (except for the tobacco shops and theaters, of whose business he disapproved) on Kansas Avenue, Topeka's main business street, and even over the long bridge to the adjacent community of North Topeka, and was turned down at every door. For four and a half days he kept up the routine, unrecognized by anyone. Finally, his empathy with the unemployed at its height, he saw a crew shoveling snow from the Santa Fe railroad tracks, and asked the foreman if he could help them without being paid. The bemused foreman agreed; Sheldon borrowed a shovel from a nearby coal yard and went to work. The simple joy of working was so great that he went on with it for half a day. The next morning he went back to the coal yard where he had borrowed the shovel and, by chance, the manager offered him a job unloading a car of coal. Sheldon went at the job with a vengeance, finishing it before noon and earning fifty cents.

Sheldon was deeply moved by his experience and based a series of eight sermons on it. He told his congregation,

> I had to confess that I, an able-bodied man, in good health, willing to do anything that a man can do with his hands, actually could not get any paying job after walking a matter of ten miles, and applying at over a dozen places where day laborers are hired. . . . Even though I knew my mother was getting a warm supper for me at home . . . I could not altogether get rid of the thought that it was a very hard world, and everybody seemed to have a job but myself. Toward the close of the day I really felt so desperate that I was willing to work for nothing, if I couldn't get pay."[9]

The problem of unemployment continued to haunt Sheldon; in 1897, for example, he published an article in the social gospel periodical *The Kingdom* that described his walking the streets with an out-of-work man, fruitlessly searching for any job, and concluded that the man had only three options left: begging, starving, or stealing. Finding all three options unacceptable, Sheldon announced that he favored making the government the employer of last resort.[10]

The unsuccessful search for work convinced Sheldon that there was a great deal happening in his community of which he was ignorant, and he pressed on with his practical sociology. He thus conceived a plan in which he would spend a week with each of eight social groups in Topeka. "It was my intention," he wrote at the end of the project, "to spend a whole week with each of these groups, living as nearly as I could the life they lived, asking them questions about their work, and preaching the gospel to them in whatever way might seem most expedient."[11] He never did explain just how he chose his eight "classes of people," but somehow he came up with these: streetcar operators, college students, blacks, railroad workers, lawyers, physicians, businessmen, and newspaper workers.

His method of study was simple, but effective: he plunged into contact with the group of the week. So the first week, he said, "I spent all my loose change in riding over the city, standing on one end or the other of the platform of the car."[12] Up and down he rode all day, talking with motormen and conductors. The next week he joined the students at Washburn College, attending their classes, visiting them in their dormitory rooms, and playing ball with them, in all enjoying the experience more than any other in the project.

The third week, if not the most enjoyable, certainly had the greatest impact on Sheldon's life and work. He spent the week—and the next two as well, because it took him that long to learn what he needed to know—with blacks in the Tennesseetown settlement just a stone's throw from Central Church. These freed slaves and their children were leading destitute lives, and Sheldon spent his first week in Tennesseetown trying to learn the causes of their destitution and helping some of them find employment—not an easy task in a city as segregated as Topeka. The second week he visited black schools, and the third week he interviewed some of Topeka's more prominent black citizens. During the last week he also conducted two interesting experiments to test the possibilities of integration: first, he went with a well-dressed black man to a good restaurant to see if they would be served; they were. Then the two went separately into two more restaurants, and the black man was served in both, perhaps to his surprise. Then they went to the YMCA, where the black man applied for membership, and at that point they discovered the color line: there the black man was not welcome.[13] Sheldon found his time in black Topeka so profoundly moving that it changed his life, as well as the lives of the people of Tennesseetown. It awakened him to the ugly reality of racism and prodded him to institute broad self-help programs in the black settlement—a story that will presently be recounted in some detail.

The fourth week (to keep Sheldon's numbering system intact) was spent on the railroad, riding mainly freight trains. A sympathetic railway superintendent gave him a pass, and Sheldon took several trips around Kansas in cabs and cabooses. As the trains rolled along he talked eagerly with the brakemen and conductors and, when circumstances permitted, with the engineers. The fifth week found Sheldon among the lawyers, attending court, reading cases, discussing briefs, and interviewing, at least briefly, every attorney in town. The sixth week was that of the physicians; Sheldon read medical books, went on hospital and home rounds, watched the performance of surgery, and attended medical society meetings. During the seventh week Sheldon spent his time mainly in stores, watching the operations and speaking with the proprietors of dry goods stores, groceries, hardware stores, real estate brokerages, shoestores, bookstores, and several others.

The eighth week had nearly as great an impact on Sheldon as had the weeks in Tennesseetown. For that period Sheldon was an unpaid reporter for the *Topeka Daily Capital*, with a beat covering transportation depots, hotels, and the suburbs. The intrepid reporter wrote several articles, one editorial, and a number of local short items, and all the while managed to learn all he could about every aspect of the newspaper business, from reporting to printing. During the week he became preoccupied with the great power that he believed newspapers held in society. People from all walks of life, he concluded, read newspapers more than they read anything else; yet the newspapers were full of shortcomings, such as a lack of moral purpose, superficial treatment of serious subjects, and inadequate discrimination concerning what to print. Since Sheldon was, as a minister, in the business of moral and spiritual uplift, he came to believe that newspapers were working counter to his most cherished values. Since his parishioners read papers every day, they needed and deserved something better. That something, he concluded, was a Christian daily newspaper, "removed entirely from political and moneyed power, and . . . strictly non-partisan and positively Christian in every department; manned by Christian men throughout, from editor-in-chief to reporters, pressmen and office-boy."[14] A Christian daily newspaper: the project would become a windmill at which Sheldon would tilt throughout his life.

The eight-week experiment intensified Sheldon's empathy with workers and helped the members of his largely above-working-class congregation understand some social problems they didn't experience personally. It also diversified the congregation; Sheldon each week invited those with whom he came in contact to come to church the following Sunday and hear his report on his week's activities, and many accepted, some staying on when they discovered that Sheldon was one preacher in a mainline church who ministered to all, not only the wealthy. Furthermore, the experience gave Sheldon renewed conviction that social gospel reform could improve, even perfect, society.[15]

Soon thereafter, around 1892, Sheldon oversaw what he considered, in the light of his strong interest in work with children and youth, one of Central Church's most important in-house social projects. A kindergarten was founded at that time—or, rather, two parallel kindergartens, one for white children at Central Church, and another for blacks in Tennesseetown. Sheldon was by then firmly committed to social betterment in Tennesseetown, and saw clearly the utility of a kindergarten there.

By 1892 the idea of kindergartens had reached the United States from Germany, where they were flourishing, and early organizational efforts were begun to establish one in Topeka. The first major public drive for a kindergarten in Topeka came in January 1893, when Sheldon penned a series of five articles on the topic for the *Topeka Daily Capital*. He earnestly described the importance of getting children off to a good start in learning during the critical formative years before the first grade, arguing that the kindergarten would soon be regarded as a social and educational necessity and that thousands of children in Topeka stood in need of it.[16]

By 1897 an addition to the church building had been built to house a laboratory kindergarten for one of the nation's first kindergarten teacher-training instutitions. The female student teachers, a local newspaper reported, had to be high school graduates who were refined, healthy, and able to sing.[17] Soon the laboratory school was turning out teachers who were eagerly snapped up by kindergartens from Maine to Texas, as the movement spread throughout the United

Central Church with kindergarten addition, 1890s. Kansas State Historical Society.

States.[18] Over the years hundreds of children attended the Central Church kindergarten; the most prominent of them was Dr. Karl Menninger, who in 1981 could still recall some of the lessons he had learned there.[19]

There was one last important social project—in this case, actually a crusade—that occupied Sheldon during those early Topeka years and throughout his life. That was the fight against alcohol. Sheldon came from a "dry" background, and there is no reason to believe that a drop of alcohol ever passed his lips. His uncle-hero Joseph Ward had been a vigorous fighter of drinking on the Dakota frontier, and Sheldon's father and grandfather had been stalwart against alcohol. According to one Topeka historian, Sheldon, although a teetotaler, was somewhat tolerant toward liquor when he arrived in Kansas and advocated "high license"—a system under which there were limited numbers of saloons paying heavy licensing fees.[20] However, Kansas was by then already a prohibition state, and Sheldon quickly came to support prohibition as the right position. He was soon Topeka's foremost dry, denouncing high license and all other halfway measures against drink.[21]

As Sheldon learned more about the illegal liquor traffic—of the existence of many speakeasies and of the fact that many drugstores were making a mockery of a legal loophole by selling enormous quantities of liquor as medicine—he became outraged at the widespread violation of the law. Even taking direct action, however, he had trouble getting the law enforced. On October 4, 1896, the night on which Sheldon read the first chapter of *In His Steps* to his congregation, he told a full house (gathered to hear of the latest news in the battle against liquor as much as to hear the first installment of the new sermon story) that he had recently gone to a "joint" on Kansas Avenue with scores of customers and asked the police to raid the place. The police, however, told Sheldon he would have to swear out a warrant, that they could not act on their own. Sheldon thundered, "Has it come to this, that officers cannot enforce the law against a bar thirty feet long, and five men pumping beer as hard as they can? . . . I know this as surely as I know anything, that there was an open saloon running back of a cigar store near the corner of Kansas avenue and Eighth street."[22]

On other occasions Sheldon tried to fight the liquor traffic in drugstores. Once he and his deacon A.G. Carruth went to the drugstores and bought several bottles of liquor without the necessary documentation that it was for medicinal purposes; the case foundered in court on the ground that Carruth, standing behind Sheldon while the purchase was made, had not actually *seen* the transaction.[23]

As one might expect, the alcohol interests tried to stop Sheldon. Some tried bribery; a bootlegger whose children were in one of Sheldon's kindergartens once offered Sheldon two hundred dollars to call off the police in his case. Sheldon of course refused, and that night the man's "joint" was raided on schedule.[24] Others were less genteel in their opposition. Threats and violence flared; Sheldon's barn was burned down, and when he rebuilt, the new one was also torched. His life was also threatened, as was his wife's.[25] Only the realization that bad publicity was no help to the wet cause halted the violence.

Through it all, Sheldon, who hated the sin, loved the sinner. In one case, after Sheldon had scored one of his greatest triumphs by securing convictions against twenty drugstore proprietors in Topeka, he got the women of his Ladies' Aid Society to visit the homes of those convicted and determine the needs of the families, and then take groceries and pay the rent for those who were destitute. Sheldon also visited in jail those he had put there, taking them books and newspapers and lending them money.[26]

The Churchman

While Sheldon's fight for social reforms brought him great publicity in Topeka and beyond, he was ever the diligent pastor, carefully tending his ecclesiastical flock. It is abundantly clear that he quickly won the hearts of his parishioners: after he had completed his first year in the position, the term of his original offer, he was reconfirmed for life.

The members of Central Church saw Sheldon as an unconventional minister, and that was an integral part of their affection for him. He tantalized them with little eccentricities, yet managed to maintain a good reservoir of ministerial decorum. Sometimes he would make his parish rounds on a bicycle at a time when the "wheel" was still a decided novelty. Sheldon was in good physical shape in those years, and occasionally would delight onlookeers with his modest physical exploits. Boys in the neighborhood found he could throw a good curve ball, and all marveled at his handsprings. He was also a juggler; Charles Sheldon Graves, who still belongs to Central Church, remembered seeing Sheldon juggle an apple, an orange, and a knife, finishing by impaling the apple, on its last fall, on the knife.[27]

He went to great lengths to deepen his parishioners' participation in church life. He encouraged, for example, the use of energetic young people in sermon research; he would make up a synopsis and assign various bits of subtopical research to his youth, giving them public credit for the information they gathered. He was an early ecumenist, moreover, suggesting that pastors in neighboring Protestant churches should canvass their territory together and thus try to end denominational rivalries.[28]

One favorite method for involving his congregation in church life was having parishioners submit questions which he would answer during an evening worship service. He did that repeatedly with his young people,[29] and at least once used the format with several local notables. On that occasion he asked ten prominent citizens (including Methodist Bishop of Kansas John H. Vincent, editors of three local papers, a prominent author, and others) to submit, in advance, questions for Sheldon to answer. Thus he found himself speaking to such questions as "Why do church people quibble over small things?" (Answer: "Frankly, I do not know, unless it is because they are not Christian enough.") and "Can we live as pure a life as Jesus lived?" (Answer: Yes. The scriptural injunction here is to "Be ye therefore perfect," something not harder today than in New Testament times.)[30]

Throughout his life Sheldon had little patience for doctrinal disputes and wanted to remove stumbling blocks to fellowship by eliminating divisive formulations of faith. Thus an 1899 ecclesiastical innovation, which raised more than a few eyebrows in Topeka, saw Central Church remove entirely the Apostles' Creed from its services and revise its covenant, which had contained traditional language about repentance, crucifixion, and the centrality of the Bible, into a document that simply affirmed the God who "has opened your eyes to see, and your heart to receive Jesus as Lord" and required members to "devote yourselves during your whole life, to the love, service, and obedience of Jesus Christ."[31] The goal, Sheldon said, was to formulate the covenant in simple, readily comprehensible language.[32]

For all of his vaunted innovativeness, Sheldon's Sunday morning worship services were quite conventional. Visitors sometimes remarked on the informality of the proceedings, but otherwise noted nothing unusual.[33] Informality extended to decor; a visitor in 1900 wrote that "The interior of this church more resembles the assembly-room of a school or a kindergarten than an ecclesiastical structure. A big map of 'the Holy Land' hung on the wall to the left of the pulpit. It had lakes in green and seas in blue. . . . It was more than uncommonly ugly."[34] Another visitor was struck by the fact that the words, "What would Jesus do?," Sheldon's then-famous motto from *In His Steps*, were stenciled on the interior walls in several places.[35]

Sheldon began his work in Topeka in an era in which preachers were groping for ways to cope with industrial America and the rising tide of reformism. As William Bos and Clyde Faries have observed, pulpit response to those new phenomena was "slow, confused, and almost disastrous."[36] The recent Protestant heritage, dating back to Second Great Awakening revivalism, had been that ministers preached personal, not social, regeneration. Although the greatest of the princes of the pulpit, Henry Ward Beecher and Phillips Brooks, had managed to escape the confines of the strict evangelical tradition, they had not broken much new ground in preaching social reform. Certainly they and other great preachers of their day had opened the doors of liberalism, with Beecher's ground-breaking acceptance of evolution and higher criticism and Brooks's optimistic emphasis on the goodness of God. But by the mid-1880s a great many ministers still opposed organized labor and preached that the poor should accept their lot. Only as Sheldon was beginning to preach did a new movement seem to be taking shape—one in which preachers cautiously began to support reform causes. Through his early years that movement grew; by the end of the century the pulpit had been revitalized by the new attention to justice rather than charity.[37] Sheldon's own development as a preacher followed what was going on around him. His sermons at Waterbury and the first ones in Topeka were cautious and evangelical, but by the mid-1890s he was using his pulpit steadily to promote his brand of reform religion and politics. He was never to achieve the artistry of Beecher or

Brooks, nor did he emulate the passionate exhortations of his fellow social gospel preachers such as Washington Gladden and Josiah Strong. He spurned flowery oratory and instead made his preaching informal, almost conversational.

Sheldon, although not a great preacher, was the very lifeblood of Central Church at the end of the century. He took on nearly mythic proportions to some of his followers: Lenore Stratton recalled in 1981 that "There was a belief that if Dr. Sheldon performed a marriage ceremony the couple would never get divorced. When one actually did, it was a great shock to the church."[38] He was loved by his flock and worked enormously hard as a pastor. In addition to leading Sunday morning and evening services and a Thursday prayer meeting, he kept up a heavy schedule of parish calling, wrote a book or two and several articles a year, often wrote seventy-five to a hundred letters a week to his parishioners,[39] and tended to countless other tasks.

Although Sheldon served his whole parish diligently, he always professed a need to spend as much time as possible with children and youth. Frequently he would make children the focus of the Sunday worship service by preaching a sermon specifically for them. In a time when Protestant churches largely reflected social class structures, Sheldon went out of his way from the beginning to make it clear that he was one pastor who wouldn't exclude anyone from his care. Blacks were welcome at Central Church, and a few did occasionally attend and participate, surely making Central one of America's first integrated churches. In a statement he read to a sociology department colloquium in 1891, Sheldon criticized the typical preacher as being classist, able to talk only to the educated: "Face him with a crowd of brakemen, street cleaners, hod carriers, and men who toil with their hands, and he is helpless."[40] By contrast, Sheldon strove to communicate with all, and tried to present his vision in their own terms. This sort of communication was really just a concrete expression of Sheldon's conviction of the universality of the gospel: all are within the compass of the church, and all humans are equally worthy children of God. His Jesus was so human that he could have been sitting in the next pew, accessible to the day laborer and the aristocrat alike.

There is no doubt that the overwhelming majority of the members of Central Church were devout Sheldon supporters. There was, however, occasional conservative opposition to some of Sheldon's social reform projects. In an era of pervasive racism, there were some who objected to Sheldon's helping the blacks of Tennesseetown. The drinkers in the church were understandably critical of Sheldon's crusades against the "joints." Marguerite Stuenkel, whose father was a pharmacist, remembered later that her father thought Sheldon unfair to druggists who sold alcohol as medicine.[41] But the majority were solidly behind their pastor. As a result of Sheldon's enthusiasm for applied Christianity, human service organizations and projects flourished within the church. Several women's groups—the Ladies' Aid Society, the Ladies' Foreign Missionary Society, the Ladies' Home Missionary Society—supported social and evangelistic projects. The Church Brotherhood, organized in 1900, provided similar outlets for the men of the church. In 1904 the Altruist Club was created, composed of young women who, somewhat like female Protestant Jesuits, took the "What would Jesus do?" pledge and committed themselves to special service at Sheldon's direction. The Willing Workers were committed to the education of young people for missionary work, a favorite Sheldon cause. Several other groups had similar outreach projects. A Central Church publication which listed such organizations quoted a young woman as saying, shortly after 1900, "I went to six services on Sunday. I attended Sunday School and Church Service in the morning; I worked with a group in Tennesseetown and sang with a group at Ingleside Home in the afternoon; I took part in Christian Endeavor and attended Church Service again in the evening."[42] One never lacked opportunities for involvement in "Sheldon's Church."

It is not surprising that membership at Central Church grew nearly twentyfold, to about a thousand, under Sheldon's leadership.[43] Although the depression of the early 1890s took its financial toll, things eventually improved, and enough money was raised to finance several additions to the original building as well as to support an ever-increasing array of social projects. Sheldon himself seemed not to care much about money; John Ripley recalled that "he would constantly go over his budget and then say, 'Well, the Lord will provide,' and the deacons were always after him."[44]

The Writer

Sheldon's busy life in Topeka never slowed the pen which had been prolific since childhood in Dakota. Throughout the early years in Topeka he turned out books, articles, poems and hymn texts, and other writings voluminously. The biggest part of his writing was directly related to his church work; early in his stint at Central he began to read his "sermon stories"—pieces of serialized inspirational fiction—to his congregation in place of Sunday evening sermons, and those stories, published as novels, formed the backbone of his literary work. Other church-related writings were also common; a perusal of old Central Church bulletins shows a plethora of Sheldon hymn texts written to familiar tunes.

How good was his writing? Throughout his lengthy literary career he was assailed by critics who found his style thoroughly pedestrian. Especially after the runaway success of *In His Steps*, critics dismissed Sheldon as a vulgarly popular writer, one whose work would never last. To be sure, Sheldon was no artist; but his works were clear and readable and, if not always deep, at least consistently interesting. The creation of lasting literature was never his goal; he always saw his writing either as something to be used for spiritual uplift or as marching orders for social reform. Those goals his writing served adequately.

The Person

Sheldon was an intensely private person, the more so because of his renown after early 1897. For all of his vigor in fighting the social

Sheldon at about the turn of the century, at the peak of his fame. Central Congregational Church (UCC), Topeka.

gospel fight, he was personally retiring, even quiescent. As far as can be determined, he never kept a diary, and no other personal materials of that kind have ever been uncovered. So his inner life to some extent remains a mystery.

Perhaps there is no inner life of Sheldon to be uncovered, or at least not much of one. That is, it appears to me that Sheldon's life was an open book. Having read most of Sheldon's published work and interviewed dozens of persons who knew him, I detect not a hint that his private life was in any way different from the kind of committed Christian life he advocated in his writings. Fight social injustice, be temperate, be loving, have a good home life—those things he wrote about at length, and, as best he could, he seems to have lived them. Carmie Wolfe of Topeka, who as a young woman accompanied the Sheldons in their latter years on cruises, reported on conversations she overheard on ships. And what were they like? She wrote that Sheldon most commonly would sit with his brother Ward (and others) and speculate about what Jesus might have done in such-and-such a situation, or discuss what Jesus might have done about some contemporary world problem.[45]

Thus we have only fleeting glimpses into his personal life. Most who spent time with Sheldon were impressed with his sincerity and earnestness in propounding his reformist Christianity, but beyond that little about his personality emerges. Perhaps his burning reformism was the truest part of his character, the key to understanding the man. When L.D. Whittemore composed a lengthy manuscript about his friend, the closest he came to revealing something of Sheldon's personality was this: "His habits are methodical. He rises early and spends the morning in his study in the church, where he dislikes interruption except by one in need of help, when he welcomes the caller at any time. The afternoon is given to pastoral duties and the evening, as far as possible, to his family."[46]

We do know a bit about Sheldon's appearance and stature in his early days in Topeka, although only a bit. One who profiled him in 1898 described the famous author of *In His Steps* as "tall, large, blue-eyed, brown-haired, brainy, gentle in manner and deliberate in speech."[47] A year later, George T.B. Davis described Sheldon in *Our Day*, a Chicago periodical, as "a typical Celt. Ruddy of countenance, tall, large. . . ."[48] Whittemore described him as "slightly above average in height and weight. He has a kindly eye which often twinkles with merriment; and expressive features, which quickly reflect his serious and earnest, or joyous mood."[49] When Sheldon arrived in Topeka in 1889 he was strong and athletic; in his early years in the city he liked to play baseball with boys and tennis with Washburn College students.

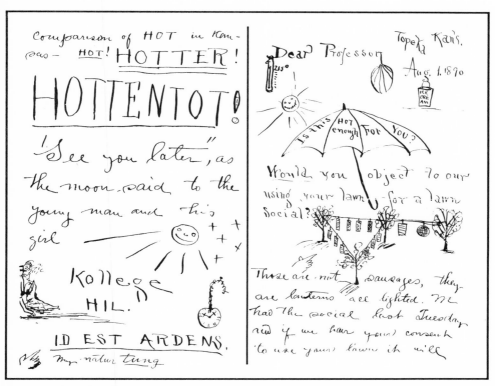

A Sheldon illustrated letter to Luther Denny Whittemore, 1890. Central Congregational Church (UCC), Topeka.

Soon after Sheldon had moved to Topeka his parents followed him there, and he set up housekeeping with them. After the long Dakota missionary stint Stewart Sheldon had returned with Sarah to the East, settling in Salem, Massachusetts, and supplying small churches there with Sunday pulpit work.[50] Moving to what proved to be their final retirement home in Topeka, they gave their son steady support in his ministerial and reformist undertakings. Sheldon's mother provided him with meals and housekeeping, and his father provided pastoral support and, most importantly, did quite a bit of clerical work for him. They were always nearby, helping out, until their deaths in 1905 and 1912, respectively.

Almost immediately after moving to Topeka Sheldon met Luther

Denny Whittemore, a Latin professor at Washburn College who lived next door to Sheldon's first landlords, the Merriams. They quickly became fast friends, and especially in the two years prior to Sheldon's marriage kept up a lively personal correspondence that started out as notes stuck in each other's doors. Sheldon's surviving epistles, many of them illustrated with line drawings, reveal a wit that doesn't show up very frequently in his published works. There are many plays on words, as well as bits of dog Latin to amuse the classics professor: "Id dabit nos magnam voluptatem habere te et tuam sororem honor now cum tua societate si gratum ad vos. Fri dies vesper, *sex temporis pacis* (time-piece). Tenesne? (Do you catch on?) (This is not slang. It is in Terence.) . . . Ignis via, et numquam animus (fire away and never mind.) . . . Vale! Ego voluntas mare te tardion. I will see you later."[51]

Sheldon met Mary Merriam, as has been detailed above, when she came to visit relatives in Waterbury while Sheldon was a pastor in that Vermont town. Although she professed disinterest in him then, they were thrown together again on his moving to Topeka, since for several months he lived in a room in her family's home. Although her parents were good supporters of Central Church, which they had helped found, they were apparently not particularly taken with Sheldon, whom they regarded as overzealous in his demands for Christian living and social reform as well as unrealisitc about money.[52] The family, founders of a bank, was wealthy; Mary Merriam Sheldon once described her paternal grandfather, Samuel Merriam, as "an aristocrat of first degree" who wanted and got the best of everything.[53] Apparently her father followed the same course.[54] But as their children's relationship prospered, the parents on both sides swallowed whatever misgivings they might have had, and the marriage took place on May 20, 1891.

Despite Sheldon's great love of children, he had only one of his own, a son whom they named Merriam, born February 23, 1897. The child was a great joy to the Sheldons in his early years, but by the time he had reached early adulthood was tired of living in the shadow of his famous father and left Topeka. He ended up in his maternal grandfather's profession, banking, in Milwaukee. His life ended tragically when, depressed by illness, he committed suicide in 1964.[55]

E.B. Merriam had a house built for the Sheldons at 1515 W. 15th, near the church, and they lived there happily for several years. Little is known about their home life or even what the inside of their home looked like; about the closest thing we have to such an account is an 1899 comment which noted that the family home was "elegant but unpretentious" and "tastily but simply furnished, pictures of Biblical and church characters and scenes predominating in the wall decorations."[56]

Sheldon family life seems destined to remain a mystery. Never in any extant record is there a hint of overt discord. On the other hand, Mary Sheldon was a difficult person; some who knew her described her as neurotic. She seems to have shared, to some extent, her parents' impatience with Sheldon, the nice guy who couldn't turn anyone away and didn't manage his money well. It seems reasonably clear, as well, that Sheldon was not particularly close to his son. But details are missing. Without diaries or other intimate resource materials, we seem destined to remain ignorant.

Perhaps little is known of the Sheldon home life because there was little of it. Sheldon was so busy with his pastorate and other projects that it is hard to see how he could have squeezed out much time for the family. His church work was a labor of love, and he never expressed an iota of doubt about the rightness of what he was doing.

Before very many years had passed in Topeka, Sheldon had pretty well gotten his social and ecclesiastical bearings and had largely started on the course the rest of his life would take. His ideas and goals never changed in a major way after he was perhaps thirty-five years old. Perhaps the clearest thing that was established by then was that Sheldon was a person of action far more than one of reflection. Those who have undertaken to analyze Sheldon's thinking have come out looking at his activities. Speculating was never his strong point; doing and urging others to do was always his specialty.

Certainly he saw himself as a social gospeler by the time he was

Following In His Steps: *A Biography of Charles M. Sheldon*

Opposite: Mary Merriam Sheldon at age forty-five, 1909. Above: Charles Sheldon and his newborn son, Merriam, ca. 1897. Central Congregational Church (UCC), Topeka.

getting established in Topeka, and he was making his presence known, at least in a minor way, to his colleagues in the movement. He had earlier contributed articles with a social gospel flavor to the *Andover Review*, his seminary's journal; now he was writing for *The Kingdom*, the Minneapolis paper that was for a few years the flagship of the movement and particularly the mouthpiece for George Herron, whose ideas Sheldon found largely congenial. Meanwhile, he was living the social gospel even as he wrote about it, undertaking projects for the uplift of workers and the underprivileged.

The Sheldon family home at 1515 W. 15th, Topeka. Much of *In His Steps* was written, Sheldon later said, on this porch. Central Congregational Church (UCC), Topeka.

In Topeka, Sheldon did have his eyes opened to concrete social problems in a way that he never had before. Never before had he had such close association with blacks as when he took up a pastorate a stone's throw from a major black neighborhood, a poor district with every possibility of becoming a festering slum. Never before had he come in contact with the fruits of unemployment, with people whose situation seemed truly desperate. In Topeka Sheldon saw real human need. He saw what seemed a staggering problem with alcohol. Yet he also came to see clearly what seemed to him the real possibility of building the Kingdom of God on earth, and determined that he would participate in that construction project.

Sheldon's theology from Andover onward was always avowedly Christocentric, but his life was truly more centered on people than on Jesus. His love of those around him was boundless and relatively undiscriminating. He called himself a sociologist, but studying people academically was not what he meant by that; what he wanted was to experience them and to help them, individually and collectively, save their souls.

3. The Tennesseetown Projects

Nothing in Charles Sheldon's early ministry so energized him as the three weeks he spent getting to know the black Exodusters of Tennesseetown. His extensive and effective innovations aimed at lifting up the neighborhood and its residents constituted the social gospel project par excellence. Here a group of determined Christians made a real impact on a concrete social problem in their immediate backyard. The work made Sheldon famous, since it was widely reported in the regional press and to some extent in the national press. It also provided Sheldon with the stuff of one of his books, a thinly disguised piece of fiction called *The Redemption of Freetown*.[1]

The Tennesseetown settlement had emerged as a result of the Compromise of 1877, which ended Reconstruction and led to massive emigration of ex-slaves out of the South. Stories circulated of cheap lands in the West, and thousands of these "Exodusters," as they came to be called, left the Mississippi Valley for unknown destinations. Kansas was as logical a place to stop as any; the state had been admitted to the Union in 1861, at the beginning of the Civil War, and was widely known as a bastion of antislavery sentiment. There were already a few blacks living more or less comfortably, if not elegantly, in Topeka, and so in about 1879 a group of ex-slaves came north to survey eastern Kansas and found it acceptable. The "Exodusters" begged passage as fourth-class freight from their Tennessee homeland to St. Louis. Because they were not wanted in St. Louis, they received charitable assistance from the natives, which sent them on up the Missouri River to the Kansas City area.[2] Equally unwelcome there, they were sent upriver to Topeka, where some of them were taken in.[3]

By 1880, some forty thousand Exodusters had passed through Topeka. About three thousand of them stayed, making their homes on the southwestern outskirts of town, where a bankrupt real estate development had left some very cheap lots for sale. The Exodusters congregated there in such numbers that the area has been called "Tennesseetown" ever since.[4]

Many people in Topeka were less than thrilled about the influx of large numbers of destitute and uneducated ex-slaves, whose clothing was little more than rags and who had no money at all. Dr. Karl Menninger has noted that white racism was rampant then: "I wish I could recall and put into words the attitude of people toward blacks in those days. It was almost as if someone had imported a lot of people with leprosy or cancer or something terrible."[5] Topeka's Republican mayor Michael C. Case and other public officials refused to spend public funds or use municipal facilities to help the strangers, stating that the time and money would be better spent sending the immigrants back to the South.

Some of the churches were not much more helpful than the government. The Board of Church Extension of the Kansas Conference of the Methodist Episcopal Church met in Topeka in April 1879 to address the situation of the Exodusters, and adjourned without providing any material relief, discussing instead "how they shall be educated and christianized and prepared for honorable citizenship."[6] But gradually help began to emerge. First Congregational Church, true to its New England antislavery roots, provided some services and helped underwrite the construction of the Tennesseetown Congregational Church building, with the understanding that it would be a relief center as well as a religious edifice.[7]

Houses began to be built, mainly by the residents, although few of them were more than shacks hardly suitable for prairie winters. Gradually other urban conveniences—small businesses, schools, churches—came to dot the Tennesseetown landscape, and it was clear even to the hardliners that the Exodusters were in Topeka to stay. In the 1880 census, blacks were found to constitute 31 percent of the city's population—a higher percentage of blacks than was found in New Orleans (30 percent) that year.[8]

Living and social conditions in Tennesseetown were abysmal from the beginning. Unemployment was rife, a fact that the local white press attributed to the incompetence of the settlers.[9] A more accurate analysis, which Sheldon was the first white Topekan to enunciate, at least in public, was that white racism kept blacks in menial, terribly underpaid jobs when jobs were available at all, and that Tennesseetown's problems stemmed mainly from the neighborhood's wrenching poverty. One history of black Topeka reports that although there was some minimal improvement in conditions through the 1880s and early 1890s (some residents began to garden and traded produce for clothing and other necessities, for example), the district had minimal, if any, medical or educational or other basic human services, and by the 1890s had become the center of a fair amount of illegal activity, with "dramshops" and "popular resorts for sports" being advertised regularly in the black press.[10] Frequent police patrols tried to contain rampant juvenile crime and gambling, and even such police duty was dangerous.[11] Perhaps the biggest symbol of Tennesseetown's freewheeling nature was Jordan Hall, a large one-story building in the middle of the settlement, built by one Andrew Jordan, a black, for use as a dance hall. Fights usually accompanied the weekly dances, and (illegal) liquor was always for sale.[12]

Sheldon's Survey

Central Church sat on property bordering Tennesseetown. That the ghetto was a seamy place was well enough known in Topeka, but Sheldon surprised many of his fellow white citizens by plunging into the settlement for three weeks while he was examining the social conditions of the eight groups in Topeka not long after arriving in the city. What Sheldon did at that time was to conduct a simple sociological study, the results of which he published in the social gospel magazine *The Kingdom* a few years later. Sheldon found about eight hundred people in Tennesseetown, divided into three "distinct classes": those raised on plantations who came to Kansas during the

Exodus; men and women who were children during the Exodus and "have been raised under a definition of freedom which uses 'liberty' and 'lawlessness' as synonymous"; and children ten years old and under, including about a hundred between three and seven who might be considered of kindergarten age. Sheldon found four black churches that "were controlled by negro preachers, and exercising considerable influence, but not very much that could be called Christian influence." He noted seeing ignorance, poverty, vice, idleness, and rowdyism. During Sheldon's three weeks there he ate, worked, and talked with the residents, spending quite a bit of time in their homes and seeing their sordid poverty up close. At the end of the period he published his conclusions about it all, protesting the closing of decent jobs to blacks and the white prejudice that seemed so pervasive, and finding that the biggest part of the solution lay in reforming the attitudes of whites: "I do not have much hope of Christianizing the negro until we have Christianized the Anglo-Saxon. It is a present question with me now, sometimes, which race needs it more."[13] Tame stuff now, perhaps, but in the mid-nineties Sheldon was a great deal more perceptive than most members of his race.

Congregational and other Protestant missionary activity was being pursued in Tennesseetown well prior to the foundation of Central Church. In Sheldon's first study of the settlement in 1891 he found four churches there, three of them with pastors.[14] One of those churches was the Tennesseetown Congregational Church, a small missionary outpost. Tennesseetown as a whole, however, was largely unchurched, and the churches that existed were feeble, unable to combat the area's towering social problems.

Sheldon's first contacts with Tennesseetown, before his three-week visit, had apparently been hostile ones: the self-described "rabid prohibitionist" had urged raids on Andy Jordan's speakeasy, for example. But by 1891 Sheldon and a nearby Presbyterian minister, a Mr. Harris, began to give lectures every other Monday night to the men and boys of the settlement. The first one was an illustrated chemical and electrical lecture on "Light"; later ones in the series were on such topics as "One Dollar and What It Can Buy," "A Quart of Whisky and What It Can Do," and "What Has Been Done for the Negro Since the War." The lectures were apparently popular, and Sheldon and Harris used them as a foot in Tennesseetown's door. They began to visit the homes of those who attended the lectures, as well as other homes where they might find other interested persons. Thus, in fairly short order, they were able to learn quite a bit about the community.[15]

This informal survey, incidentally, was only the first of several serious efforts on the part of Central Church members to find out in detail about the needs of their black neighbors. The most important such effort was a probing house-to-house survey undertaken by Leroy Halbert and Mrs. M.L. Sherman in 1898. They visited 146 families, inquiring about religious preference (61 families each for Baptist and Methodist; 6 each for Catholic, Christian, and Congregational), earnings (the average was $6.15 per week for men, $3.22 for women), average house size (3 1/2 rooms), health, marital status, birth situation (167 had been born slaves), educational level achieved (generally quite low), and a host of other things. They discovered a very few fairly prosperous Tennesseetown residents, notably John Williams, who lived in a five-room painted house with a piano, made twelve hundred dollars per year, subscribed to a newspaper, and owned two hundred books. But at the other end of the spectrum, and closer to the norm, was the Wallace family, with twenty-three children all living at home, no assets, and virtually no income. The census document recording these findings makes for fascinating reading.[16] But we are getting ahead of our story.

The Kindergarten

Sheldon's early and less comprehensive survey led him to the conclusion that several important social services needed to be supplied to the settlement, and he determined that the first would be a kindergarten. Andrew Jordan, the dance-hall and speakeasy proprietor, readily agreed to lease his building for two years for the project (one must presume that the price offered him was more lucrative than income from the dance-hall business), and in the summer of 1892 fund-raising was undertaken in earnest. Some of the children who would be in the kindergarten helped raise money for it; Leroy Halbert's history of the Tennesseetown projects reports that a choir of "fifteen little darkey boys" sang a program of plantation songs at Central Church and made some money for the project.[17] More substantial amounts of money were raised from white charitable organizations and from individuals.

The renovation of Jordan Hall (which for the duration of the kindergarten's stay there was known as Union Hall) was a first step; the building had never been properly finished and was in poor repair. Many Central Church young people spent long evenings working on the structure and then plastering and painting.[18] By spring the work had been finished, and the first black kindergarten west of the Mississippi opened its doors on April 3, 1893, in the hall on Lincoln Street between King (now Munson) and Twelfth. There were three teachers: Carrie R. Roberts, the principal, and assistants Jeanette Miller and Margaret Adams. By the time the lease with Andy Jordan expired two years later, the kindergarten had become such a resounding success that more permanent quarters were established for it in the Tennesseetown Congregational Church building down the street to the north.

Many of the people of Tennesseetown had misgivings about the white intrusion into their community: some of them, quite naturally, saw it as an enemy invasion. But many Tennesseetown mothers had a desperate need for day care, and the kindergarten was a lifesaver for them. The children immediately liked the kindergarten, and their parents began to appreciate the colorful craft projects their children were carrying home. Soon acceptance of the kindergarten was total, and Sheldon had gained a foothold in Tennesseetown.[19] Dozens of Tennesseetown children were enrolled from the first; by 1900, there had been 287 of them altogether, including 57 enrolled that year. The school stayed in business for eighteen years, until 1910, by which time the city of Topeka had decided to support kindergartens and this one was moved to nearby Buchanan school.[20] Some of the alumni became important leaders in the Topeka black community, using the kindergarten as a first step toward formal education that would help lift them out of poverty. Probably the most prominent alumnus was Elisha Scott, in whom Sheldon took a special interest, years later arranging financial support for him to attend law school at Washburn University. Scott became a leading Topeka attorney, as did his sons John Scott and Charles Sheldon Scott. The Scotts argued many early civil rights and school desegregation cases. Their most illustrious moment came in 1954 when Charles Scott argued the winning side of the landmark *Brown v. Board of Education* school desegregation case before the U.S. Supreme Court. The Scott family law firm continues to handle civil rights cases today.

Little information has been preserved about what actually was done on a daily basis in the kindergarten during its first five years. In February 1898, however, an assistant in training, Mrs. June Chapman, was promoted to the head teachership when her predecessor resigned, and she kept that job for twelve years—as long as the kindergarten lasted.[21] A good deal of information has been preserved from her era.

Chapman's first morning on the job, it appears, was chaotic, with children running everywhere. As their first task, the teachers undertook to clean up their charges, washing them and putting clean aprons over their dirty clothes. Evidently Chapman's cleanliness program infiltrated the children's homes, because by 1900 they were reported to be arriving neat and clean.[22] Making an impact on Tennesseetown home life, in fact, seemed to be a main point of Chapman's program. For example, she had the children eat lunch at the kindergarten every Friday in order to drill them in table manners, and once she made each child a set of cardboard keys, writing on them such things as "Good morning," "Good night," "If you please," and "Thank you."

But Chapman didn't limit her interest in home life to instructing her pupils; she also made a regular practice of visiting Tennesseetown homes in the afternoons, and soon became a welcome visitor. Several of the women of Tennesseetown joined her in the program of home extension visits. Among them was "Aunty" Ransome, an

Sheldon kindergarten class at play with June Chapman. Kansas State Historical Society.

Kindergarten pupils celebrate Friedrich Froebel's birthday. Kansas State Historical Society.

elderly ex-slave who also visited the kindergarten from time to time to tell stories of slavery days.

The warm response Chapman received in response to her home visits led her to create an organization, a sort of PTA, for the mothers of the pupils. On one Wednesday afternoon a mothers' meeting was held at the kindergarten, and so many mothers attended and voiced their enthusiasm about the project that a permanent organization was formed.[23] A December 1900 count showed forty-three Tennesseetown mothers in the Sheldon League of American Mothers;[24] by 1906, at least, the Sheldon Congress of Mothers, as it was then called, was planning its monthly meetings so carefully that an annual brochure listing meetings and topics was printed.[25] Meanwhile Chapman organized yet another group, the Tennesseetown Kindergarten Auxiliary, from outside the settlement to provide volunteer help with the class and to help raise funds for equipment and supplies.[26]

In the summer the kindergarteners got lessons in gardening. An undated clipping from the turn-of-the-century era describes the young students as getting ready to harvest the produce of their garden at King and Lincoln streets: cotton, watermelons, and popcorn, "as well as a number of other garden and field products."[27] They also

Opposite: The Sheldon Kindergarten Band. Above: Kindergarten class on Washington's birthday. Kansas State Historical Society.

grew flowers, and at least once took advantage of a *Topeka Daily Capital* seed giveaway designed to promote flower gardening among children. Chapman marched her charges down to the newspaper office to pick up the seeds, and the paper reported that "they yelled with a vim, and the boys swung their caps in the air over their heads while straining in their lungs to the utmost. They brought with them some handsome tulips which they raised on the kindergarten grounds from bulbs planted last fall."[28]

Yet another Chapman project was a kindergarten band, an ensemble of twenty-five cornets, which specialized in marches.[29] There were other outings as well, including one to the state capitol, where the class visited Governor Edward W. Hoch.[30] There were also frequent special observances at the kindergarten building. In 1898,

The Tennesseetown Projects   55

for example, the kindergarten had a celebration of the birthday of Friedrich Froebel, founder of the kindergarten movement, with lots of colorful decorations, a new picture of Froebel, and a grand march around the classroom with the children carrying American and German flags.[31] Once a year there was a "crumb party" for feeding birds and animals in the winter.

The verdict on Chapman's leadership seems to be unanimous: she did marvelous work for the kindergarten, and probably played no little part in convincing the citizens of Topeka to fund kindergartens in all the elementary schools of the city. Twice Chapman and her charges received recognition from other parts of the country for their work. In 1904 she packed up some of the children's arts and crafts and sent them to a kindergarten competition at the St. Louis World's Fair (the Louisiana Purchase Exhibition), winning second place in the nationwide contest (first place was taken by a white kindergarten). Another bundle of similar materials was sent to the Jamestown Tercentennial Exposition in 1907, and another national second prize was awarded to the Topeka youngsters. Incidentally, the name of the preschool was changed at the time of the St. Louis competition; the proud Kansas sponsors of the entry feared that those attending the fair might confuse Tennesseetown with the state of Tennessee, and so the name of the kindergarten was changed from "Tennesseetown" to "Sheldon."[32]

Sheldon himself was held in near-reverence by the children. His frequent visits were favorite occasions in the classroom, and at least once, in 1905, when Sheldon was ill, the students made a wicker basket, filled it with a pumpkin, popcorn, vegetables, and flowers they had raised, and rolled it over to his house in a wagon. Sheldon repaid the compliment by writing a verse in honor of the pupils:

My brother of whatever tongue or race,
  Whatever be the color of thy skin;
Tho' either white or black or brown thy face,
  Thou art in God's great family—my kin.[33]

In 1981 there was at least one surviving student from the Sheldon kindergarten, Minus Gentry, then eighty-five. His memories of Sheldon were positive in the extreme: "He was a fine man, he was.

He'd come on down here to the kindergarten, to visit the kids, you know. He would talk to us and play with us, come shake hands with us. He was very generous, he was, a kind and generous man. Everybody loved him, everybody. If everybody in the world was like him, why, it would be a good world."[34]

The Library

Once Union Hall had been rented and the kindergarten established, it occurred to someone that the classroom space could be used in the evening as a library. The young people, especially the college students, of Central Church were enthusiastic about the idea and agreed to volunteer to staff the library. About the only need was for books, so Sheldon announced that a social would be held, the admission price to which would be a book. The social was thronged, and the books thus collected, along with others donated by the city library, enabled the library to open soon after the kindergarten did in 1893.[35] The book social became an annual affair, and the library's holdings eventually numbered in the thousands of volumes.

At first B.C. Duke, a member of the Tennesseetown Congregational Church, was put in charge of the library, but from the outset he had trouble riding herd over the clientele, and the library quickly became a hangout for rowdies—of which Tennesseetown still had plenty at that point. Finally one night he called the police and had six boys arrested for disturbing the peace. The publicity following that incident was disastrous, and, as Leroy Halbert reported, "the parents kept their children from the Library and it soon closed."[36]

But Sheldon never said die. In October 1894 the library opened again, this time with volunteer attendants from Central Church. A small social, with apples and donuts, was held for the boys who were the library's main patrons, and Sheldon gave them a pep talk, explaining why libraries had to be orderly places. Halbert dryly reported that Sheldon's earnest pleading, plus the memory of the arrests, kept the boys "to an endurable standard of order for a while." However, at least on the nights when lenient caretakers were in charge, "sometimes the Hall resembled a circus about as much as a reading room."[37]

When the lease from Andrew Jordan ran out in the fall of 1895, the library moved with the kindergarten to the Tennesseetown Congregational Church. Discipline problems continued; so far was the library from being a typical reading room that Minus Gentry rembered the library evenings as "game nights" where not-so-sedate activities, such as playing caroms, were the rule.[38] Halbert said that one volunteer staffer "needed a bottle of Paine's Celery Compound to restore his nerves after each experience in the Library." Apparently the youngsters continued, throughout the history of the library, to expand their minds mainly by throwing paperwads, pieces of coal, and books, and by blowing out the lights and rattling the blinds. Periodic Sheldon lectures on order may have helped, but the level of decorum was never high. Nevertheless, Halbert, like Sheldon, was optimistic about the library's usefulness: "It is the refractory boys who attract most of the attention, but there has always been an element of well behaved and studious patrons of the Library," some of whom read many books. Moreover, if they hadn't been in the library, what mischief might they have been causing elsewhere?[39] The library was, in fact, well patronized, and during two winters in the late nineties, Henry Burt, at that time the Washburn student hired to head the library, actually enticed a number of the young patrons to join a literary society featuring debates and recitations.[40] The library apparently lasted for many years; William H. Guild in 1981 recalled that he had surely worked in the library as late as 1909 and possibly as late as 1913, earning fifty cents a night for his efforts.[41]

Other Educational and Cultural Projects

Yet another use made of Union Hall was as a place to hold sewing classes for the schoolgirls of Tennesseetown. Ten women from Central Church, and one from a nearby Presbyterian church, supervised the project and furnished materials for the Saturday afternoon classes. By the fall of 1896 the project had become a substantial one, and Mrs. F.E. Sherman was hired to take charge of the class. By the fall of 1897 attendance was up to sixty, including virtually every girl in the neighborhood.[42]

In the meantime, the boys were not neglected. Basket-weaving classes were instituted for them; the boys could buy the necessary materials for about five cents and had no trouble selling the baskets they made for fifteen. The dime profit was a powerful motivator, and the basket-weaving classes led to the establishment of a manual training department at the Buchanan (public) school in Tennesseetown, with some of the classes conducted at the Tennesseetown church.[43] In November 1894, a Boys' Brigade was founded, featuring military marching and drilling, but discipline problems quickly did it in.[44]

Vocational education did not triumph in Tennesseetown at the expense of culture. Special musical and other entertainments were regular parts of the program for the uplift of the ghetto. Some of the performances involved nationally known ensembles, as in 1913 when the Fisk University Jubilee Singers gave a series of concerts to integrated audiences.[45]

Nor was the spiritual life of the settlement neglected. When Central Church was organized in 1888, some of the members were already helping with the Sunday school at the Tennesseetown church. Halbert wrote that "the first thing Mr. Sheldon ever did for Tennesseetown was to sing tenor in a quartet for the Sunday school." By the end of 1891, attendance was averaging fifty at the Sunday school; by 1899, it topped one hundred, helped in part by a series of interclass attendance competitions. Gradually some black leadership emerged, joining the white Central members in running the program. And members of the Sunday school began to raise part of their own support, Halbert told a touching story in this regard: "One poor boy may be seen from week to week going around picking up old iron, rubber, etc. These he sells to the junk dealer to get money for the Sunday school. Some times he spends considerable time in this way so as to get at least two pennies to bring to his class on Sunday. . . . An example of sacrifice like this furnishes inspiration enough to overbalance a great many discouragements." Meanwhile, services were held at the church itself, as distinct from the Sunday school, sometimes with the help of a black resident minister, but more often with preaching supply from Central or other churches. Also, a Christian Endeavor Society was started in August 1899, letting thirty or so Tennesseetown children become a part of that enormous nationwide youth movement.[46]

Social Services for Tennesseetown

Even as the various educational and cultural programs were being instituted, Sheldon saw the necessity for direct social services to the destitute residents of the settlement. Many such services eventually emerged. Some of them were offered on an organized basis— for example, several physicians provided free medical care, a lawyer gave free legal help, and E.B. Merriam, Sheldon's father-in-law and a prominent banker, made small interest-free loans to individuals in need.[47] Sheldon and a group of Central Church men organized a successful effort to find jobs for the men of the settlement,[48] and Sheldon's assistant pastor Leroy Halbert helped to found a Monday-morning nursery, freeing the mothers to do their laundry in peace.[49]

In many cases, such assistance was rendered by individuals, acting privately, and of course these instances cannot be enumerated fully. Many, for example, took to making regular Sunday afternoon calls on the elderly and ill of the settlement, sometimes staying for hours. Distribution of food and clothing took place frequently as well. Special efforts were made to check up on persons in need during the winter. A few reports of such home visitation have survived; one is Mrs. F.E. Sherman's account of recent activities to a Central Church annual meeting:

> One place I found a very old lady, nearly blind, to whom I carried a Thanksgiving dinner and read to her from the Bible. Another place I found a woman and two little children living in one small room without a window. The only light she had was from leaving the door open or lighting a lamp. I gave her clothing for the baby and food for herself and the other litle one. She was doing the best she could with what she

had. Another place I found an old lady nearly 100 years old, very destitute. I supplied her with warm underclothing and shoes. She was very cheerful; she showed me the only dress she had, a calico wrapper all worn to pieces. She said, "Can you get me a dress?" I told her I would. She was grateful for all the help she had. Another place an old man was very sick, a woman also sick and two little children. They were lacking almost anything to make life happy. With money received from the Ladies' Society, the whole house was cleaned, washing done and they were made more comfortable. The Christmas presents from Central Church made many hearts happy, filled many wants and were gratefully received.[50]

Sheldon personally, without fanfare, did as much as any member of his congregation to help where he could. His aversion to personal publicity undoubtedly caused many altruistic acts to go unnoticed, but sometimes word of them got out, as in the case of a Tennesseetown woman who was run down by a streecar and had her leg amputated: Sheldon sent her a wooden prosthesis, one early biographical article reported.[51] The works of mercy were manifold, and they were gratefully received.

The Village Improvement Society

One project that was relatively late in inception but that had a major impact on the settlement was the formation of the Village Improvement Society. Despite several years of a kindergarten, other educational projects, social services, and cultural and religious programs, Tennesseetown remained physically quite unattractive, with shabby houses and yards which were "for the most part, covered with tin cans, dead cats and rubbish."[52] A.B. Whiting, Sheldon's loyal and energetic deacon, stepped into that breach in January 1898 with the suggestion to Sheldon that prizes be offered to Tennesseetown residents to encourage them to improve their property. Sheldon responded by calling a meeting at the Tennesseetown church the next month to discuss Whiting's ideas, which had been refined into a fairly clear plan of action. The church was nearly full; most of the ministers and other leaders of the settlement were there. Sheldon and Whiting described the physical problems of Tennesseetown and then suggested their plan to attack them.

At first the reaction was mixed, although it is difficult to imagine that by 1898 Tennesseetown would have rejected any Sheldon plan. Some rose to say that they were already working on problems relating to houses and yards and did not need any special program. There was some resentment, naturally, toward the idea of whites' coming into the settlement once again, this time telling the residents how to live. Halbert said that "one woman spoke saying that she was as clean and neat as anybody and she did not need to be told to improve her place." She also worried that the do-gooders would want the people to quit keeping hogs, an important part of their winter food supply. But many others argued for the plan, and, on a vote, it was adopted.[53]

On March 7 another meeting was held and prizes were set up in such categories as gardening, beautification of premises, building repair, and housekeeping. In all, twenty-seven different individuals entered the nine competitions, many entering more than one. Garden seeds were provided for contestants in the gardening divisions, as well as for other Tennesseetown gardeners. The contestants took to their work with real spirit, and on October 18 a meeting was held to award the prizes. Thirty-five dollars in cash and that much or more in merchandise had been raised from local merchants, and there was a general call for another competition in 1899, so successful had the first one been.[54] Houses had been painted, yards had been sodded, alleys had been cleaned of trash, and the spirit of the settlement was much improved.

The competition was indeed repeated in 1899, and for several years thereafter. Many new categories of improvements were added, including some for food preservation. Several categories were also created especially for children. The *Topeka Daily Capital*, reporting on the fall festival at which the 1899 awards were given, counted eighteen categories of competition, covering gardening, neat premises, improvement of buildings and fences, interior house cleaning, flower gardening, and fresh and preserved garden produce for adults, and gardening, sewing, baking, and oratory for children. The second awards ceremony played to an overflow crowd that sat amid exhibitions of embroidery, quilts, fresh garden produce, preserves, handicrafts, and other such things. The boys between twelve and eighteen gave their orations, the winner in that competition receiving one dollar. Typical first prizes ran from one to four dollars in cash, or other awards such as six silverplated forks, a rocking chair, a pair of shoes, an umbrella, and a one-year subscription to the *Daily Capital*.[55] Halbert, describing the evening, wrote that

> the place looked like a county fair in miniature. . . . The whole exhibition was a credit to the community. In the evening a meeting was held at the church, where the declaimers competed and all the prizes were awarded. The church was packed with people and the enthusiasm ran high. About $50 in money was given out and a considerable amount of merchandise. After the prizes were given out, the woman who had spoken against the project the first year came around and said, "How is this? I entered for three things but I didn't get but two prizes." . . . The results of the plan in the improvement of the town are plainly visible.[56]

Two years later, in 1901, at the spring meeting of the Village Improvement Society, Sheldon delivered a speech in which he suggested that the positions of leadership in the Society, filled mainly by whites from Central Church, be turned over to blacks living in Tennesseetown. The transfer of power was quickly completed, although Central members remained active in their support of Society projects.[57]

The End of the Projects—What They Achieved

No single date marked the end of the Tennesseetown projects. Some of them faded away as local interests and needs changed; more of them never vanished at all but were taken over by governmental bodies as permanent public responsibilities. The kindergarten and various vocational training projects are good examples of the latter. After the legislature in 1907 authorized public kindergartens, the Topeka Board of Education took over the Sheldon original; and it thus may be said to be very much alive today, minus his name. Eventually the Tennesseetown Congregational Church, which had never been especially strong, came to be seen as less and less necessary in light of the development of several other strong churches, notably Shiloh Baptist, in the settlement. Finally the mission church building was sold in 1911.[58]

At the obvious level, the great success of most of the Tennesseetown projects is the measure of the worth of the effort poured into the settlement. The kindergarten was a pioneering, triumphant success story in that it served hundreds of families and ushered kindergartens into the Kansas public schools. The Village Improvement Society certainly contributed to the physical beautification of the neighborhood. The library undoubtedly made a noticeable contribution to literacy and the appreciation of good books. The sewing and manual training classes helped young people earn some money and trained them for jobs they desperately needed. On that level alone one must conclude that the effort Sheldon initiated was very much worth while.

Much of white Topeka was most impressed with the effects of the Village Improvement Society's cleanup program. In 1903 a Topeka newspaper beamed, "Tennesseetown has a prosperous look. Where formerly weeds grew in luxuriance, there are cane patches or cornfields or gardens. Where a few years ago there were a few old boards nailed together to represent a house, there is now a respectable little cottage. Where there was once a bare lawn of weeds, there is now often a lawn of blue-grass with park in front. There is a general look of enterprise instead of dilapidation."[59] Another booster a year later noted that even though Tennesseetown's streets were not paved, and there was no sewer in the neighborhood (the taxes for such things would, after all, "be a virtual confiscation of the property assessed"), nevertheless "the little district has more of a thriving look and is fast losing its tumble-down appearance."[60] A 1906 visitor took delight in the fact that an active interracial baseball game was in progress near Huntoon and Lincoln streets, where a dozen years earlier one could have expected to see only crap games on the sidewalk.[61]

But there were other results as well, less obvious ones. Although statistics for the period are hard to come by, several sources report that the crime rate in Tennesseetown dropped substantially during the 1890s—a result in which Sheldon took great pride.[62] And given that other white churches eventually came to see the merit of the projects and joined in working on them, it can be fairly said that Tennesseetown provided an early, practical demonstration of social reform through ecumenical outreach. Churches proved they could work together on worthwhile projects, and the Topeka congregations involved—at one time or another they represented most of the major Protestant denominations—practiced the social gospel at the grassroots level.

There was always a small undercurrent of resentment at the condescension implicit in the spectacle of whites entering a black neighborhood to improve it, but on the whole Tennesseetown welcomed its benefactors. Sheldon himself was nearly deified by those who had been lifted up from destitution to mere poverty; one of them once paid him the ultimate compliment: "Brother Sheldon, your face may be white, but your heart is just as black as mine!"[63]

To the twentieth-century historian, who has the benefit of having observed a century of social change programs, Sheldon's uplift of Tennesseetown still stands as a good, intelligent, balanced approach to community betterment. It didn't just provide gifts, but seriously promoted self-help. It wasn't just a palliative program, but an integrated mix of relief and educational endeavors, with a strong emphasis on helping people get jobs in a time and situation when they were hard to come by. The program certainly had its naive moments and some relative weaknesses, but on the whole it was more coherent, and did a lot more good, than a great many more costly and elaborate programs do today.

4. The Astounding Success of *In His Steps*

The publication and phenomenal sales of a simple but perceptive little novel called *In His Steps* catapulted Sheldon from local prominence as a crusading social gospel minister to world renown. Ever after 1897 he was eagerly sought out for interviews (which he rarely granted), his mail came in torrents, and his permanent marketability as a public speaker and writer was assured. For this unassuming novel—only one of many Sheldon wrote, the rest being modest successes at best—sold millions of copies, probably tens of millions, and was read by Christians and others the world over.

The story of the writing, publication, and circulation of *In His Steps* has been told many times, several of them by Sheldon and many more by his biographers and critics. But relatively rarely has the story been told accurately. Many exaggerations and myths quickly grew up around the book, and many of those who have written accounts marveling at its great success have never stopped to separate fact from fiction. Indeed, until Topeka historian John Ripley did a good deal of spadework in the mid-1960s and published two articles that demolished most of the more egregious myths, the story was apparently never written accurately.[1]

In His Steps was the seventh in a series of "sermon stories" which Sheldon had begun reading to his congregation in 1891. That sermonic form emerged from a problem familiar to more than a few pastors: low attendance, in this case at the Sunday evening services. The Central Church neighborhood was still thinly populated, and the stalwart souls who made up the membership were often not very inspired to turn out for an evening service after attending Sunday school, morning services, and the Christian Endeavor meeting in the afternoon. Other ministers might have considered discontinuing the service, but Sheldon felt challenged to fill the church. He identified as the problem his preaching of two sermons in one day; as he said in 1935, "I told all I know in the morning, and besides why should I preach another sermon to people who did not live up to the first one?"[2] Fairly quickly, in the summer of 1891, he hit upon his answer: he would write a story to be read to the congregation in place of a sermon, reading a chapter a week; and he would end each chapter at a critical point in the action, so that people would want to come back to see how the crisis was resolved. His sermon story format found some inspiration in Jesus' own methods of teaching, and Sheldon thought of his stories as resembling parables—that is, putting important ideas into the form of easily remembered stories.[3]

He began to work on his first story, which he called "Richard Bruce, or The Life That Now Is," that summer. The reading of it began in September, and the young pastor was so intent on making his project work that he had a synopsis printed each week summarizing the story to that point. Within three weeks the church was packed on Sunday nights. People came from many other churches as well as from Central. Sheldon went on to read thirty sermon stories to Sunday evening audiences, all the way until his retirement in 1919. The normal pattern was to begin a story in September and read it in twelve installments, ending it just before the Washburn College students were due to leave for the holidays. Interest never flagged; the church remained packed throughout the thirty years. Sheldon always believed that people were inherently religious, and that religion was an exciting topic, and that those facts, plus the novelty of what he was doing, attracted the crowds. But beyond that the draw was great because of Sheldon's narrative techniques: his ability to leave stories hanging at the ends of chapters, hinting of future developments; his consistent inclusion of a happy love story in each tale; his clear social commitment, hinting at the social gospel radicalism he could never bring himself to advocate in the nonfiction world; and his ability to communicate simply and clearly.[4]

And so the stories, all eventually published as novels, poured

Read in Central Church, beginning Sunday, evening, October 4. 1896.

In His Steps.

Chapter I.

For hereunto were ye called: because Christ also suffered for you, leaving you an example, that ye should follow his steps.

It was ~~Saturday~~ Friday morning and the Rev. ~~John Raymond~~ Henry Maxwell was trying to finish his Sunday morning sermon. He had been interrupted several times and was growing nervous as the morning wore away, and the sermon grew very slowly towards a satisfactory finish "Mary," he called to his wife, as he went up stairs after the last interruption, "if any one comes after this, I wish you would tell

The first page of the manuscript of *In His Steps.* Humanities Research Center, University of Texas.

out. After "Richard Bruce," which was the 1891 story, came "Robert Hardy's Seven Days," "The Twentieth Door," "The Crucifixion of Philip Strong," "John King's Question Class," "His Brother's Keeper"— and then, in 1896, "In His Steps." (If the reader is counting years, be advised that two sermon stories were read in either 1893 or 1894— the record is not quite clear.) Several of the earlier stories were among Sheldon's best work. *Robert Hardy's Seven Days*, for example, was the story of a man who was told he had only a week to live— and chose to make it a week of committed Christian living. *His Brother's Keeper* was set at a strike in the iron mines of Upper Michigan. *The Crucifixion of Philip Strong* was the story of a crusading social gospel minister who gave up all for the cause.

Before we proceed with the story of *In His Steps*, it would be well to mention that Sheldon's novel belonged to a genre quite popular at the turn of the century. Like many other noble social movements, the social gospel produced its own popular propaganda. Thus the social gospel novel emerged as a type of fiction that analyzed the social problems of the nation from a social gospel point of view, typically touching on the inequities between the rich and the poor, assessing labor-management conflicts, and identifying individual activities, such as drinking, that were seen as interfering with social progress. These novels went on to offer a social gospel solution to the problem or problems specific to the book—usually an exhortation to Christians to clean up their personal lives and go to work reconstructing the social order, working to bring in the Kingdom of God on earth—almost invariably in the spirit of optimism and idealism which so characterized social gospel thinking. The novels tended to be overly sentimental, theologically sloppy, and literarily forgettable (Sheldon's were all of those things), but they do reflect the sense of crisis that the churches were feeling in an era in which modern science was threatening evangelical faith, and urbanization and industrialization were changing the American way of life.[5] As Wallace Davies has noted, the novels at least document the extent of guilt feelings among the middle class over the growth of poverty, economic injustice, and the churches' neglect of the working class.[6]

It is difficult to date the birth of the genre precisely, but it certainly began a decade or two before Sheldon started composing his sermon stories. Henry F. May points to *The Silent Partner*, published by Elizabeth Stuart Phelps in 1871, as being one of the first, characterizing the novel as a "ghastly and detailed picture of labor conditions in a New England textile mill town," in which a frivolous society lass inherits the mill and, with a newly serious attitude, works to improve conditions there.[7] One of the first such novels to gain widespread recognition, in this case because of the eminence of its author, was *The Christian League of Connecticut*, by Washington Gladden. Published in book form in 1893, the novel told the story of a minister and one of his prominent parishioners who formed a "Christian League Club of New Albion" (the fictional Connecticut city where the novel was set) to do mighty works of evangelism, relief, ecumenism, and social reform in the poorer parts of town, succeeding so spectacularly that the work of the League finally spread to cities throughout the land.[8] Soon there was a flood of social gospel novels, including such works as *The Union League Club*, a sequel to Gladden's *Christian League*, by R.E. Porter; *How They Lived in Hampton*, by Edward Everett Hale; and *Murvale Eastman, Christian Socialist*, by Albion W. Tourgee.[9] The genre probably reached its highest literary development with the works of William Dean Howells, an active social gospeler who joined W.D.P. Bliss's Church of the Carpenter in Boston; his most compelling social gospel novels were the utopian *A Traveller from Altruria* (which inspired the founding of several communes and a string of Altrurian Clubs based on its principles), *A Hazard of New Fortunes*, and *Annie Kilburn*.[10] C. Howard Hopkins, the historian of the social gospel, analyzed this literary outcropping thus: "Fully awake to the social emergency, its evangelistic fervor yet failed to project social goals and techniques commensurate with the demands of the crisis. Nevertheless, the social-gospel novel brought social religion to the attention of millions of laymen who might never have heard of it otherwise."[11]

Sheldon was certainly familiar with other social gospel novels; indeed, some of his ideas seem to have been adapted from them. Clarence Gohdes in 1954 argued that Sheldon's project of donning old clothes and going out to look for a job came directly from the British social gospel novel *Robert Elsmere*, by Mrs. Humphrey

Ward,[12] a book that began by illustrating the ugly underside of rural English life, where absentee landlords exploited poor tenants, and then shifted to London, vividly showing the gap between the rich and the poor, and the work social reformers were doing to try to close it.[13] A popular nonfiction social gospel book, *If Christ Came to Chicago*, by W.T. Stead, must have had an impact on Sheldon's thinking, since in places *In His Steps* strikingly resembles it. Indeed, in a reissue of his 1894 book, Stead in a new preface virtually accused Sheldon of stealing his ideas:

> Not only is the watchword ["What would Jesus do?" was Sheldon's version of it] of the two books the same, but the same remedy is propounded in both cases. Mr. Sheldon dwells more on the evils of the saloon than I saw any reason to do, and he lays much stress on Sunday journalism, of which I said little or nothing. But with these exceptions, "In His Steps," alike in its diagnosis of the disease and in the remedy which it prescribes, might have been written for the express purpose of popularizing the teaching of "If Christ Came to Chicago."[14]

Actually, Stead overstated his claim. The watchword of his book was not "What would Jesus do?" or "In His Steps," but "Be a Christ!" The closest he came to Sheldon's motto was at the end of his book, when he urged his readers, "For what He would have you to do is to follow in His footsteps and be a Christ to those among whom you live, in the family, in the workshop, in the city and in the State."[15] Nevertheless, he and Sheldon were very closely aligned ideologically, having been shaped by similar environments, and were both effective propagandists for the social gospel.

Whatever can be said of the rest of the genre, Sheldon, with a single volume, became the king of it. His was the only social gospel novel that saturated the reading public of the English-speaking world.

In His Steps: The Story

The story was set in the fictional small midwestern city of Raymond. Its chief hero, the Rev. Henry Maxwell, was the pastor of the

First Church of Raymond. The novel opened on a Friday morning, when Maxwell was trying to finish his Sunday sermon, using for a text 1 Peter 2:21—"For hereunto were ye called; because Christ also suffered for you, leaving you an example that ye should follow his steps." Suddenly he was interrupted by the doorbell; a tramp had stopped, asking the minister for help in finding a job. Maxwell, irritated at the interruption, replied that jobs were tight and that he could not help.[16]

On Sunday morning the fashionable First Church held its morning service, and Maxwell preached earnestly on following in the steps of Jesus. When he finished he sat down and the choir rose to sing, but suddenly there was an interruption—a man was speaking aloud from the back of the sanctuary. The startled church fell silent as the interloper walked down to the space in front of the pulpit and turned to face the congregation, announcing that he wanted "the satisfaction of thinking that I said my say in a place like this before this sort of crowd." Maxwell recognized that his tramp from the previous Friday was back again, still wearing the same shabby clothing, still unkempt in appearance.

No one made any move to stop the tramp, and so he launched into a speech. The speech was an eloquent one, one that challenged Raymond's elegant Christians to mean what they said when they talked about discipleship. After several minutes of speaking the tramp collapsed, and soon thereafter died. By the next Sunday, though, Henry Maxwell and fifty of his parishioners pledged to remake their lives by asking themselves, "what would Jesus do?" when faced with a moral decision.

The rest of the book illustrates the manner in which the experiment in Jesus-like living was carried out. The first episode is that of Ed Norman, editor of the Raymond *Daily News*, who applied the "What would Jesus do?" test to his paper. He banned objectionable news (including that for liquor and cigars) and stopped publishing his Sunday edition. The paper went broke, but at a critical moment was bailed out by an heiress and eventually prospered. Another character, singer Rachel Winslow, turned down a lucrative offer from a touring opera company in order to sing at revivals in the slums.

Henry Maxwell simply devoted himself more firmly to his pastorate, preaching fearlessly, aiding great causes (such as prohibition), and helping the poor. Several of those who took the Pledge began to hold revivals in the Rectangle, Raymond's slum district. A few souls began to be saved, but in a tense moment some of the Rectangle's sinners started to throw things at the revivalists, and one of the newly saved Rectangle dwellers, a young woman named Loreen, was killed by a thrown "heavy bottle"—clearly a liquor bottle. Still the reformers pressed on. Virginia Page, the heiress who saved the newspaper, devoted much of her fortune to housing and other improvements in the Rectangle.

Word of the reform of Raymond began to spread, and visitors from afar, notably Chicago, came to see the good works. When they returned to Chicago they initiated similar projects there, helping the poor and redeeming wretched souls. The last third or so of the book is set in Chicago, with a faithful band carrying out projects and making converts despite harassments and shortcomings. The story ends with Maxwell, in Chicago to to tell the Raymond story to a large church audience, praying and having a vision of people walking In His Steps. Throughout the story are concrete descriptions of a multitude of social-gospel projects, from feeding the poor to finding jobs for the unemployed. There is a personal side to the book as well, especially in the love stories which peek out at several points as some of the characters court and marry each other.

Sheldon began to write *In His Steps* in the summer of 1896, composing much of it on his front porch on hot summer days. There was apparently only one draft of the novel; the manuscript, which now resides at the University of Texas, reads like the published work and contains few changes.

The original reading of the story, which took place on consecutive Sunday nights beginning on October 4, 1896, was relatively uneventful. The church was packed on the night of the first installment—not only because a new sermon story was beginning, but because the crusading social gospel minister had promised to reveal the names and locations of illegal bars that evening. The *Topeka State*

Above: Loreen, tragic heroine of *In His Steps*. Illustration by Stereopticon and Film Exchange, 1900. Opposite: Loreen. Illustration from Ward, Locke and Co. edition, 1899. Central Congregational Church (UCC), Topeka.

Journal saw fit to cover the happenings at Central Church that night, concentrating exclusively on the antiliquor revelations, save for a throwaway line, "After this prelude the pastor began his story-sermon upon the subject: 'In His Steps.'"[17]

But even as Sheldon was reading it on successive Sundays, the story was reaching a wider public. Shortly after Sheldon began reading the story at Central Church, *The Advance*, a private weekly magazine published "in the interests of Congregationalism," purchased serial rights to the story for seventy-five dollars, and on November 5, 1896, began publishing it chapter by chapter. The purchase price

was a generous one; the magazine with a relatively modest circulation of twenty-one-thousand usually did not pay its authors.[18] But James A. Adams, the editor of *The Advance*, must have thought he had a hot property on his hands. In fact *The Advance* had similarly serialized two of Sheldon's earlier sermon stories (*Robert Hardy's Seven Days* and *The Crucifixion of Philip Strong*), and, according to John Ripley, all six previous sermon stories had been serialized and then published as books.[19] So *The Advance* knew it was working with an established writer and made a good bet. The response was strong; readers, *Advance* publisher John Caleb Kilner said in 1897, were sending a "great quantity of letters, from all parts of the country" praising the story and urging its publication in book form.[20]

Soon thereafter Sheldon tried to sell the book to major publishers in Chicago. He approached at least two of them, the McClurg Company and Fleming H. Revell. They both (or all) turned him down cold. In 1920 Sheldon said of the publishers, "They never told me" why they rejected the book,[21] but by 1938 he was reporting that "the editors and readers of each company politely regretted that, as the public was not interested in a religious story, it would not pay to publish it."[22] That hardly rings true; the best-selling book of 1897 in the U.S. was *Quo Vadis?*, by Henryk Sienkiewicz, and other thoroughly religious best sellers, including Hall Caine's *The Christian*, were also in circulation then. Writers in this century have generally assumed that the editors at the publishing houses simply found Sheldon's work not good enough, and tried to give him a gentle rejection. About the best insight we have into the situation comes from another memory, this one from George Doran's autobiography, written in 1935. Doran, who was an office boy at the Fleming H. Revell Company in Chicago when Sheldon turned up there, wrote, "About that time we all of us made an unusually bad guess in publishing. . . . Sheldon brought the book, *In His Steps: What Would Jesus Do?* to us and literally begged us to issue it in book form. But no, it was too revolutionary, too intensely practical. Evangelical as was our effort, this did not extend to the point where we would present Jesus as Sheldon did, as the intimate and concerned personal friend of mankind. Thrice we declined the publication. . . . We had missed

THE
ADVANCE

Published Weekly in the interests of Congregationalism.

Volume xxxii   CHICAGO THURSDAY Nov. 5. 1896   Number 1617

REV. CHARLES M. SHELDON.
Central Church, Topeka, Kan.
Author of Our Serial.

THE ADVANCE PUBLISHING CO
215 MADISON ST CHICAGO ILL.

Sheldon featured on the cover of the *Advance* on the occasion of the publication of the first installment of his new serial, *In His Steps*. Kansas State Historical Society.

The Astounding Success of *In His Steps*   77

a golden opportunity. We were approaching 1896, politics was seething, religion was pushed somewhat into the background. We were entering upon a new phase of social and religious life."[23]

Giving up on the big time, Sheldon returned to *The Advance* and its company to issue the book. It did, with two simultaneous first editions, a twenty-five-cent paperback and a cloth book for a dollar, in June, 1897. Sales of the Advance company's editions fairly quickly reached up into the hundreds of thousands; the book was popular from the first and might well have approached a million copies in sales without any further help. However, in 1899 the dam burst. Other publishers figured out that Sheldon's copyright—the Advance editions carried a standard copyright notice—was invalid, and the first of dozens, perhaps hundreds, of unauthorized editions emerged. The copyright defect was caused by *The Advance's* practice, common among small periodicals at the time, of never copyrighting any of its issues; the contents of the entire magazine were thus in the public domain. Sheldon's two earlier sermon stories published in *The Advance* (*Robert Hardy's Seven Days* and *The Crucifixion of Philip Strong*) were similarly not protected by copyright and, following the phenomenal success of *In His Steps*, also appeared in pirate editions. When it became clear in 1899 that the Advance company was losing its most valuable property, publisher John Kilner began to copyright the magazine—but no other such heavyweight properties ever turned up for him again.

The lack of a valid copyright cut deeply into Sheldon's royalties, as one would expect. Over the years wildly varying stories—including several different ones from Sheldon himself—have portrayed him as making nothing at all, very little, or a small fortune from the book. Since Sheldon's own accounts vary, exact figures will never be obtained, but it is fair to say that his receipts were exceedingly modest in relation to the success of the book. On the other hand, the oft-repeated assertion that he got nothing at all—best exemplified in a Ripley's "Believe It or Not" syndicated cartoon (picturing the pastor-author in front of a veritable mountain of copies of the book), which appeared in newspapers on August 5, 1938, asserting that Sheldon "never received a cent in royalties!"—is also wide of the mark.

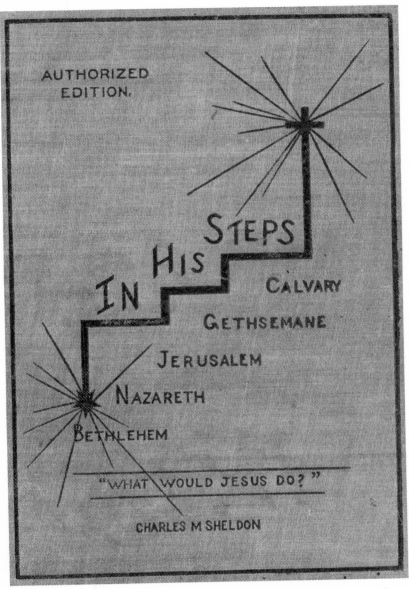

AUTHORIZED EDITION.

STEPS

IN HIS

CALVARY

GETHSEMANE

JERUSALEM

NAZARETH

BETHLEHEM

"WHAT WOULD JESUS DO?"

CHARLES M SHELDON

The cover of the first edition of *In His Steps*, issued by the Advance Publishing Co. Collection of Timothy Miller.

NEW EDITION.

IN HIS STEPS

"What Would Jesus Do?"

BY REV. CHARLES M. SHELDON.

Now ready—a new and authorized edition of this, the most famous book of the century.

5 CENTS PER COPY, BY MAIL, PREPAID.

Pamphlet edition, printed from new type, on good book paper, profusely illustrated with new and original engravings, heavy enameled paper covers with handsome engraved design.

Also, a Library edition, on extra heavy paper, cloth back and corners, ornamented sides. By mail, prepaid, 25 cents per copy.

Either of above editions sent by mail, prepaid, to any address, on receipt of price.

DAVID C. COOK PUBLISHING CO., 36 WASHINGTON ST., CHICAGO.

A fair guess is that Sheldon probably got at least ten thousand dollars in royalties from the book—not much less, but possibly quite a lot more. Grosset and Dunlap published an edition of *In His Steps* for many years and alone among American publishers of the book kept paying Sheldon royalties; by the time of Sheldon's death these payments had totalled about seven thousand dollars.[24] The David C. Cook Publishing Company claimed that it paid Sheldon a 10 percent royalty on its five-cent edition, which sold over half a mil-

Advertisements for *In His Steps*, ca. 1899. Shawnee County Historical Society.

lion copies, that would have come to over $2,500.[25] Sheldon wrote in 1933 that a British publisher who sold 3 million copies of *In His Steps* and other Sheldon works once sent him twenty pounds (then about a hundred dollars).[26] A reporter who interviewed Sheldon in 1926 reported that Sheldon had told him that Ralph Waldo Trine had on his own initiative gone to the various publishers, asking them to pay Sheldon something, and Sheldon received some small checks from that effort; for example, Henry Altemus reportedly sent $150.[27] An undated letter in the Sheldon Room announces that the Afrikaans edition of the book is selling well and that the publishers are enclosing a check for $297.75 and will send another "within a few months."[28]

The biggest unknown in this equation is the money Sheldon received from the Advance company. He admitted to getting only $275—$75 for the original serial installments and $200 in 10 percent royalties on 20,000 copies of the book, which sold for ten cents each.[29] But the early copies of the book sold for twenty-five cents and one dollar, and sales surpassed 20,000 long before the copyright defect had become known. At the end of 1898 the Advance company reported sales of 397,000; Sheldon should still have been receiving royalties then, and no dime books had yet been issued. At the beginning of 1900, a few months into the pirate-edition era, Advance sales were reported to be nearing 600,000.[30] Even if Advance quit paying Sheldon when the novel was known to have entered the public domain, he should have got quite a tidy sum before that time. Sheldon says in his autobiography that Advance "paid the author ten per cent royalty on all sales as long as they continued in the business."[31] If that is true, he was paid well over $6,000 on Advance's sales of over 600,000. Thus a guess of a minimum of $10,000 from all sources seems fair; if Advance paid its contractual royalties, and if it reported sales accurately, Sheldon's income should have reached several times that figure. Given his loud complaining later in life about being shorted, it would seem unlikely that his remuneration was many tens of thousands of dollars. On the other hand, the money trickled in slowly; the $7,000 from Grosset and Dunlap came in over several decades. Perhaps the lack of a large sum all at once made Sheldon feel less adequately paid than he really was. Whatever he made, though, fame far outdistanced fortune as Sheldon's reward for writing a blockbuster.

Proliferation

The first mass-market publisher to print the book was Street and Smith, a big reprint house. The first Street and Smith offer for rights to the book (even though the firm was apparently aware that the copyright was worthless) would have resulted in an edition of the book that would have carried the copyright notice and would pay the usual royalties. J.C. Kilner of the Advance company, however, had gone to Europe, and his staff would not give the permission for the reprint without Kilner's go-ahead. Then Street and Smith learned that J.S. Ogilvie was aware of the copyright defect, and so they went ahead and issued their edition—without the copyright notice. When Kilner returned he contacted lawyers in New York and Chicago; they all advised him not to sue for breach of copyright.[32]

It didn't take long for other publishers to get on the bandwagon. Sheldon wrote in 1933 that within a year the book had been issued by sixteen publishers, at prices ranging from a nickel to fifty cents.[33] By 1902 Sheldon was claiming that his two most popular books (the second was *The Crucifixion of Philip Strong*) had "been published and sold by over one hundred different firms in the United States and Europe."[34] His count may be slightly exaggerated, but several publishers issued multiple editions—gift editions, holiday editions, cheap paperbacks, and expensive clothbound books. There were many other publishers in foreign lands; no one really knows how many there ultimately were.

A number of special editions were printed for the exclusive use of particular firms. Possibly the biggest of such editions was one issued by the Woolworth company and sold in dime stores; Sheldon said that it sold for ten cents east of Chicago, and fifteen west of there.[35] In addition, the book turned up in countless millions of copies of newspapers and magazines. In 1899 and 1900, the American Press Association, a feature supplier to more than half the nation's sixteen thousand daily and weekly newspapers, offered *In His Steps* to its subscribers, and a great many of them surely used it. Some printed it as a serial; others printed the whole novel at once, typically as a special section of the paper.[36] Such reprinting was not confined to the United States; newspapers throughout the English-speaking world did the same thing.[37]

As well as the book was received in the United States, it probably did even better in Great Britain. British editions began to pour forth in 1898, ranging in price from six shillings downward to a penny. Sheldon wrote that there were over twenty-five British and continental publishers of the book, and that he had in his collection in 1933 forty-seven different foreign editions.[38] One publisher was reported to have sold one and a half million copies in two months, and within a year some 6 million copies were believed to have been sold in Great Britain.[39] Again there were several special editions, such as one commissioned by a Scotch grocer who had the name of his store printed at the bottom of every page.[40]

One report of Sheldon's success made his books out to be very popular indeed in Great Britain:

> A reporter of an English paper who went into a book store says: "The name loomed up everywhere in the shop. In front shilling editions, then nine pence editions, then four and one half pence editions, and then piled up heaps of the irreducible penny edition. In what dark unswept corner did 'John Ward, Preacher,' and 'Robert Elsmere' hide? Where were 'The Christian'? 'The Sorrows of Satan'? Not a trace of them to be found, all of them snowed under by the drifting masses of Sheldonian literature. There never was such an opportunity for the enterprising book seller. The books are coming out weekly, daily, according to the enthusiasm of the publisher. Mr. Bowden has sold very nearly one million copies of 'In His Steps,' and considerably more than a million of the other stories. Nothing half so wonderful has happened before in the publishing trade. Even Uncle Tom's Cabin, sold in the fifties, wet from the press, did not approach the colossal figures of Sheldon."[41]

The question of morality and proper theology was apparently a serious one in Great Britain; Sheldon claimed in his autobiography that

> several expurgated editions were published correcting the author's faulty theology by inserting the orthodox teaching of Christ. One of these, which the author cherishes as a literary curiosity, is entitled "The Rescue of Loreen," and it is interspersed with conversations and preaching intended to counteract the very dangerous influence of the original story. The compiler of this interesting amended edition was a Mrs. J.B. Horton. Her pamphlet sold by the thousands alongside the original "In His Steps," and was read by the extreme conservatives as an antidote to the first story.[42]

No one has any idea how many copies of In His Steps have been printed. If the count includes serial and periodical publications of the book, the total would surely be many tens of millions, at least. If one counts only book printings, the total might be as few as 8 or 10 million, or as many as 30 million. Given the circumstances of the book's proliferation, no one will ever have anything approaching an accurate count.

Sheldon himself claimed on several occasions that the circulation of the book was something over 20 million copies. In 1930, for example, he wrote,

> As to American and British editions, it is a question I am not able to answer with exactness as the different publishers of the book, whom I have written occasionally purely out of curiosity, refuse to report the sales. . . . But the Editor of the *Atlantic Monthly* [Edward Weeks] is my authority for stating that over eight million copies have been published and sold in the United States and over twelve million in Great Britain and Europe. The same estimate has been given by Mr. [Gilbert] Seldes [a prominent literary critic] in the *Saturday Evening Post*. These figures do not include the sales of translations of which there are over twenty. According to these men, the book has had the largest sale of any book ever printed with the exception of the Bible.[43]

But how did Edward Weeks and Gilbert Seldes get their estimates of Sheldon's book sales? From Sheldon himself! John Ripley has described how it happened:

> In the introductory paragraphs of his *Saturday Evening Post* article about best sellers, "Over the Tops," (Apr. 25, 1936), Gilbert Seldes gives full credit for his sales figures to Edward Weeks' "A Modern Estimate of American Best Sellers, 1875–1933," a paper presented at a meeting of the Institute of Arts and Sciences, Columbia University. Mr. Weeks' compilation of the sales records of sixty-five best sellers was also published in *Atlantic Monthly*, May 1934. *In His Steps* was placed at the top of the list with 8,000,000 copies. . . .

> Because Mr. Weeks was the first authority ever to include *In His Steps* in a recognized list of best sellers, let alone honoring it with the top spot, curiosity prompted this writer to try to obtain a copy of Mr. Weeks' paper to learn the source of his figures on *In His Steps*. In that respect we have not had any success, but no matter. Only recently we learned that many years ago Mr. Weeks himself revealed the source of his statistical information about *In His Steps*. In "The Best Sellers Since 1875" which appeared in *Publisher's Weekly*, April 21, 1934, Author

Weeks states that "—Charles Sheldon himself supplied me with the American sales of *In His Steps* [8,000,000] and added that world sales of the book must come close to 24,000,000."

Now there is a revelation that should go into the records as a rarely executed literary triple play, Sheldon to Weeks to Seldes and back to Sheldon.[44]

Weeks's estimate, however inaccurately derived, has been the basis for other reports of sales of 22, or 23, or 24 million copies—or maybe 30 million, if one adds the sales in foreign languages. In 1947, however, Frank Luther Mott, the dean of the school of journalism at the University of Missouri, questioned such totals, arguing that they were merely anecdotal. He got sales estimates from five U.S. publishers, totalling 540,000 copies, and concluded that 2 million American plus 6 million British copies might make a good guess.[45]

But my own guess is that Mott is too conservative. It seems to be fairly well established that Advance sold upwards of 600,000 copies, and very likely a million or so; Sheldon had a penny copy of the book from London which was imprinted either "969000th" or "971000th."[46] If there is no deceit here, then two publishers accounted for perhaps 2 million copies. Mott surveyed five publishers of the book and found that they averaged over 100,000 copies apiece; since there were over sixty publishers of the title at the time in the U.S. and Britain, several million sales are likely there. Moreover, the book was published in dozens of foreign languages and must have had substantial sales in at least some of them. Sheldon once wrote that he had been informed that over a million Japanese copies were sold.[47] But who will ever know the truth of it all?

The book's actual readership is even more difficult to estimate than the number of published copies. Clearly many of those millions of copies were each read by several persons. John Ripley has told of a woman who described to him just what rounds had been made by the copy she read in the first decade of the twentieth century:

> She remembers so well her school teacher's announcing that he'd bought a copy, a paperback of *In His Steps*. And after he read it, he passed it around to each family, where the children would take it home and Momma and adults would read it by daylight. And Father would

bring it out at night and read it by the lamplight after doing the chores. We were way down the line and that book was in bad condition, and the dog had torn it, but it went the rounds of eighteen families. Now just figure out the readership of that.[48]

Sales of the book, incidentally, continue to be as strong as ever. Peggy Greene of the *Topeka Daily Capital* reported that average annual sales during the 1960s were about 100,000.[49] At this writing some nine American publishers carry the book in eleven editions in English, including two large-print editions and a gift edition, and another publisher markets a Spanish edition. A comic book version was in print until recently. One presumes there wouldn't be so many in on the action if it were not worthwhile. When a special edition of the book was issued by the Shawnee County [Topeka] Historical Society in 1967, *Capper's Weekly*, a paper serving a predominantly rural and small-town midwestern audience, offered to sell copies to readers, and immediately got over a thousand orders.[50]

Just as the number of copies cannot be determined, so the number of translations seems destined to remain a mystery. In his latter years Sheldon told a reporter that he had thirty-two different translations in twenty-four languages but that he did not have a copy in Russian.[51] Just before his death he told Glenn Clark, who was interviewing him about a possible sequel to *In His Steps*, that he believed there had been forty-five translations.[52] But there is no hard evidence for such a claim. Several writers have offered lists of translations, but they rarely go beyond fifteen languages. By collating such lists, and presuming that they are founded in fact, one can come up with a master list of twenty-five to thirty languages. Even so, an exact count remains elusive, because some of the lists are vague or confusing. But certainly among the translations were ones into the major languages of Western Europe and several from Eastern Europe and the Middle and Far East. There are a few surprises: some lists, including Sheldon's, say that the book was translated into two constructed languages, Esperanto and Pasilaly. There were multiple translations into some languages. According to the best evidence I could find, *In His Steps* has been translated into the following languages: Arabic, Armenian, Bulgarian, Chinese, Czech, Danish, Dutch, Esperanto, French, Gaelic,

Cover of a 1977 comic book version of *In His Steps*. Spire Christian Comics, Fleming H. Revell Co. Copyright © Al Hartley. Used by permission.

A commercial advertisement from a Topeka firm playing on the fame of *In His Steps*. Sheldon sternly disapproved of such appropriations of his concept.

German, Greek, Hungarian, Italian, Japanese, Norwegian, Pasilaly, Persian, Polish, Portuguese, Russian, Spanish, Swedish, Telugu, Turkish, and Welsh. There were also, apparently, translations into one or more (East) Indian languages and into more than one African language.

In His Steps was a story begging for dramatization, and various dramatic adaptations have appeared over the years. One of the first

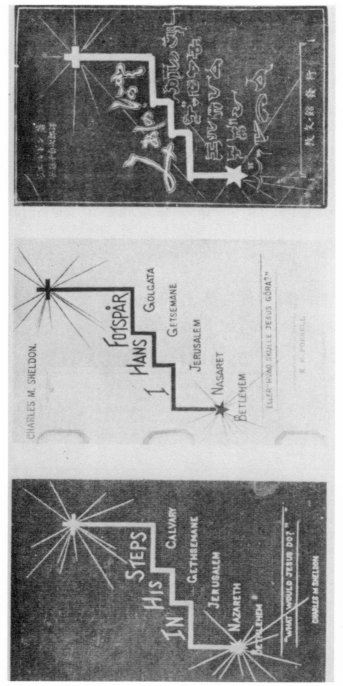

Covers of English, Swedish, and Japanese editions of *In His Steps*, all based on the original cover design by Myron Waterman, Sheldon's brother-in-law. Shawnee County Historical Society.

was handled by Sheldon himself, in collaboration with Professor F.H. Lane, the head of the theater department at Washburn College. The play was performed many times at Central Church, and on some occasions Sheldon himself appropriately took the role of Henry Maxwell. Another dramatic version received wide play—a radio adaptation consisting of twenty-six half-hour programs. The series premiered on KTSJ in Topeka on Easter Sunday, 1947, and was subsequently carried on many other stations in the United States and Canada.[53]

Perhaps the best dramatic version from an artistic standpoint, and certainly the most innovative, was a lantern-slide version that appeared in 1900. George Bond, a prominent Chicago lantern-slide photographer, produced a "photo play" of *In His Steps* which consisted of 150 hand-colored glass transparencies, together with a script. The pictures were posed by professional actors and were of remarkable quality. Sheldon never complained about Bond's appropriation of his marerial; indeed, he wrote Bond a letter commending the good work. Gerald D. McDonald of the New York Public Library once opined that Bond's version of Sheldon's novel was "the very first photographic screen adaptation of an American novel, and would set the pattern for the most successful type of Hollywood movies."[54]

In His Steps even made it into the musical world. The Sheldon collections at Central Church contain several pieces of sheet music entitled "In His Steps" and based on the book.

Of all Sheldon's experiences related to *In His Steps*, none was so frustrating, or expensive, as those involving the attempt to make a film version. The story begins in 1899, when Sheldon, needing money, sold all of his rights to *In His Steps*—at that point the rights were presumably virtually worthless—to the Advance company for one hundred dollars. It then jumps to 1916, when Sheldon began negotiating with a motion picture company for a film version of the book. By then the Advance Publishing Company had gone into receivership, and the receiver, hearing of the film project, claimed that he held the rights to the film, even though, as Sheldon later lamented, "at the time of the sale to the *Advance* the motion picture had not been invented."[55] Sheldon undoubtedly could have contested the claim, but he was not of a litigious nature, and so he borrowed five hundred dollars, the amount demanded by the Advance company receiver, and bought back his rights, which were actually in the public domain. Then the final irony: "Before further negotiations were completed with the screen company, it went bankrupt and the entire matter was dropped."[56]

There were several other false starts on the movie-making project over the next decade or two. Then, in 1936, the Grand National Film Corporation made and distributed a cinematic *In His Steps* without Sheldon's knowledge or consent. Sheldon was irate: "They advertised it as being suggested by the story. It was a cheap melodrama that did not have a single character, scene or lesson that is in the book. They even went so far as to advertise the film—'You have read the book, come and see the picture.'"[57] When Sheldon's comments were widely quoted, Grand National threatened him with a libel suit. Sheldon appealed to the Federal Trade Commission to remove the title from the film on the grounds that it was false and misleading; eventually, without FTC action, a successor company, Grand National Pictures, Inc., retitled the film *Sins of the Children*.[58] When the film reached Topeka, Sheldon conspicuously stayed away from the Jayhawk Theater where it played, but he had already seen the show in New York. The film portrayed a young couple who defied a feud between their fathers and eloped to the country to learn how to support themselves. The *Topeka State Journal* reported that "most of the Topeka pastors and their wives who saw the preview agreed that it was a fine show. None of them, however, saw any resemblance between the picture and Dr. Sheldon's book."[59]

The Book's Appeal

Many have explained the success of *In His Steps* as deriving mainly, or entirely, from the copyright problems and consequent flood of pirate editions; but of course its mere availability does not account for the book's success: people had to be waiting to buy all of those copies. Several things contributed to the book's enormous audience. For one, Sheldon was a hero to the millions of members of Christian Endeavor, the great ecumenical youth movement which at the turn of the century was at the peak of its influence, and the book made a perfect gift for Endeavor members to give to each other. One publisher, in fact, brought out a "Christian Endeavor Illustrated Edition," boxed, which sold for $1.50. There were other special editions as well. Since it could be procured very cheaply, some merchants used it as a premium, and a good many firms distributed copies to their employees.[60]

Peggy Greene has pointed out that "many church people disapproved of novels" in the 1890s, "but because *In His Steps* was called a 'sermon story,' they could enjoy it without feeling guilty."[61] Thus Sheldon may have located a unique market. It was certainly an easily comprehensible work that spoke directly to the average churchgoer. The social gospel, as propounded by intellectuals, had been around for several decades, and the religious public was aware that some religious leaders were critical of social inequity and injustice; but this was the book that really brought the social crisis home to the masses in direct fashion. The novel pointed out social problems which people could see immediately. For example, it attacked drunkenness; and by any standard liquor was viewed as a major social problem at the turn of the century, one which enormous numbers of Protestant church members felt it necessary to fight. Many laborers were obligated to work long hours, including Sundays; thus they could empathize with a book that called for just treatment of employees and observance of the sanctity of Sunday.[62] Gerald McDonald summed up well the appeal of the book

> as a novel of practical Christianity, with simple solutions offered for complex problems. It came out of an age of reform when idealists wanted to clean up politics, rid the cities of their slums, and find a personal answer to the moral confusion they knew existed in their own lives. Without reading at all like a sociological treatise, the book managed to touch briefly upon such topics as technological unemployment, trade unionism, monopolies, "the new woman," the single tax, socialism, temperance, pure foods, settlement houses and city missions, the cooperative movement and "the mess in city hall." It was timely, you see, and some of it was timeless."[63]

In His Steps had an impact far beyond the curiosity of its huge sales; millions among the readers were affected to a greater or lesser extent in their daily lives by their reactions to the book. Eric F. Goldman quite properly included Sheldon's novel on his list of thirteen books that have changed America, along with such other titles as *The Federalist Papers* and *Uncle Tom's Cabin*.[64] The writer who in 1899 asserted that Sheldon during the course of a year "preached to about ten times as many people as all the other Congregational ministers in the country put together" was not far off the mark.[65] In England, an unnamed town council, according to one report, took the pledge to make "What would Jesus do?" the test for its decisions.[66] And some readers were inspired to attempt action beyond the purely local sphere: the *Topeka State Journal* reported in July 1899 that a new United Christian Party was holding its first convention in Des Moines, nominating candidates for state and national offices, having adopted a declaration of principle which said, "We believe in direct legislation of the people, and in order to make a government from God through Christ, we should be governed in all things, lawmaking included, by the standard, 'What would Jesus do?'"[67]

Nowhere was there a stronger embrace of "Sheldonism" than in the Topeka preacher's own church. Before he had even finished reading the sermon story in the fall of 1896 a group had been organized in the church to try to live up to the motto, "What Would Jesus Do?" Most of Central Church's Christian Endeavor Society members and many other church members, including Sheldon, took the pledge to try to live up to the slogan.

By 1899 Sheldon had become a prominent public figure in the United States and in Great Britain, somewhat to his chagrin. He consistently declined interviews with the press, claiming that he wanted his book to stand on its own with its message, that he wanted people to know about his ideas, not about himself. For over two years he refused requests for interviews and declined to write for publication, except that he continued to write and publish his annual sermon stories.

Sheldon also became the eventual recipient of a torrent of mail, for years averaging hundreds of letters per week, and hundreds per

day at times. At first the letters were welcome; Sheldon greatly enjoyed receiving "scores of thousands" of them "from persons who
told him the story had changed their lives."[68] But as the flood grew
there were more and more letters asking for specific advice on
matters of moral urgency, as if, as L.D. Whittemore observed, people
felt that "a new and infallible rule of right had been discovered and
that moral questions could now be satisfactorily answered. And who
could better tell what Jesus would do than the writer of 'the book'?"
Sheldon's basic answer was, "I can not tell you what Jesus would do
in your place. It is for each one of you to ask what Jesus would do if
he were in your place and then do unhesitatingly what it seems
probably that he would do."[69] As the letters became a torrent, he was
unable to reply to them. Eventually a dominant theme appeared in
the letters: Sheldon was obviously a rich man, since he was the author of a runaway best seller, so he should do as Jesus would and
send some money to the letter-writer or to the writer's favorite Christian project. Sheldon, ironically, could not have afforded the postage
it would have taken to reply to such letters. But on they came, re-
questing thousands of dollars for a settlement house, or copies of all
of his books, or assistance in a project.

Critical Response to the Book

Any manifesto calling upon its readers to change their ways of
living is bound to inspire controversy, and Sheldon's certainly did
that. Newspaper editors, church leaders, and other opinion-makers
criticized the book soon after it was published, and the criticisms
have continued to surface over the years since. One might have
thought that the book was almost beyond criticism—except perhaps for its naiveté or less-than-brilliant literary style—since its advocacy of living a life in imitation of Christ simply revived an ancient
theme, one that had always been popular in the literature of all
branches of Christianity. But criticism there certainly was from the
first, and much of it came from the churches.

The most common criticism was to the effect that Sheldon was not a good writer. Although many of the more elegant critics disdained reviewing Sheldon's work at all, just as serious music critics would ignore Liberace, some did find it necessary to come to grips with this immensely popular writer. Yes, he could tell a simple story, they agreed, but his books were flat, lifeless, implausible. An 1899 article more or less summarized that line of criticism in two sentences: "The stories are not badly told, but, though they are trimmed up with some exciting incidents, they are not exciting. They do not contain a single epigram, and hardly a grain of humor."[70] Certainly few would argue that Sheldon's books were literary masterpieces. On the other hand, it had to be conceded that he managed to hold to a story line and keep the interest of the reader. In any event, Sheldon's goal was not to produce literature, but to prick consciences. It is also instructive to recall that *In His Steps* and the other sermon stories were all composed for oral, not written, presentation to young Protestant church audiences.

Some critics, focusing on content rather than style, went on to maintain that Sheldon couldn't literally have meant that we should try to act like Jesus, because the way Jesus lived was not necessarily the way he intended his followers to live. After all, they argued, we can't all be prophets and leaders and moral examples. One sympathetic critic, William E. Barton, gently pointed out that a lot of things very widely done—including many done by Sheldon himself—are perfectly compatible with the teachings of Jesus, even though Jesus didn't do them. For example, marriage and family are appropriate parts of life for most people, even though Jesus did not indulge in them.[71]

Some saw Sheldon's ideas as hopelessly simplistic. He exhibited a theology that invariably rewarded the virtuous and damned the wicked immediately. "For Mr. Sheldon is not one to let the virtuous man suffer for more than a moment of time," a British critic wrote in 1899:

> The wicked man has no chance of escape. . . . One poor girl, for no better reason that that she is selfish and has friends of the aristocratic name Vaspaile, dies most miserably mad. . . . It is also soothing to know, on the authority of Mr. Sheldon, that no accident and no dis-

ease can prove fatal to the truly virtuous. . . . It has been said that he knows no more of life than of the English language, that his morals are a kind of spiritual blackmail, as who should say, "Smoke a cigarette and you will be smashed up in a railway accident."[72]

Although Sheldon's writing does not excite the interest it once did, he continues to be criticized—and defended—today. For the last several decades the commentary has come principally from the groves of academe, as scholars continue to try to figure out the puzzle of the simple book that sold millions of copies. The passage of nearly a century has opened up the possibility of evaluating Sheldon in the context of his era; thus critical analysis of Sheldon in recent decades has tended to be more penetrating than the flood of shoot-from-the-hip criticisms that appeared when the book was at the peak of its popularity.

Probably the most incisive reappraisal, and one often harsh in its judgment of Sheldon's ideas, was that of Paul Boyer. After making the ritual acknowledgment of the book's "abysmal literary quality,"[73] Boyer opened up a whole new line of criticism of *In His Steps*: his thesis was that the novel is "concerned only minimally with religion, social justice or reform, but that it *is* concerned, almost obsessively, with certain psychological and emotional problems troubling the American middle class at the close of the 19th century."[74]

So what is the novel really about? Boyer proposes that the book's true significance lies in its demonstrating the fear and fascination that WASPs were experiencing over the immigrant workers crowding into their cities, as well as their own insecurity about their inadequacies as persons. Thus Sheldon's working-class neighborhoods are always "brutal, coarse, impure," reflecting the WASP fear of violence boiling up from the seething immigrant cauldron. Moreover, the book promotes the then-popular (among WASPs) idea that this potential violence is closely related to alcohol: "alcohol is a shorthand symbol for all that is menacing in the lower classes, so Prohibition becomes the all-important first step in defusing the working class's explosive potential.[75] In the face of this threat, the middle class has a secret weapon: "its moral fiber and force of character."[76] Thus *In His Steps* "holds out hope that the revolutionary potential of the slums—

though menacing and fearsome—may be eliminated if the middle-class virtues are transmitted to the working class in time."[77]

The characters of *In His Steps*, in Boyer's view, long for intimacy and a sense of community in their lives, and their real fulfillment comes when they experience passion and intimacy (several love stories surface now and then throughout the novel) and when they experience a sense of community that comes from their association with the poor. Thus *In His Steps* is significant, Boyer says, for its excellent glimpse into middle-class life at the turn of the century. The book may be weak in its social ideas, but "its grasp of psychological reality is firm and unerring."[78]

Other recent critics have followed Boyer's line of thought, and built upon it.[79] But the critics and revisionist analysts do not entirely control the current scholarship on Sheldon. Several have undertaken spirited rejoinders to the new critics. Sheldon's most vigorous defender in the last few years has been James Smylie, who has taken several of the major critics to task one by one:

> It is very easy, of course, to make a case against Sheldon for what seems to be a preoccupation with the liquor question and Sabbatarianism. It may be convenient to do this and overlook the fact that he was trying to give some direction in dealing with many of the major issues confronting people in his middle-class congregation and which were on the hearts of many Americans. Henry May is right when he calls attention to Sheldon's insistence upon a change of heart, but wrong when he implies that Sheldon left the matter there. Charles Hopkins is right when he sees that Sheldon makes a place for the works of charity, but wrong when he implies that Sheldon was not interested in justice too. Paul S. Boyer is right when he calls attention to the psychological fear which may be found in the novel. But he is wrong when he does not see the cases of conscience as genuine attempts to contribute to the public good, and not just attempts to insure a dominant role in society.
>
> Although it is very important to assess these various cases of conscience, we must keep in mind what seems to be Sheldon's primary purpose. He wanted to motivate his hearers and his readers and to give them an option for a life style not very popular in the "Gilded Age."[80]

In his own day, Sheldon rarely replied to his critics; he wanted people to read the book and make their own decisions about it, and he was well aware that whatever the critics might say, far more people were reading him than were reading them. On a very few occasions, however, he did come out of his shell to respond to criticisms he thought particularly unfair or ill-founded. After several critics had said that Sheldon was guilty of sacrilege because his book, in trying to get individuals to take Jesus into their daily decision-making, dragged the sacred down to the mundane level, Sheldon finally felt moved to reply:

> I will allow no man to go beyond me in reverence for Jesus Christ, whom I honor and love more than I honor and love any being ever born into this world. But I wish to utter my tremendous protest against the attempt to keep Jesus out of daily human life on the plea that it is sacrilege to bring Him into it. The real sacrilege consists not in asking every day, "What would Jesus do in my place?" but in *not* asking it. . . . The cry which the last century has heard very often, "let the preacher stick to the gospel, and not attempt to mix gospel and politics and business," is the cry of the spirit that does not reverence Jesus, and does not want to have him rule in the marketplace, or in any of the daily money-making or power-making walks of life. . . . The real sacrilege of human life is to exclude the Son of Man from man's life. The real reverence for Him is to place Him humbly, unostentatiously, but firmly, on the throne of every day's conduct."[81]

On his loss of royalties when the book went into the public domain Sheldon's attitude was inconsistent. Several times he complained rather harshly that the publishers doing well with his book were acting immorally, if not illegally, in not sharing their profits with him; but he was well aware that the lack of copyright was the reason why the book did so well, and he was extremely pleased at its circulation. His autobiography well summed up his thoughts:

> If the book had had a clear title the probability is that it would have had a small audience. The very fact that over fifty different publishers put the book out gave it a wide reading, and established its public as no one publisher could possibly have done.
>
> The only regret the author has perhaps felt as the years have gone on has been his helplessness to minister to the pitiful needs of those who have held up beseeching hands for help. . . .[82]

Before this chapter is closed it should be noted, again, that Sheldon wrote more than one book, even if a single title did far outsell the others combined. Publishers mindful of the success of *In His*

Steps readily issued the others, and, although lightning never struck again, several of the other books had respectable sales. Ironically (did Sheldon not learn his lesson?), several other books also had defective copyrights and ended up in multiple editions, although never nearly as many as *In His Steps* had. British sales were always strong; at least one other Sheldon novel (*His Brother's Keeper*) ended up being published in a cheap, mass-market edition in England, where it sold for a penny.[83]

Three of Sheldon's later books, *Jesus Is Here!*, *In His Steps Today*, and *In His Steps To-day* (why he gave two volumes virtually identical titles he never explained), were three different kinds of sequels to *In His Steps*. *Jesus Is Here!* drew by far the most notice of the three. It was set, initially, in the thoroughly reformed town of Raymond, fifteen years after the original church members had taken their pledge to ask, "What would Jesus do?" Suddenly Jesus returned to earth—in Raymond—to bring his message to the world once again. Jesus, who looked "like an average man—only—different"[84] to people who saw him, but whose image mysteriously didn't show up on photographic plates, spoke boldly against alcohol and tobacco, convinced the rich to roll up their sleeves and help the poor, led an audience out of a theater featuring a "notorious actress," and even stopped by to give some advice to the president. Sheldon received a great deal of criticism for his portrayal of Jesus as a man in a business suit; some found it all irreverent.[85]

The other two sequels received little attention. *In His Steps Today*, a very short novel, described the doings of the Ward family after Mr. Ward read *In His Steps* again and the family decided to take the "what would Jesus do?" pledge. *In His Steps To-day* was a longer book in which each chapter was a round-table discussion on a specific topic. The topics include such things as politics, farming, labor, the press, and the theater; in each case various speakers discussed the situation, and then Jesus, present at the discussion, told them what society should be doing about the matter in question.

The many other sermon stories tended to cover many of the sorts of themes dwelt on in *In His Steps*—themes such as race, immigration, social conflict, the rights of labor, political corruption, urban housing, newspaper publishing, corruption in business, observance of Sunday, war and peace—and, of course, gambling, smoking, and above all drinking. *The Narrow Gate*, for example, concerned a young crusading newspaper editor who fights the saloon in the town of Colby (Sheldon noted in a preface that the story was based on real events). *Paul Douglass, Journalist* dealt with a favorite Sheldon theme, a newspaper editor who tries to Christianize his paper. *The Redemption of Freetown* concerned a community's attempts to improve conditions in its black ghetto and was a very thinly veiled account of Central Church's activities in Tennesseetown. *Who Killed Joe's Baby?* was another tract against liquor, a short novel that was especially popular in Topeka.[86]

These stories, like *In His Steps*, encountered a fair share of criticism. Characteristic of the criticism was an article that appeared in the *Spectator* in 1899, which complained that "the plan of all the stories is much the same. The reader is introduced to the hero . . . just when he has made up his mind to apply this test, 'What would Jesus do?' to all his public and private actions; and the stories describe the many changes and sacrifices which his new rule of life forces upon him. . . . With these stories before us, we cannot but wonder what has induced three millions of people to buy and read them."[87] The criticism of sameness of plot is certainly a valid one, and in some cases the resemblance between the stories is even closer. For example, *Malcolm Kirk* and *Howard Chase, Red Hill, Kansas*, were both stories of young socially conscious ministers who took marginal parishes in rural Kansas, survived various threats and adventures, and finally succeeded in cleaning up the town. Several chapters of the two novels could be interchanged without doing much damage to the plot of either. One doesn't have to read all thirty books to hear what Sheldon had to say.

In later life Sheldon wrote several books other than sermon stories, including compendiums of short, inspirational paragraphs, books of Bible stories retold, an autobiography, an anthology of his articles, and numerous short tracts and essays on various subjects. Probably the best received of his later works was *The Everyday Bible*, which was much like the *Reader's Digest Bible* that was to follow half a century later: a recompilation of the Scriptures, which set forth the main narrative in such a way that it could "be readily followed as in any other book intended for ordinary perusal," and omitted long lists of laws, genealogical tables, and the like. *The Everyday Bible* was adopted for use in some public schools in Kansas and elsewhere and found a market among people who wanted to read a simplified Bible.

Some of Sheldon's fans also attempted, in essence, to expand the master's corpus. Probably the most ambitious effort was a book by Glenn Clark, an ardent Sheldon admirer, entitled *What Would Jesus Do?* That book was a sequel to *In His Steps* in which the characters were grandchildren of the originals. The story began in 1945 when the Rev. Charles S. Maxwell, a minister in Raymond, proposes that his parishioners take the same pledge their grandparents did half a century earlier. The story is much the same as that of the original: a newspaper is reformed, social problems are attacked, the city prospers.[88] Sheldon died before Clark's book had been published, but he endorsed the concept shortly before his death and would have liked the finished product.

5. The Christian Daily Newspaper

In March of 1900, Charles Sheldon conducted the best-publicized experiment of the entire social gospel era when he spent a week editing the *Topeka Daily Capital* according to the "What would Jesus do?" principle. A Christian daily newspaper—the establishment of which Sheldon had been urging for nearly a decade—became a reality, if only for a week. For that week his newspaper out-circulated virtually every other in the country. Christian Endeavor Societies took in thousands of dollars in commissions for promoting the project; some shrewd publicists carefully orchestrated what may well have been the most successful newspaper promotion in history. The most written-about week in Topeka's history made the already famous writer more prominent—or notorious—than ever.

The idea of a Christian daily paper, giving believers uplifting news while sparing them from having to look at degrading advertising, was clearly percolating in Sheldon's imagination in his first years in Topeka. His first known written appeal for a Christian newspaper appeared in his first sermon story, *Richard Bruce*, which was published in 1893 after being read at Central Church in 1891. In chapter 8 of the novel, the saintly Rev. John King tells Tom Howard, a high-minded young journalist who has recently had a conversion experience, that he is trying to start a Christian daily paper that will be issued simultaneously in New York, Boston, Philadelphia, Chicago, and San Francisco. King says that while there will be some communication of the news of the day, "Our main purpose will be to furnish a distinctively religious paper, so that it shall be totally different from every other daily published."[1]

Sheldon was certainly not the originator of the concept. More than six decades before his project, the first of several religious newspapers appeared in Philadelphia—the *North American*. Its editorials were largely moral essays; it carried no advertising for saloons, and neither news of nor advertising for the theater. In the face of heavy losses, however, it was soon sold to a secular publisher. Nevertheless, others later tried to create other explicitly religious dailies. In June 1860, the *New York World* was established on such a basis, featuring church notices on the front page and rejecting all theatrical news and advertising (although it did accept patent medicine ads). It too lost money and about a year later merged with a secular paper. Meanwhile, however, in August 1860, the *New York Sun* had been made over into a religious paper whose owners tried to make it "a daily lay preacher to the poorer classes of New York."[2] It carried no ads for liquor, cigars, the theater, and the like, and the day's work began with a prayer in the editorial rooms. But financial disaster hit once again, and in December 1861 the *Sun* became secular again. Still, interest in committed Christian journalism persisted; the *Boston Daily News* opened as "a moral, religious daily" in 1869. Its end came abruptly in 1876, when a minister closely associated with the paper fled the country in the wake of the revelation that he had committed forgery.[3]

Amid the failures, however, was one success story for Christian daily journalism in North America. The *Montreal Witness* was founded as a weekly in 1840, made into a daily twenty years later, and run successfully in that fashion for over half a century. Sheldon was well familiar with the *Witness*, which refused all objectionable advertising (such as for liquor, tobacco, theater productions, and professional sports) and still made a profit; indeed, he gave a story about its success front-page space in his own Christian daily in 1900. What Sheldon may not have realized was that the *Witness* was the only strongly Protestant English-language paper in Catholic Montreal and thus had a strong base of support in the Protestant minority; when the *Witness's* owner, John Dougall, established a similar *New York Witness*, he lost fifty thousand dollars on the venture in the four years it operated as a daily.[4]

Although most of the experiments in Christian daily journalism failed, the nondaily religious press was vigorous in Sheldon's day. Certainly Christians had no shortage of uplifting reading material and religious news and analysis, even if it didn't arrive daily on the doorstep. The unquestioned leader in religious journalism after the Civil War was the *Independent*, a nominally Congregational weekly to which Sheldon frequently contributed. In second place for many years was the *Christian Union*, founded shortly after the war and edited for twelve years by Henry Ward Beecher, who had earlier had a brief stint at the helm of the *Independent*. The *Christian Union*, whose name was changed to the *Outlook* in 1893, remained quite popular until after World War I. Beyond such general-market religious periodicals were a host of more specifically targeted journals, many of them denominational (the Congregationalists alone had more than a dozen periodicals in the closing years of the century). The social gospel spawned several publications of its own, including *Dawn*, the *Kingdom*, and the *Social Gospel*. There were several interdenominational Christian magazines, such as the popular *Christian Herald* and the *Ram's Horn*. And, of course, there were plenty of periodicals published by Catholics, Jews, Mormons, Theosophists, New Thought advocates, and others. Sheldon's era was in fact the heyday of religious journalism in America.[5]

Within the social gospel movement, most of Sheldon's colleagues supported the idea of a Christian daily as firmly as Sheldon did. Several social gospel publications pushed Christian journalism as an integral part of the campaign to Christianize society and usher in the Kingdom.[6] Sheldon's campaign was thus neither lonely nor original.

In any event, by 1895 Sheldon was carrying the banner for the project. On April 21 of that year he preached a sermon outlining a plan for a newspaper that would carry moral news and advertising and be operated by committed Christians. "A Christian daily would have to be a real newspaper," he proclaimed. "It could not be conducted on any namby pamby, goody goody basis." Sheldon claimed to have endorsements from many Protestant leaders for the idea, and said that the right staff would not be difficult to find. A more detailed analysis appeared in two parts in the *Kingdom*, the social gospel weekly out of Minneapolis, two months later; Sheldon at that time bemoaned the fact that the *Topeka Daily Capital*, although it was one of the "cleanest, most reputable papers in the United States," was still nothing that "could truthfully be called Christian." When the *Capital's* business manager, Dell Keizer, a friend of Sheldon's, asked the pastor to blue-pencil everything he considered not Christian from a typical edition of the *Capital*, Sheldon went to work:

> I read that paper through and it certainly contained nothing glaringly objectionable, from a moral point of view. But the entire front page was given up to the glorification of the Republican party which had just held a convention in the city and had failed to say a word about the shameful neglect of the governor to enforce the prohibitory law of the state. I drew the pencil across the whole front page on that account. . . . Then I turned over the pages and found advertisements of chewing tobacco and slang reports of baseball games and several accounts of criminal trials and columns of society doing which could not possibly be allowed so much space in a Christian daily. And about the only thing . . . untouched by the blue pencil, were the market reports and the weather bulletins,—and I had some misgivings about letting these stand, as two-thirds of the time they are misleading and so untrue and so unchristian.[7]

In place of that, Sheldon argued, since people read newspapers all the time, they should be given the kind of thing they ought to be reading rather than the trash placed before them by the existing papers.[8]

In 1895, Sheldon got a chance to put some of his new ideas about Christian journalism to a practical test. Arthur Capper, who was later to become a major daily newspaper publisher, sat Sheldon down in an editor's chair in the autumn of that year.

Capper had purchased the *Topeka Mail* in 1893, and the *Kansas Breeze* not long after that. In 1895 he merged the two papers and set out to use various gimmicks to boost the circulation of the *Mail and Breeze*. One gimmick was to use famous Kansans as one-issue guest editors.[9] Sheldon was among them, and his contribution, which appeared on October 11, 1895, was a blend of gentle humor, serious advocacy, short verses, and a gaggle of one-liners. The articles were by no means all religious or moralistic. He pushed civic improvement: for example, he demanded a replacement for the dangerous old Kaw River bridge. He devoted an article to kindergartens, his two in Topeka having already proved great successes. Another article encouraged better sanitation through systematic garbage collection. He argued for better enforcement of the Kansas prohibitory law, and urged people to live their religious convictions every day of the week. He even—audaciously, in a conservative state and town—defended Christian socialism, albeit a mild variety of it: "Christian Socialism is no more, no less than the answer to the Lord's Prayer in an attempt to make the kingdom of God a reality in the every day life of the world."[10]

Sheldon's stint at the *Mail and Breeze* only whetted his appetite for a Christian paper, and he continued to talk about the idea whenever he could find an audience. In July 1896, he outlined his thinking on the subject at a weeknight church meeting, describing a paper that would be clean, nonpartisan, and honest, the product of committed journalists whose work would always be signed.[11]

That fall's sermon story was "In His Steps," and Christian journalism was a major focus of it. The book's Edward Norman, editor of the *Raymond Daily News*, who took the pledge to run his paper on the "What would Jesus do?" principle, began by rejecting news of a prize fight, at which time his managing editor predicted, echoing a prediction Arthur Capper had made to Sheldon earlier, that the paper would soon go belly up. But Norman pushed on, cancelling liquor and tobacco advertising and dropping the Sunday edition, finally taking a half-million-dollar infusion from an heiress before the Christian public managed to rally and push the paper back into the black.

With the runaway success of the novel, Sheldon's ideas about Christian journalism received worldwide publicity, and in 1899 the newspaper idea attracted still greater notice. The occasion was the Eighteenth International Christian Endeavor Convention at Detroit in July. Sheldon was one of the great heroes of the 4 million American and many more foreign Endeavorers. He held several question-and-answer sessions with his young audiences during the convention; they usually focused on *In His Steps* and the taking of the "What would Jesus do?" pledge. Finally a question about Ed Norman's newspaper was asked, and Sheldon allowed that he hoped the "ideal in the book will be real in a few years. . . ."[12]

Christian Endeavor was a powerful movement in those days, and its convention doings were widely reported. Sheldon, because of his popularity with the crowd, received generous coverage. But still no one was ready to start such a paper; Sheldon had always disclaimed wanting to make it a personal project, since he preferred to stay in the pastorate, and certainly no heiress had stepped forward with the necessary funding, as had occurred in the novel.

Enter Frederick O. Popenoe. In August 1899, shortly after Sheldon had made such a hit in Detroit, Popenoe, an ambitious man, had, at the age of thirty-seven, purchased the *Topeka Daily Capital* from the Bank of Topeka, which had taken over the paper in 1895 when its founder, editor, and majority stockholder, Joseph K. Hudson, had got himself into a financial corner. The enterprising Popenoe was eager to turn Topeka's only morning paper from a money-loser into a profitable enterprise. However, he could do little to change the content of the paper, since banker David Mulvane had secured, as a condition of the sale, a long-term contract for Hudson as editor-in-chief. Hudson and Mulvane were closely allied in a faction within the Kansas Republican Party, and Mulvane wanted the paper to have the right political slant on things.[13]

It was on the afternoon of November 3, 1899, that Popenoe, apparently acting on impulse, offered Sheldon the chance to take over the *Capital* for a week and show just what his Christian daily newspaper might look like in print. The two were with a party watching a military parade that day, and the conversation had drifted to the Ed Norman episode in *In His Steps*. Apparently the basic outlines of the project were hammered out on the spot. Sheldon's only restrictions were that he would agree to keep the paper's staff intact; out-of-town subscription rates would be upped (from ten to twenty-five cents for the week) for the special edition; and Sheldon agreed not to endanger the property or its future.[14]

Preparations began almost immediately. The news hit Topeka on January 23, 1900, when the entire front page of the *Capital* was

Frederick Popenoe in his office at the *Topeka Daily Capital,* ca. 1900. Kansas State Historical Society.

given over to a dramatic announcement of the project, which by then had been given a date: the week of March 13. An enormous banner headline read, "Rev. Charles M. Sheldon to Edit the Capital." Reproduced were a letter from Dell Keizer, the *Capital's* business manager, making the offer, and Sheldon's handwritten acceptance of it. An article entitled "Unique Idea in the History of Journalism" told of Sheldon's ideas about Christian journalism, and there were many endorsements of the project from clerics and politicians.

Much groundwork had to be done quickly. Arrangements had to be made for printing the vastly expanded press run. Clerks had to be hired to take subscriptions. A great expansion of the mailing operation would be necessary. And the *Capital's* management had one thorny legal problem to solve: the paper had a number of longstand-

The Christian Daily Newspaper   109

Above: Bags of copies of the Sheldon edition being mailed out. Central Congregational Church (UCC), Topeka. Opposite: *Topeka Daily Capital* staff in newsroom, 1900. Kansas State Historical Society.

ing national advertising accounts that were secured by time and space contracts, specifying day of week and position in the paper, and the *Capital* might be legally liable for damages if the contracted firms could not run their copy during Sheldon week; certainly they would want to take full advantage of this enormously publicized event. But Sheldon had been promised full control of the paper, including the right to censor any ads he chose. Moreover, the S.C. Beckwith Agency of New York owned the "foreign" advertising rights and was thus in charge of such sales; but Popenoe had given Herbert Houston those rights for the Sheldon edition as a part of the special promotion going on. How to handle such awesome potential legal liability? Popenoe purchased some expensive legal advice in New York, and was presented with what was apparently a workable solution: he would lease the *Capital* plant and Associated Press franchise to Sheldon for the week. That way if any liabilities arose, they would be Sheldon's.[15]

The *Capital*'s press could print 120,000 eight-page papers a day if it ran around the clock, but fairly soon it became apparent that circulation would go much higher than that. Arrangements were made for the paper to be printed by the *Chicago Journal*, the *Staats Zeitung* (a German language newspaper in New York City), and the *Westminster Gazette* in London. Four sets of printing matrices were made each day in Topeka; one set was sent to Chicago, where the paper appeared a day after its publication in Topeka, another to New York, where it was two days late, and the last set to London.[16]

The post office did its part by assigning six clerks to the *Capital* office to spend twelve hours daily weighing the papers to be mailed out. The post office also had to add a clerk to handle money orders, since hundreds (or thousands) of them were arriving daily in Topeka.[17] Clyde Reed, the superintendent of railway mail service for Kansas (and later governor and U.S. senator), went to Topeka to oversee the operation. The Santa Fe and Rock Island railroads each parked a special mail car daily on a siding to use as a temporary post office and then to carry the mail on its way.

Why was the Sheldon edition such a phenomenal success? Partly, of course, because Sheldon was by this time a household name; *In His Steps* was just then selling millions of copies. But there was more to it than met the eye. Behind the hundreds of thousands of subscriptions also lay a sharp and successful promotional campaign. Without Sheldon's knowledge or consent, Popenoe had decided to hire special help for the promotion, and retained two men who turned out to be excellent drumbeaters, Herbert S. Houston and Auguste C. Babize. Sheldon was slow to catch on to Popenoe's grand plan, and thus never really had a chance to object to it, but he clearly disapproved of it all when he did find out. Ever afterward he retained some bitterness about the commercialization of his religious project; it is not accident that even twenty-five years later Sheldon chose not to mention Popenoe's name anywhere in the chapter on the Christian daily in his autobiography.

Houston, a Kansas native, was familiar with Sheldon's reputation and had read *In His Steps*; when Popenoe signed him up, he took a leave from *Outing* magazine, where he was advertising manager. He was hired to sell advertising for the Sheldon edition, but he ended up also promoting circulation, since it turned out that advertising rates were to be tied to circulation and not actually computed until the experiment was over. In this second project he joined Babize, who had been specifically hired as a secret press agent for the project. Babize was seemingly caught in a conflict of interest, since he was a correspondent for the *Chicago Times-Herald* who was covering Sheldon week in Topeka as well as the chief publicist for the project (although his latter job was never publicly announced). But he pulled it off—very effectively.

The biggest and most successful part of the promotion went through Christian Endeavor, that mighty army of Christian youth whose idolization of Sheldon was already complete. Babize and Houston offered them a lucrative deal: sell the subscriptions for twenty-five cents and keep ten cents of it for your local CE society. The plan was first unveiled to the Endeavorers in the February 8 issue of the *Christian Endeavor World*, their national weekly, where

A weary editor Sheldon shakes hands with the printer's "devil." Kansas State Historical Society.

the back cover was given over entirely to the promotion of the project. The ad featured a picture of Sheldon and a letter from William Shaw, treasurer of the United Society of Christian Endeavor, telling of the plan, and then provided specific directions for making up the list of subscribers to send in.[18] Quickly, similar offers were

A mound of letters bearing orders for the Sheldon edition. Kansas State Historical Society.

made to other youth groups through their periodicals; thus the offer also appeared in such journals as the *Epworth Herald*, the *Baptist Young People's Union*, and the *Christian Herald*. A young sales army was created over night.

The other main avenue of promotion was the use of the Sheldon edition as a premium. Many newspapers took out bulk subscriptions and offered the week's run as a bonus for new subscribers. Apparently no one recorded how many copies were sold in that manner, but it was surely in the tens, if not hundreds, of thousands.

Many newspapers and magazines, religious and secular, also printed their opinions about the scheme, which a number of them derisively tagged "holy week." The secular press was by and large critical from the first. One of the most frequent criticisms (perhaps

Dr. T. De Witt Talmage, D.D., Editor · NEW YORK, MARCH 14, 1900 · PRICE FIVE CENTS

CHRISTIAN HERALD

AND SIGNS OF OUR TIMES

OFFICES: BIBLE HOUSE, NEW YORK · COPYRIGHT 1900, BY LOUIS KLOPSCH · VOLUME 23—NUMBER 11

1. D. L. McEachron, S. S. Sup't.
2. Rev. F. M. Ellis.
3. Mr. Sheldon and His Baby Son
4. His Tennesseetown Chapel
5. His First Church (upstairs)
6. Pastor Sheldon's Home
7. Mr. Sheldon's Present Church

The cover of the *Christian Herald* for the week of the Sheldon Edition.
F. M. Ellis was a Washburn College professor who occasionally filled the
Central pulpit when Sheldon was away. Kansas State Historical Society.

first voiced by the editors of the *Chicago Tribune*) was that a week wasn't long enough to run an honest experiment.[19] The second most frequent complaint was that Sheldon did not have the background for the job, that newspapers should be operated by newspaper-men. Others simply didn't care for Sheldon's type of religiosity and told him to quit meddling and get back to his pulpit. Among the more charitable critics was Sheldon's fellow Kansan, the renowned William Allen White:

> No one can doubt the absolute sincerity of Chas. M. Sheldon. He is not striving after notoriety. He is trying to make the world better, and such men succeed in their purposes.
> But he isn't an editor and his attempt to publish a model Christian newspaper seems to be a lamentable failure. There are today in America a hundred daily newspapers whose editors are daily having a wider influence for good than Chas. M. Sheldon, editor, has. Their papers are more interesting and hence do not repel men. . . . Their newspapers come nearer being Christian newspapers than the Sheldon Capital comes, because their editors are better editors and just as good Christians. . . . Editor Sheldon's faith is all right but his works are poor."[20]

More critical, almost apoplectically so, was Ed Howe, the well-known editor of the *Atchison* [Kansas] *Globe* and a professed agnostic. He offered to turn the tables and take over the pulpit at Sheldon's church. Then he went that one better and proposed to run a series of lay sermons in the *Topeka State Journal* during Sheldon week at the *Capital*. The lay sermons, which were run not only in the *State Journal* but in a number of newspapers elsewhere, will be discussed in greater detail below.

The newspapers may have been largely critical of the project, but quite a few members of the clergy were more supportive, as were some politicians who saw a bandwagon to jump on. In Wichita a candidate for Congress declared he would run on a platform he thought Jesus would endorse.[21]

Sheldon was plenty busy from the time of the announcement in late January until the scheduled debut of the Sheldon edition on March 13. For several weeks he spent half of every day learning the ropes of the newspaper business and preparing some of the material he would use. Meanwhile, he tried to cope with the flood of mail, much of it advising him on the proper path to follow in his project and a good deal more containing job applications from persons, many of them ministers, who tried to "impress upon him that they know just what sort of news Jesus would print."[22]

By the time Sheldon week had rolled around, the pastor had adopted a set of rules both for the newspaper itself and for the conduct of the staff during the week. As for editorial rules, Sheldon announced several unusual ones. For one, bylines were to be used in all stories in order to encourage reporters to do reliable work, to reward them for good work, and to locate responsibility in the case of error. Slang was to be avoided; Sheldon instructed his staffers to write "populist," for example, instead of "pop." After a person had been interviewed, the reporter was to show the article to the subject and then return the interview to Sheldon with the subject's written permission to use it. Moreover, a first refusal to be interviewed was to be taken as final. Sports news was to be downplayed: the only sporting events to be covered at all were those which would fall under the heading of "clean, healthful amateur athletics."[23] Crime news was to be similarly tempered, and such items were always to be accompanied by a short piece of analysis pointing out the reasons for the crime and how it might have been prevented. There was to be no partisan political news, and no reporting of the theater. As for staff deportment, Sheldon "respectfully asked all the employees not to drink, swear, or smoke while on duty."

Finally Sheldon week arrived. On Monday morning the pastor-editor showed up at the *Capital* offices to begin work on the Tuesday paper (the *Capital* did not publish a Monday edition). The next morning the first paper rolled off the presses. To say the least, it was not a conventional newspaper. During Sheldon week the editorial content as well as advertising in the *Capital* was as unusual as everyone had anticipated.

Sheldon's ideas about what the thirty-six news columns in the eight-page paper should contain had been spelled out prior to the experiment in some detail. In addition to moderating reports of crime, vice, or human depravity and accompanying them by editorial comment, Sheldon had also decided not to include news of prize fights, scandals, or other objectionable activities. Most stock market reports were excluded, since Sheldon regarded most market activity as nothing more than gambling. Moreover, there was no sensationalism; Sheldon always attempted to devote space to items in proportion to their importance. To maintain proper control, Sheldon announced to his staff that he would read every line in the paper, right down to the filler items. At midnight on his first night Sheldon found himself in need of six inches of filler. Finally *Capital* associate editor Harold T. Chase found an item about a jockey who refused an offer of $10,000 to race on Sunday.[24] Sheldon's response: "I suppose that you have some way of knowing this story is true?"[25] So he sat down and composed the needed fifteen lines in thirty minutes.[26]

The Christian daily newspaper was notably short on news. In part that was because Sheldon happened to encounter a light week for news, especially on the foreign front; the Boer War had just ended, and things were still. But Sheldon told his staff that the main reason for using a good deal of material that really wasn't current news was that the point of the week's experiment was to illustrate his ideas as fully as possible; an ongoing daily newspaper would not be a showpiece and could concentrate more on news.[27] To help fill the space Sheldon in advance had secured gratis contributions from many prominent religious writers and two cartoons from nationally known artists.

The first day's paper, on March 13, looked at first glance like a regular issue of the *Capital*, only grayer. In the top left-hand corner was "A Morning Prayer and Resolve." The headline story was "Starving India," an account of a famine to whose relief the editor encouraged his Christian readers to contribute. Although the only wire reports which had reached the *Capital* were weeks old, Sheldon led with the story, arguing that "the press has neglected this great matter of the news of the world."[28] The other front page articles were "The War Spirit," a spirited denunciation of war; "The Cry for Work," an indictment of the liquor industry as a disproportionate contributor to unemployment; "Prohibition Tested," testimonials to the success

The Sheldon edition attacked war through pictures as well as words. Kansas State Historical Society.

of prohibition; and "Colorado's Burden," a plea for help for a Colorado YMCA that was trying to build a tuberculosis sanitorium.

Page two, the editorial page, carried, among other things, Sheldon's statement of purpose, in which he announced that his paper would be nonpartisan, would advocate prohibition, would focus on greed and other social evils, would oppose war, and mainly would try "to influence its readers to seek first the Kingdom of God." Page three contained "telegraphic and Kansas news," ranging from an account of the apparent end of the Boer War to news of the Methodist Church conference in Chanute, Kansas. The most riveting item was entitled "Death in a Fire Trap" and told of a Newark tenement fire that had killed fourteen. Sheldon concluded the item with his

Part of a page from the Sheldon edition. Central Congregational Church (UCC), Topeka.

promised editorial note: "How long will men continue to build 'veritable fire traps' (see words above) for other human beings to inhabit? The greed of men who own and take the rent of such tenement property as this is a greed for which they will have to give account in the last Great Day.—Editor."

Page four was reserved for local news and was mainly predictable. There were stories of prohibition and antismoking rallies, of meetings of the YMCA and charitable social organizations. Page five consisted of feature articles on a variety of topics. On page six there was a livestock market report, along with two columns of classified ads and several display ads for items ranging from buggies to tracts to nail clippers. Page seven was all advertising, the largest ad being awarded to the *Christian Herald*. Finally, page eight was also all advertising, including a half page ad for featherbone (being promoted for dress stays and skirts).

The rest of the week's issues followed in a similar vein, with articles on topics ranging from Sunday observance to prison reform, encouraging settlement houses, municipal ownership of utilities, and other worthy projects.

The Saturday paper carried a caveat for Sheldon's readers: the Tuesday paper had carried an ad for a cream separator that Sheldon had since been informed was not as advertised; Sheldon warned his readers that, contrary to his policy, he had not "had time to examine the separator and pass upon its merits." Much of page two was given over to church notices—including one for the "Divine Science and Apostolic Congregation" led by Charles F. Parham, the former Methodist pastor who would a few months later start one of the most remarkable religious movements in history when his young followers began to speak in tongues for what was believed to be the first time since apostolic days, thus giving birth to the Pentecostal/Charismatic movement.

The Saturday evening paper was the most unusual of all. Sheldon had decided that no printing or local delivery of the paper would take place at any time on Sunday, and so a special paper would be printed on Saturday evening. And his Saturday night paper was to be no normal Sunday-type edition; instead, what

Sheldon did was to provide a paper loaded with material he deemed suitable for family Sunday reading. Thus page one was all biblical. The lead story was an article entitled "The Bible: The Basis of Our Christian Civilization." Also on the front page was the Sermon on the Mount in the revised version. The rest of the paper was much the same.

Two examples of Sheldon's special approach to reporting have been held up repeatedly by Sheldon scholars as especially noteworthy. One was his subdued reporting of the suicide of J. Sherman Peffer, the son of former U.S. Senator W.A. Peffer of Topeka. By the press standards of the day it was a newsworthy event, the most sensational piece of local news that week. The younger Peffer had been working as a Linotype operator for the *Capital*, and in fact had set, in advance, a good deal of advertising copy for the Sheldon edition, but had been fired on Saturday just before Sheldon week. Despondent, he went to Kansas City and after a hard weekend gave himself an overdose of morphine. (Many newspapers elsewhere tried their best somehow to connect the suicide to Sheldon, who had in fact been utterly unconnected to Peffer's firing.)[29] Sheldon's reporters wanted to dash out to the Peffer home to interview Sherman's parents, but Sheldon stopped them. Instead, he adhered to his policy of avoiding sensationalism, running a short paragraph on an inside page giving the bare circumstances of the death and offering the paper's sympathy to the bereaved parents.

Sheldon's other case of unusual coverage involved the society page. The minister had long been critical of the serious reporting of what he considered frippery and frivolity. So he ordered the society editor, Miss Jessie Garwood, to "take an average day in Topeka, and write about the wasted time and money spent in social frivolity on that day, concluding with an itemized statement of the cost of such frivolities going on." Garwood, apparently relishing the unusual assignment, on her assigned day located two receptions, three thimble parties, eight card parties, six dinners, five luncheons, and two club dances, with expenses totalling $716. There was also on that day a thousand-dollar theatrical performance that had become an imporant social event. An editorial followed the story; it suggested that all of the $1716 should have gone to famine relief for India.[30]

During his week on the newspaper, Sheldon put in thirteen to sixteen hours of work each day, arriving at the office each morning within six hours of the time he had left the night before.[31] He rented a room at the nearby Copeland Hotel for the week, collapsing there at the end of each long day. After a few hours of sleep he would make a brief morning trip home to see his wife and son and then hurry back to the job.[32] He ate his meals at a restaurant. The only exception to the rigid routine came on Thursday, Central Church's regular prayer meeting night, when Sheldon went out to the church to perform his role as leader. Then it was back downtown to work.[33]

Sheldon's week as an editor might have been far easier had not a bevy of out-of-town reporters overwhelmed his every moment. Given the *Capital* management's determination to promote the experiment aggressively, it isn't surprising that it turned into the media event of the year. Correspondents for out-of-town newspapers and magazines began showing up in Topeka well before Sheldon week, and they were prominently present while Sheldon did his work. There were apparently about twenty of them in all. Fending off their persistent searching for exclusive material kept Sheldon hopping.

On the other hand, his relations with the *Capital's* staff seem to have been quite cordial. One of Sheldon's democratic gestures stood newspaper tradition on its head: on the masthead, instead of listing only a few of the paper's top officials, Sheldon listed the name and position of every single employee of the *Capital* right down to the janitor and galley boy, excepting only the owner and de facto publisher of the paper, Fred Popenoe.[34] Why was Popenoe omitted? The best guess is probably that by this time Sheldon realized that Popenoe had made a carnival of Sheldon's sacred project and didn't want to glorify the man who was using him.

Considering the magnitude of the venture, the printing and distribution of the Sheldon edition went fairly smoothly. As planned, the press at the *Capital* was worked to capacity, printing some

Newsboys leaving to sell the Sheldon edition. Kansas State Historical Society.

120,000 copies per day, and similar press runs were undertaken in Chicago and New York. Meanwhile the crew of mailers "had to wrap like mad to keep up with the press."[35] Only once was the smooth production operation interrupted in Topeka, and that was by design. While the Saturday evening paper was still in the middle of its run, Sheldon went to the press room at 11:30 P.M. to check on its progress and was told that it was not yet finished. He told the foreman Robert Maxwell and the rest of the pressmen to quit and go home. "Print the rest of them Monday morning," he said.[36] Thus the no-Sunday-work principle stuck. The crew returned shortly after midnight on Monday morning, and from 1 until 10 A.M. the press cranked out the rest of the edition.[37]

The main mystery in the Sheldon edition's distribution centers on the British printing of it. Given Sheldon's enormous British popularity, there seemed to be little reason to doubt that the London version would sell like hotcakes. At one point in the planning, in fact, the *Capital* owners were said to be pondering other European editions in languages other than English.[38] Apparently the London edition was printed as arranged, by the *Westminster Gazette*; a story in that paper on April 4, 1900, told of a crowd of men and boys in Tudor Street (just off Fleet Street) waiting to get copies of the paper, and of newsboys carrying off bundles of them.[39] The *Capital* on April 1 ran a report on the London edition, saying it was meeting "with more ridicule than anything else."[40] But for some reason no copies of the London paper seem to have been preserved anywhere. Even the British Museum's newspaper archives contain none.

If the British edition was in many respects, including its breadth of circulation, an enigma, reliable circulation figures for the American version are readily available. The *Capital*'s average circulation in 1899 was 11,223 (on Sundays, 12,298);[41] during Sheldon week that daily figure shot up to an astounding 362,684. For Sheldon week as a whole, 2,176,100 papers were printed in the United States.[42]

One of Sheldon's basic precepts for a Christian newspaper was that it should run only advertisements that were honest and for meritorious products, and he was true to his ideals in rejecting advertising that failed to meet his standards. According to one account, Sheldon spent at least two weeks before the week of the experiment going over advertising contracts and making essential decisions.[43] At first he apparently feared that he would damage the paper's revenue by rejecting ads, but as things turned out, the advertising space was all filled and in fact demand for it was so high that he could have filled the paper several times over.[44]

Topping the list of rejected advertisements were those for alcohol and tobacco. Patent medicine ads were rejected as well, even though Sheldon admitted that "some patent medicines have good qualities," because many of them he regarded as frauds and he didn't have time to sort the good from the bad.[45] Similarly eliminated were electric belt and magnetic healing ads, and even a liquor-cure ad, because Sheldon did not regard alcoholism as a disease and therefore something needing treatment. Corset ads were refused, because "he believes tight lacing is injurious to women" and besides, "a picture of a woman fitting in a corset is suggestive and coarse."[46] Theatrical advertisements were completely forbidden. Ads for books or magazines were accepted only after Sheldon had inspected and passed on the item in question; he would not advertise magazines which carried "whisky ads or ads containing suggestive cuts."[47] Ads of the "agent wanted" variety were turned down, along with all land and mining promotions and advertising for sales of stock. Sheldon even rejected advertisements from several building and loan associations because he "did not personally know the officers, and was uncertain about the financial condition of the concerns."[48] He went so far as to reject all ads from Kansas City merchants, on the grounds that they were in direct competition with their Topeka counterparts; Sheldon believed "that a home paper should protect home merchants."[49]

Even ads that were within all the above guidelines were not guaranteed space. Sheldon turned down at least two Bible ads. In one case, a Bible publishing house wanted to advertise its three-dollar Bibles for one dollar; Sheldon "wired the firm how they could sell Bibles thus, but received no answer."[50] Another ad submitted offered a five-dollar Bible on thin paper for three dollars; after examining a copy, Sheldon decided that three dollars was the usual price and declined the ad.[51] Similar ads promising other phony discounts were similarly rejected. In a few cases Sheldon simply changed the ad copy. John W. Ripley, Sr., father of the present Topeka historian, was chagrined when he saw the copy of his standing ad for the Topeka Laundry Company changed from "Strictly High Grade Work" to "Claims to do Strictly High Grade Work."[52]

Sheldon naturally rejected ads which seemed to make a mockery of his ideas, such as one which claimed, "If Christ were on earth he would buy his clothing from So and So," as the *State Journal* reported it.[53] But he was burned on others. Startling today are two classified ads, in the first two days' papers, for specifically white employees; Sheldon was no racist, but in this case he apparently did not question prevailing social policy. Even more surprising was an ad from the Perine Plow Works which ran on March 16 under the headline STIR THE SUBSOIL DEEP:

> To let in the rains that refresh the earth. Otherwise a large portion of moisture graciously sent by our Heavenly Father is wasted by running off from the surface.
>
> Perine's Subsoil Plow accomplished the stirring, as we believe would please JESUS, who said let nothing be lost.
>
> Also, Perine's improved Potato Digger, designed to work well, even in unfavorable conditions of soil, which induces good words instead of bad, by which we desire to honor JESUS.

The next day the offensive ad had come to Sheldon's attention, and he apologized for it: "I regret that an advertisement of a plow was accompanied with certain phrases which contain the name of Christ in connection with the business, worded in such a way as to be offensive to several readers as well as myself. It was through an oversight that the advertisement appeared, and as soon as it was brought to my attention it was rejected."[54]

Trying to figure out how much to charge for advertising was at first an enormous problem, since no one had any idea what the circulation of the paper would be. Moreover, a huge circulation could make for prohibitively expensive ads. Houston came up with a plan that suited both Sheldon and the *Capital*'s owners: the usual rates would be preserved for Topeka advertisers, but a precedent-shattering scheme was laid down for "foreign" advertisers, in which the ad rates would not be determined until the press run had been completed. The formula, as Houston reported it, was two-fifths of a cent per agate line per thousand copies, "the bill to be accompanied by a statement signed by Doctor Sheldon showing the actual net circulation." Those advertisers who so chose could specify a limit as to the number of copies in which their ads would appear, in order to keep a lid on their costs.[55]

It is fortunate that the Sheldon edition was published back in the heyday of competitive journalism, for Topeka's other daily paper, the *State Journal*, gives us invaluable information from an indepen-

A cartoon lampooning Sheldon's banning of advertising for certain products. Among the forbidden products were liquor, corsets, and patent medicines, including Lydia Pinkham's Compound. Kansas State Historical Society.

dent viewpoint. Frank MacLennan's afternoon paper provided a healthy mix of straight news reporting on the Sheldon edition, editorial criticism of it all, and a big dose of satire.

Soon after the plans for the Sheldon edition were made public, the *State Journal* had announced a journalistic experiment of its own. It had engaged Ed Howe, the well-known editor of the *Atchison* [Kansas] *Globe* and anticlerical activist, to write a series of "lay sermons" to be published in the *State Journal*. Other American newspapers, eager to cash in somehow on Sheldon week, snapped up the rights to the sermons, and thus on the eve of Sheldon week MacLen-

The meeting to decide whether the paper shall go on as a Christian daily, or be run as Hudson would run it.

Topeka Daily Capital directors and staffers argue over thea paper's future. Kansas State Historical Society.

nan was able to boast that Howe's lay sermons had been contracted to papers with an aggregate circulation of over 600,000, and would therefore reach far more people than Sheldon's words would.[56]

Sheldon's failure to provide much of what was generally construed to be news was all to MacLennan's benefit. The *State Journal's* circulation soared by 40 percent for the week. MacLennan interspersed his coverage of the Sheldon experiment with tidbits designed to embarrass the pastor-journalist; when Sheldon one day complained of wealthy tax dodgers, the *State Journal* responded by running a list of 259 firms and individuals paying high dollar sums in taxes.[57] After the first Sheldon *Capital* had appeared, MacLennan pointed out that there had been "not a line of news on the front page" and noted that the bypassed stories that most papers would have regarded as newsworthy included that of a fighter killed in the ring by Jim Jeffries and an outbreak of bubonic plague in San Francisco.[58]

Ed Howe's lay sermons turned out to be an embarrassment to the papers that had so eagerly signed up to run them. Most of the subscribing papers had understood that Howe would be defending secular journalism, but what he actually wrote were, as John Ripley has characterized them, "long, tedious diatribes, supercharged with bitter and unjustified attacks on Christianity in general." Even Mac-Lennan apologized to his readers for them, saying that they were not what he had expected and that they should have been drastically cut. The four main out-of-town papers carrying Howe's "sermons"—the *Chicago Tribune*, the *New York Herald*, the *St. Louis Republic*, and the *Indianapolis Press*—all dropped the series after printing the first installment.[59]

Although Howe's project self-destructed, other slightly more light-hearted satires of the Sheldon edition were actually fairly entertaining. The *Atchison Champion*, the other paper in Howe's city (ordinarily a weekly, but issued daily during this momentous week), announced that it would publish its paper for the week of March 13 "as the devil would run it." The first page (of four) of each issue that week, while weak as satire, at least intended to provide comic relief and thus was far more readable than Howe's dreary polemics.

Any chance of the Sheldon edition's concluding its run quietly and with dignity was scotched on Friday night when Popenoe showed up in the newsroom to announce that the *Capital* would be permanently turned into a somewhat modified Christian daily. He had decided that he could permanently retain at least 100,000 of the subscribers to the Sheldon edition, and he had decided to go that route with Auguste Babize as editor.

But he destroyed what had been good relations with his staff with his Friday night bombshell. The *State Journal* eagerly reported the battle which ensued. Although Popenoe's announcement had said that there was "complete unanimity of sentiment among the stockholders," that was patently untrue. Dell Keizer, owner of a major block of *Capital* stock, simply said, "The proposition is absurd."[60] Hudson, although he owned no stock, reminded Popenoe that "I have a contract for $5,000 per year for a stated number of years in which it is stipulated that I am to have full editorial management of the *Capital* and shall control its policy and I do not propose to conduct the paper as a Christian daily."[61]

The battle continued over the weekend. The *Kansas City World* speculated that it would all end in a lawsuit, with Keizer alleging that the value of his stock would suffer if the paper were to become a permanent Christian daily, and Popenoe replying that under Keizer's business management the paper had been losing money fairly consistently.[62] Finally on Monday morning the stockholders met and agreed on a compromise in which Hudson would remain in place as editor, but that the paper would be run on a "high plane." Babize would join the staff as news editor rather than managing editor, and some kind of ground between secular and Sheldonian Christian journalism would be found.[63] Thus the *Capital* continued to be published as a secular paper, and itself never mentioned the fight. Babize did finally join the staff as associate editor, but the paper didn't change noticeably.

In fact conflict was far from resolved. For two months the feuding continued; finally, after Popenoe had become angered by a Hudson editorial, Keizer and Hudson quit the paper on May 29.[64] Popenoe continued to struggle to make it profitable, working with Babize, who had become business manager after Keizer's resignation. But business deteriorated, and finally, on March 12, 1901, one year after Sheldon had begun his famous experiment, it was announced that Popenoe had relinquished control of the paper, turning it back over to the Bank of Topeka, and that in fact he was no longer even in Topeka. He had gone off to check on his gold mining holdings in Costa Rica, and later turned up as a nurseryman in California, introducing the Fuerte avocado and Deglet Noor dates.[65]

Despite the furor with which it all ended, the Sheldon edition certainly had an impact on American life, in some ways an enduring impact. Perhaps the most obvious and immediate effect, and certainly that of which Sheldon was most proud, was the relief project for the famine in India, which came as a direct result of his appeal for help. He urged his readers to contribute at least ten cents, and many sent in more than that. Many thousands of dollars were sent to Sheldon directly, and finally something over $100,000—one report says that Sheldon provided the inspiration for a continuing campaign that eventually raised $700,000[66]—was contributed to help end starvation. Moreover, the *Christian Herald's* publishers orchestrated a campaign asking farmers to donate grain, and Kansas farmers responded with a carload of corn. The Frisco and New York Central railroads carried the grain free to New York, and the *Christian Herald* chartered a boat to carry it to Bombay.[67] Thereupon the British Secretary of State for India announced that he would pay all transportation charges for food donated by Americans, and another $100,000 in cash and grain came rolling in.[68] The grain thus sent was vitally helpful to India.

Sheldon also made an impact in the field of advertising, where his ideas quite probably helped to shape an emerging consensus that the press had to make a commitment to truth in its ads. The first major set of truth-in-advertising principles to gain much prominence emerged from a press convention in 1911. Herbert Houston, Sheldon's advertising manager and later a leader in the truth movement, credited the pastor's influence: "It is not for those who were part of that interesting experiment [the Sheldon edition] to claim any credit for the Truth Movement in Advertising—and they never claimed any. But this much is true—some of the fine things now fixed firmly in the practise of advertising were carried out in Topeka over ten years before the Boston Convention of 1911."[69]

Although there is every reason to believe that the Sheldon edition turned a solid profit, just how much it came to is open to speculation. The *State Journal* and the *Mail and Breeze*, citing informed sources, said that the *Capital's* earnings for the week were around

$30,000. Other papers apparently reached into the air for higher estimates. Ripley wrote of such fantasy:

> With admirable restraint, Ed Howe in the Atchison *Globe*, March 19, stated that "women and children" (when he yearned to say "widows and orphans") contributed largely to the $65,000 profit. The Chicago *Tribune* of March 13 called Ed Howe's estimate and raised it to $70,000. Then the Kansas City *World* on March 19 upped the pot to $95,000, whereupon the Council Bluffs (Iowa) *Nonpareil*, March 14, gave the kitty a hefty boost to $150,000. But a gentleman from Tipton, Nev., made pikers out of the Midwesterners. The editor of the Tipton *Gazette* disqualified the *Capital*, and on March 8 awarded the entire profit of at least a quarter of a million dollars to the Rev. Mr. Charles M. Sheldon.[70]

The truth is that in this case Sheldon really did not receive a cent for his efforts; that deal had been made with Popenoe in advance. However, the sum of $5000 from the Sheldon edition's profits was placed at Sheldon's disposal for charitable purposes. He donated it to projects ranging from Indian famine relief to a public drinking fountain in Topeka.

Just as there had been plenty of press comment on the project before its commencement, there was a torrent of evaluative writing afterwards. Everyone, it seems—especially journalists and clergy— had opinions about the Christian daily.

The country's newspapers on the whole considered the project a decided failure, although their reasons for that evaluation differed. Certainly they found that it made good copy; every newspaper in the country, one is tempted to believe after sifting through the enormous piles of press reactions, had its say about the project at length. Some found the whole concept blasphemous or at least sacrilegious. Others dismissed the paper as hopelessly boring. Some just didn't like Sheldon's ideas. Only a few thought Sheldon had anything to offer the secular press.

The most masterful satire of the episode came from Finley Peter Dunne, whose fictional Mr. Dooley was keenly interested in the Sheldon edition. A few excerpts from a long and clever ramble:

Sheldon's goal: "'Give me,' he says, 'a chanst, an' I'll projooce th' kind iv organ that's be got out in hiven,' he says."

Editor to staff: "'Gintlemen,' he says, 'I find that th' wurruk ye've been accustomed to doin',' he says, 'is calc'lated f'r to disthroy th' morality an' debase th' home life iv Topeka, not to mintion th' sur-roundin' methrolopuses iv Valencia, Wanamaker, Sugar Works, Pax-ico, an' Snokomo,' he says. 'Th' newspaper, instead iv bein' a pow'rful agent f'r th' salvation iv mankind, has become something that they want to r-read,' he says."

The contents of the paper: an "article on sewerage an' wan on prayin' f'r rain, an' another on muni-cipal ownership iv gas-tanks."

Pious ads: for "Th' Christyan Unity Five-cint See-gar" and "Nebuchednezzar grass seed, f'r man an' beast."

"'Twas nice to r-read. It made a man feel as if he was in church—asleep."[71]

On the other hand, many clerics were supportive. Many of those who shared Sheldon's antiliquor and antiwar activism, or his mild brand of Christian socialism, eagerly praised the experiment. Of all of Sheldon's ecclesiastical and clerical supporters, none did such a thorough job of arguing the case as the social gospel leader Washing-ton Gladden. Gladden first attacked Sheldon's detractors, noting that "the banality of most of these criticisms is rather pitiable." Many critics accused Sheldon of claiming to be "the accredited represen-tative of Christ," when in fact Sheldon clearly disclaimed any such role. Sheldon had "a clear and laudable purpose, and it is as far from any assumption of exclusive or superior Christliness as the East is from the West." Gladden flatly contradicted those who said it was "absurd to suggest that the business of a daily newspaper should be conducted on Christian principles." As for Sheldon's content, he went with "subjects of real importance," and "the ethical aspects of all such questions have been clearly and strongly presented; the ap-plication of the Christian law to problems of society and politics has been fearlessly made. . . ." Gladden saw Sheldon as right in downgrading "gossip and rumor and scandal and the disgusting de-tails of vice and crime . . . there are thousands of bright and beau-tiful things which would be the best kind of news if the reporters were trained to look for them." Could there be a permanent Christian daily? Yes, said Gladden, "Such a newspaper can be made," and it could support itself. "There are people enough in every considerable community who would hail it as the harbinger of the millennium, and whose patronage would make it self-supporting."[72] In short, Sheldon had no stronger or more eloquent supporter than Gladden.

And apart from all the published reaction to the project, Sheldon had a private flood of mail that was overwhelmingly supportive of what he had tried to do. Hundreds of letters, he wrote, asked him to establish a Christian daily permanently—but, alas, no one "came forward with the millions necessary to establish it."[73]

Just as Sheldon had been reticent about commenting on *In His Steps* during its ascent to international fame, so did he decline to defend himself extensively against criticism about his editorial venture. Thus his responses to his attackers were relatively few. However, to the end of his life Sheldon continued to criticize the daily press. Many more articles on problems in contemporary journalism were yet to emerge from his typewriter. Given that unending stream of criticism of the press, it is hardly surprising that Sheldon continued to hope for the establishment of a Christian daily until his dying day. In article after article, interview after interview, he clung to his ideal. "It is a bewildering and astonishing fact that Protestantism with its 26 million church members in America has no voice speaking every day for its faith. . . . Every other human energy has one," and "it would do more to help evangelize the world than all the denominational magazines put together.[74] Had he lived a few years longer, he might well have taken pride in the development of Christian television, although he wouldn't have much cared for the theological conservatism which has come to dominate that medium. Sheldon was always the true believer among social gospelers, but he was no fundamentalist.

He did have plenty of opportunities to undertake Christian journalism on a more limited scale, but he would never leave his pastorate for it until, after retirement, he finally went to work for the *Christian Herald* as nominal editor-in-chief (actually a contributing editor). One report says that Sheldon was offered astronomically high salaries—as high as $15,000 in the early years of the century—to serve as the religion editor of one or another daily paper.[75] He even turned down an offer to recreate his great 1900 experiment on a smaller scale; one day in 1934, after Sheldon, by now well into retirement, had been criticizing the press again, this time in an article in the *Christian Century*, the publisher of the *Topeka State Journal* offered "a full day at The State Journal helm without restriction." But Sheldon turned the offer down, remarking, "The editors are right in saying one day would not prove anything. I wish I had a paper of my own."[76]

6. The Social Reformer

S heldon's favorite role, after pastor, was that of social reformer. The peak of his career coincided with the peak of the social gospel movement, and he considered himself a loyal member of Protestantism's reformist faction. For years he corresponded with George Herron, Washington Gladden, and other social Christians, although his thinking was at many points distinctly different from theirs. He enthusiastically visited many settlement houses and institutional churches, and he endorsed Ralph Albertson's social gospel commune—the Christian Commonwealth Colony—in Georgia. As its most successful popularizer, Sheldon's contribution to the movement was an important one. Although he failed to provide a detailed blueprint of a thoroughly reformed society—one which discussed such things as the ideal economic structure of society and the role of private property in the new age[1]—he firmly believed in the concepts most central to the movement, such as the basic tenet that religion involves relationships between and among human beings as well as between humans and God and the precept that it is possible and necessary for the kingdom of God to be built on earth.

This chapter will not analyze Sheldon's role in the social gospel movement; perhaps the information provided here will help others do that in the future. Instead, the following pages will explore Sheldon's ideas and his own sense of context for them. His distinctive theme, as should be clear by now, was that of living according to the ideal of *imitatio Christi*: What would Jesus do? Other social gospel leaders may not often have employed that terminology, but they certainly embraced the concept. As Sheldon himself pointed out, he invented neither the concept nor the catch phrase[2]. By the time

Sheldon took it up, the idea of pledging to live a life of following Jesus was widespread in several evangelical Protestant social reform organizations.[3] His version of it was simple: if only people would try to follow the Master, such basic human problems as selfishness, greed, and attention only to self-interest would melt away. That people by and large rejected the path puzzled him, he maintained: "I live in a constant state of wonder over the stupidity of the human race in refusing to apply the teaching of Jesus to everyday life. It is not so much what we call wickedness that refuses to make religion practical. It is just sheer foolishness."[4]

His critics found one stumbling block, however, that Sheldon never really surmounted satisfactorily: how does one know just what Jesus would do in a given contemporary situation? Perhaps it is to Sheldon's credit that he never tried to give sweeping answers, recognizing that no single formula could cover every situation.[5] All we can do, he argued, is to keep in mind the basic themes Jesus taught—such fundamentals as seeking first the Kingdom and loving one's neighbor[6]—and then make the best decisions we can. Sometimes studying the lives of notable Christians might be useful for guidance; in any event we can always call on the Holy Spirit, our "one unfailing source."[7] Sheldon was loath to make decisions for others; when, after *In His Steps* had begun to achieve widespread renown, letters seeking specific advice began to pour in, Sheldon always answered, "I can not tell you what Jesus would do in your place. It is for each one of you to ask what Jesus would do if he were in your place and then to do unhesitatingly what it seems probable that he would do."[8] It was situation ethics: each individual had decisions to make.

Sheldon fully recognized that without detailed legislation on behavior, well-meaning persons would make different, and sometimes diametrically opposed, decisions. That never seemed to bother him, so long as the decisions were made conscientiously. In one case in which Sheldon was asked for advice, two young men were wrestling with the question of military service. One enlisted and resolved to take the Gospel to his fellow soldiers; the other felt conscientiously moved not to participate. The pacifist Sheldon blessed them both, even the one who went to war, because both had examined their consciences. The fact that Jesus could not have followed both courses of action was apparently no problem for Sheldon.[9]

In at least one matter, Sheldon, in the name of following the master, actually contradicted the record of Jesus' behavior. Sheldon was a lifelong prohibitionist who based his opposition to drinking, he said, on his perception of what Jesus would do, even though he conceded that Jesus drank wine. Times had changed, Sheldon said, and now Jesus would neither drink nor tolerate drinking. Why? Because times had changed. Specifically, the despicable institution known as the saloon had come into existence. Jesus would address his environment in any age; the Sermon on the Mount preached in Sheldon's day would have been different from what it had been two thousand years earlier. Jesus, after all, did not apparently oppose slavery, but Sheldon could not imagine that he would have approved of the American variety of it. So "we are not to be guided by what Jesus actually did or did not do in Palestine, but we are to try to bring Jesus down to our own times and adapt his spirit to the action that we are called upon to do."[10]

Given this kind of thinking, it is not surprising that Sheldon had critics within the social gospel movement. John W. Chadwick, pastor of the Second Unitarian Church of Brooklyn at the turn of the century, put one line of criticism succinctly:

> The author of "In His Steps" plays fast and loose with the standard he professedly adopts. Jesus is merely the personification of his own personal ideals. . . . He does not believe in Sunday papers, and consequently has no doubt what Jesus would do about them. At every point the standard works this way. . . . He asks, "What would Jesus do if he were Charles M. Sheldon?" And very naturally and properly answers, "He would do what Charles M. Sheldon, acting according to his best light and knowledge, does."[11]

Such criticism is surely valid, and Sheldon apparently never fully came to grips with it. However, Sheldon's most important point was that one should engage in moral reflection before acting; someone else's Jesus might not have acted like Sheldon's, he conceded.

Sheldon did believe that the "what would Jesus do?" test was applicable to every station in life, every profession, every personal situation. In his 1931 novel *He Is Here*, he had a mysterious stranger enter the lives of ten very different kinds of persons—a surgeon, a farmer, an admiral, a politician, a store clerk, and so forth—and tell them how to apply the right principles to what they were doing.[12] Sheldon believed that one's choice of vocation was no small matter, and that that decision should be made in light of committing oneself to service to society;[13] but whatever one's choice of profession, the rule of following Jesus applied equally to all.

Sheldon's behavioral model focused on individuals, not institutions or social structures. About the closest he came to advocating systemic changes was in his advocacy of cooperatives in business and manufacturing, and of public ownership of utilities.[14] But social salvation would proceed from individual salvation and social reform projects.[15]

Sheldon believed implicitly in the practicality of following Jesus. To those who thought otherwise he simply retorted that many were proving it practical by doing it.[16] If by calling such a life impractical his critics meant that it might cost money or interfere with one's job, then they needed to learn that living the wrong sort of life also had its price.[17] Sometimes Sheldon would veritably thunder against those who alleged the impracticality of a life led in imitation of Christ:

> This is the everlasting and contemptuous whine of the man who wants Christianity to protect his property and his civilization but does not want to be a real Christian himself because he knows he will stand a chance to lose some of his property if he really does the Christlike thing.
>
> But in heaven's name, if doing as Jesus would do is not practical, what *is* practical? The things that hard-headed business men call practical have all failed to make a better world.[18]

The theme of the cost of discipleship, of the need for suffering to reach one's goals, eventually became pervasive in Sheldon's writings on the "what would Jesus do?" precept. Apparently that theme emerged most strongly after Sheldon had begun to read the works of and correspond with George Herron, in the 1890s at the zenith of his considerable social gospel influence. Herron, perhaps the most brilliant of social gospel theorists, taught that the redemption of society would come only through sacrifice on the part of individual Christians.[19] Thus Sheldon eventually stressed that following Jesus carried a high price but that nothing worth having could be gained without sacrifice.[20]

The theme of suffering as the price and consequence of discipleship cropped up in several of Sheldon's novels after the mid-1890s. Certainly it was prominent in *In His Steps*.

Underlying Sheldon's social thinking was a fundamental and undying faith in two social gospel staples: optimism and idealism. He was an optimist who really did believe that the kingdom of God could be created on earth. And he was an idealist who had a clear vision of what the future ought to look like.

Sheldon seems to have espoused a virtually uncritical optimism throughout his life. In 1895 he wrote to the members of his church, "Every day I have more and more confidence in the wonderful results which I believe God is going to bring about in the social and political life of the world, using us who are Christians as instruments to do his great will."[21] Those were the heady days of rose-colored vision among the social gospelers, and like the rest of them Sheldon seemed really to believe that human society could be reformed, that through sacrifice and dedicated labor not only the world but individual human behavior could be overwhelmingly improved, that the kingdom of God really could take shape in this world. Actually, Sheldon never directly argued for human perfectability; as Ronald White has put it, he recognized that there was a "curious mixture" of good and evil in persons, churches, and societies.[22] But he did look for the best in people and urged those around him to look for the best in their own circumstances. Thus he could talk to a farmer who was losing money in a declining farm market and point out that the farmer owned 160 acres of God's green earth, had a house and car and other possessions, had a fine family, and never got sick—in short, the farmer was loaded with blessings, even if his debts were killing him. He could talk to a politician who feared that the opposition party was leading the nation into ruin, and point out that things really weren't so bad in the country, that the politician's life was still prosperous, that better days lay just ahead. He could talk to a minister who bemoaned a dead church and point out personal and ecclesiastical blessings the minister never noticed. "The goodness of life is greater than its evil, if we will only seek for it," he preached."[23]

He carried that optimism right into old age, far beyond the point at which many abandon their youthful view of things. Thus at eighty he was still declaiming, "There are more good people in the world than bad ones, and in time the good ones are going to overcome the evil. If I didn't believe that, I would bid my audience farewell and spend the rest of my life sitting in the chimney corner and railing at a humanity that does not want to be saved."[24] He believed that he had evidence justifying his optimism; several times during his latter years he compiled lists of the ways the nation and the world had improved during his lifetime as sure evidence of the inevitability of progress. Typical items on those lists were the abolition of slavery, the enactment of national prohibition, the suppression of child labor, better conditions for laborers, the control of some unjust practices on the part of big business, the rise of social services, the spread of democracy around the world, the emancipation of women, the growth of antiwar sentiment, and a growing interest in religion.[25] He seemed constitutionally unable to see that things like the continued existence of unjust governments, bloodier wars than ever before, and new forms of business corruption and of oppression had replaced the vanished evils.

The theme of Christian idealism was never-ending: Sheldon had ideal solutions for just about every problem the human race could ever face and clung to them no matter how utterly impractical they may have seemed to those around him. And the source of this idealism was, naturally, Jesus. "Jesus was the most idealistic person of the earth. Jesus has started more practical deeds for earth's betterment than anyone else."[26] That theme pours from Sheldon's sermons and essays and recurs repeatedly in the sermon stories.

Social Services

Given such philosophical and emotional underpinnings, Sheldon had plenty of specific ideas about how the world needed to be reformed, and he worked diligently on a great many of them. One of the most important fields for committed work was in the simple provision of essential goods and services to the poor. He urged his hearers and readers to open their bounty to those less fortunate. In novel after novel his greatest heroes and heroines were those who provided the most basic kinds of social services to society's outcasts—feeding the hungry, clothing the naked, housing the homeless.

Sheldon relied on traditional methods for serving the poor: such service came chiefly through institutional churches and settlement houses. Early in his career Sheldon surveyed the methods of successful institutional churches in big cities, and ever afterward Central Church functioned according to that model, especially through its provision of a broad array of services to Tennesseetown. The proper course for a socially conscious church to take was to provide both in-house services and outreach programs. Central Church provided both; services within the church building began in a major way when the kindergarten addition was erected, and Sheldon steadily expanded the facilities, eventually overseeing the addition of a gymnasium, a theater, and many other amenities. "Gymnasiums have a place in the parish house," he told a reporter, "because physical development goes hand in hand with the spiritual. Clean amusements and entertainments keep the mind clean and permit of spiritual development."[27] Institutional churches seemed to work well in Topeka, at the turn of the century a city of only thirty thousand. For larger cities, Sheldon advocated the use of settlement houses as well. But the vehicle employed was of less importance than the fact that services were delivered to those most in need.

Labor

Sheldon, following the lead of other social gospelers, focused a portion of his reformist energies on the labor question. The social gospel period was one of rapidly increasing union sentiment among workers, and the social Christians helped provide workers with a reasoned ethical basis for pursuing unionization and basic human rights in the workplace.

Sheldon believed deeply in the dignity of labor, and he never missed an opportunity to remind his parishioners, most of whom were not of the working class, that laboring people were just as important before the law and in the sight of God as their self-styled betters. "It is better to earn one's bread by the sweat of one's brow than to try to make a living by making other folks sweat," he would remind them. "It is the common work of the human hand that keeps us all from starving to death." [28] To a large extent he knew whereof he spoke having worked hard himself as a boy in Dakota and throughout his academy, college, and seminary years in a wide variety of quite menial jobs. He urged workers to be diligent and proud in their labor, and employers to reform labor practices in the interest of fairness and human decency. He demonstrated his concern for the laborer whenever possible: one summer, for example, Sheldon wrote an article advising those who would go on cruises and sojourn at resort hotels not to forget that real people worked at terrible jobs—stoking the engines of ships, for example—to make it all possible. [29]

One of Sheldon's more engaging short stories was a testimony to the importance of manual labor. At the beginning of the story, entitled "The Great Catastrophe of 1913," a coal-shoveler developed a strange inability to open and shut his fingers, and when he got to the hospital he encountered a long line of other workers with the same affliction: their hands had become totally useless, and there seemed to be no medical explanation for it. The disease spread rapidly until New York came to a standstill. Only laborers were affected; managers and executives were spared. People not used to manual work suddenly were forced to do it, but many things went undone; the city's utilities failed and services such as garbage collection and janitorial work came to a halt. Food quickly ceased to be available, and the city was threatened with starvation. As the epidemic continued, privileged persons had to do more and more manual work—and, as they did, their hands also became useless. At the end of a week suddenly all were healed, and the city sprang back to life. But all had had quite an object lesson in just how important seemingly trivial work could be.[30]

Although he was not very fond of strikes—they were confrontive, and Sheldon always urged conciliatory solutions to problems—Sheldon's ideas on labor were influenced by a mining strike he witnessed in 1895. He had gone to Negaunee, in Michigan's upper peninsula, to visit his brother Ward, who was a surgeon there. An iron miners' strike was in progress when he got there, and he was impressed from his first glimpse of it because of its religious elements. As he recounted a typical strikers' rally, a band would play a stirring march while five hundred miners marched into the town square. Then the miners all took their hats off while a leader prayed for God's blessing and asked God to keep them from such enemies as lawlessness and drunkenness during the strike; the prayers even asked that God "bless the other side—may they do right." The prayer was apparently the centerpiece of the rally; shortly afterwards the band would play again and the miners would disperse. Sheldon found a great uplift in this injection of faith into a critical human situation.[31]

Labor issues were much on Sheldon's mind for several years thereafter. He was especially concerned with the plight of those thrown out of work in the economic depression of the 1890s and on several occasions tried to help out-of-work men find jobs, usually with little success. Seeing how hard it was to find jobs in the public sector, Sheldon proposed public works as the answer of last resort—road-building projects, if nothing else.[32] In 1896, he made the plight of an unemployed printer the springboard for *In His Steps*.

For all of his concern for the hardships of distressed individuals, Sheldon's solutions were seldom more profound than suggesting that brotherly love be applied to labor problems or that Christian principles guide both labor and management. As usual, Jesus was the true solution. "The workingman will never be satisfied until he goes to him who said, 'Come unto me all ye that labor and are heavy laden and I will give you rest,'" he wrote in 1895.[33]

Strikes and unemployment were Sheldon's early labor concerns, but eventually his vision broadened. He became a firm critic of child labor. One of his better short stories, entitled "Of Such Is the Kingdom," featured a nine-year-old girl who had to work even on Sundays in a factory owned by upstanding church members. The contrast he sketched between the horrible conditions in the factory and the elegance of the churches where their owners went was appalling. In case the reader miss the point, Sheldon eventually stated it bluntly: child labor was "one of the greatest and most inexcusable wrongs of which a civilized nation was ever guilty."[34]

On the matter of unionization Sheldon was less clear. He supported the right of workers to organize to seek redress of legitimate grievances, but his misgivings about the inherent divisiveness of strikes also applied to unions. Although he had only good things to say about the activities of the union strikers in the iron-mine strike of 1895, a visit to a mining strike in the vicinity of Cripple Creek, Colorado, nine years later produced some different perceptions. Sheldon saw plenty of violence and said that almost all of it was perpetrated by union members against nonmembers.[35] After that he generally shied away from taking a stand on unionization; his ideals and what he perceived to be the reality of the situation must have been in serious conflict.

One special labor situation in which Sheldon had a lifelong interest was that of female domestics. The Sheldon family had hired help most of the time, so he knew the situation well. In many articles and one book, Sheldon hammered at the theme of fair treatment for domestics, or "hired girls," as the terminology of the day had it.

That theme first cropped up in In His Steps; near the end of the novel, Felicia, one of the dedicated Christian workers in the Chicago portion of the story, took on as her special project a training school for hired girls that would help to dignify and uplift the profession.[36] A year later, in another sermon story, Malcolm Kirk, Sheldon addressed the problem at much greater length: the last third of the story focused on a domestic-help tale in which a diligent and faithful young woman performed her menial tasks flawlessly but was kept in low status by the lady of the house. This discrimination was finally overcome, and the hired girl had a grand vision of reforming domestic service through applied Christianity.[37] Another brief but vigorous defense of domestics appeared in the next sermon story, *John King's Question Class*,[38] and then the following year the sermon story of 1899 (published as a book in 1900) was an entire novel devoted to the issue. *Born to Serve* is the story of Barbara Clark, a young woman who wanted to work as a domestic, despite her mother's protest that the job was too lowly for her. When she proceeded to enter service, she found that the work was indeed underpaid, that her living conditions were miserable, and that her social status was roughly that of an Untouchable. Through perseverance and persuasion, however, she eventually prevailed and at the end of the book was the proprietress of a thriving school giving professional training to domestics and raising their social status.[39]

The issue was of sufficient importance to Sheldon that at one time he even tried to organize something of a union of domestic workers, an organization which would promote the kind of elevation of their lot described in *Born to Serve*. John Ripley later recalled that Sheldon actually got a few women signed up for an informal organization that would represent them, but that the effort was not very successful because "the domestics were coming in from Sweden and Ireland and Norway, and there were black domestics as well, all just hungry for work at three or four dollars a week."[40]

Perhaps because the Sheldon family was always fairly dependent on domestic help, perhaps because Sheldon simply saw a flagrant injustice at close range, he continued periodically to write on behalf of better wages, better working conditions, and humane treatment for domestics. He urged that they be considered socially as worthy as those for whom they worked[41] and argued that their pay should be upgraded greatly.[42] "When we have made the service of the hand in the kitchen as honorable as the service of the hand with the typewriter, or the loom, or the counter, or the piano, or the pen, then, and not till then . . . can we expect young women of ability, of ambition and of power to enter the home for service there as readily as they now enter in other departments of human labor."[43]

Christian Socialism

The manifestly widespread injustices perpetrated upon workers during the Gilded Age, together with a traditional Christian concern for human brotherhood, led many of the social gospelers to advocate socialism as the economic system that would best promote justice. But it was socialism with a difference: Christian socialism. There were probably as many definitions of that compound term as there were social gospel activists. Broadly speaking, there were two types of impulse identified with Christian socialism: one was a relatively vague sense that Christians should support social justice (sympathizing with the poor and with laboring people) and clean up their own lives; the other was an aggressive, politicized commitment that tended to lead to alliances with Marxists and other political socialists. There were many more self-described Christian socialists in the vague camp than in the aggressive one, and Sheldon was solidly in that majority party.

However mild Sheldon's brand of Christian socialism, he was using the term sympathetically by 1895, when he wrote a series of four articles for *The Kingdom*, the social gospel weekly, entitled "Short Talks with a Workingman." In one article the reference was fleeting, with Sheldon's noting that one of the "vital principles" of Christian socialism was "the real unselfish love of one's neighbor."[44] In another he discussed the need to overcome selfishness and argued that the masses had to get involved in selfless struggle if Christian socialism were to triumph.[45] Not a very profound brand of socialism, to be sure. Indeed, some of the more seriously committed of the social gospelers criticized Sheldon and others who shared his views for claiming to be Christian socialists when in fact their analyses were so moderate. For example, the editor of the *Social Forum* scolded

Sheldon for calling himself a Christian socialist when "his plea was for charity rather than justice, whereas the Christian Socialist looks for the remedy of the poverty and distress caused by social conditions not in the palliating and aggravating application of pauperizing charity, but in the removal of the conditions."[46]

Sheldon's claim to the title of "Christian socialist" was indeed a thin one if his statements for general consumption are taken at face value. When asked if he were a Christian socialist, the formula he often used to reply was, yes, if you define the term as "one who applies the teachings of the Sermon on the Mount to daily life."[47] While it is true that Sheldon was a gradualist, it is also difficult to perceive just how far his socialist convictions went, since most of his pronouncements on the matter were intended for public consumption at home as well as abroad, and Topeka at the turn of the century was a rock-ribbed Republican town, conservative to the core. My own conclusion is that he may have been a bit more thoroughgoing a socialist than he let on to his immediate associates. He did resist any temptation to turn his ideas in a political direction, however; when in the early twentieth century a newly formed Christian Socialist party asked Sheldon to be its vice presidential candidate, he declined the offer.[48]

Sheldon apparently made only one lengthy statement defining exactly what he meant by Christian socialism; it appeared in his novel *The Heart of the World: A Story of Christian Socialism*. The novel probably was more autobiographical, at least in its early pages, than Sheldon ever would have admitted. The hero, the Rev. Frederick Stanton, was the pastor of a fashionable church and a closet socialist whose views suddenly became known. Stanton then gave a lengthy speech on his (and presumably Sheldon's own) understanding of Christian socialism. Christian socialism, he said, is first of all Christian and demands Christian conversion; it involves abandoning material prosperity as one's goal in life, adopting instead the objective of helping to realize the Kingdom of God; it entails the collective ownership of the basic necessities of life, and a turning away from large personal fortunes; it involves the spending of public monies only on important things, especially schools; it stands firm against the liquor trade; it regards the church as of great importance, supporting Sunday observance, missions, and the like; it supports marriage and the Christian family; it opposes class hatred, racism, sectarianism, and machine politics.[49] In short, Sheldon's vision of Christian socialism indeed involved some elements that might truly be labeled "socialist," but more properly, as his critics have asserted, were merely reformist Christianity. Only in his advocacy of public ownership of utilities was Sheldon certainly a socialist.[50]

Recognizing that most of his readers and listeners were not quite ready to abandon capitalism, Sheldon had other ethical ideas about the proper conduct of private business and the use of money. Against those who argued that private business was no one else's concern, Sheldon inveighed that the use of all property was a public matter.[51] On some occasions he sweepingly condemned "our pagan industrial society" for producing unemployment and inhumane working conditions.[52] More frequently, however, he focused on the individual business proprietor—such as were the backbone of his congregation—and demanded highly ethical conduct on the part of all parties. Over and over again he postulated that the cornerstone of ethical business practice should be the Golden Rule. The theme ran heavily through his fiction, where unethical businessmen were frequently the villains and honest ones great heroes.[53] Business ethics to Sheldon went beyond simply providing a fair deal for consumers in stores; the very nature of the business had to be productive and ethical. Sheldon had harsh condemnation for speculators, for example, whom he considered simply leeches on society.

Sheldon readily admitted that applying his strict standards to business life in the real world might well mean hardship or even bankruptcy. However, he wrote, "this fact would not prove that Christianity cannot be applied to modern business; it would simply prove that modern business does not square with the teachings of Christianity." He didn't shrink from the implications of that, going on to say, "If the men of New York or Philadelphia should find the immediate result of obedience to Jesus' teachings to be the partial or entire loss of their business, the ultimate result would be of far greater value to them and the world in a readjustment of commercial life on a basis of love to mankind."[54]

For someone who married into a prominent banking family, Sheldon's antipathy toward money was surprisingly broad. He did have clear ideas on how to use it; he was a great believer in stewardship and faulted would-be Christians for spending money on trivialities. "The first thing that is the matter with America is the way she is spending God's money," he wrote in 1922, listing the nation's expenditures for such things as cosmetics, tobacco, movies, and even chewing gum.[55] Sheldon remembered with fondness the poverty of his own youth and wrote, in an article aimed at a financially comfortable audience, "I am not arguing for a general condition of poverty for the human race, but I do think the human race needs to be reminded that the lack of things is not in itself a curse."[56] He lamented the fact that those all around him seemed to place the quest for wealth above all else, because, he believed, the acquisition of wealth and the seeking of the kingdom of God were "diametrically opposed."[57] He believed, in the time-honored Christian tradition, that material wealth was nothing more than a handicap to spiritual development.[58]

Sheldon's biggest salvos against material acquisitiveness were directed at the biggest fortunes. He doubted that any person of considerable wealth could have got to such a position honorably and believed that big fortunes were inherently bad for society. Apparently (perhaps only incidentally) promoting a labor theory of value, Sheldon argued that it would be better to avoid accumulating the money in the first place. Justice would be better served by the distribution of profits to workers than by the accumulation of big sums which might be used philanthropically.[59]

Problems of the Cities

The social gospel was centrally concerned with urban problems, and Sheldon was as committed as anyone to trying to improve life for the poor in the cities. For the most part his ideas were not very unusual or innovative; here he was clearly of service mainly as a publicist of the ideas of others. But some of those ideas, notably those concerning settlement houses, got heroic support from

Sheldon, especially in his novels. He did believe that the awful problems of Gilded Age urbanization needed to be solved before any progress could be made toward establishing the Kingdom of God on earth. He worked on a broad spectrum of social ills in Topeka and supported those fighting the same fight in the bigger cities. And he urged philanthropists to focus on alleviation of urban problems: "I wonder why Mr. Carnegie instead of founding hundreds of libraries all over the country doesn't go into Chicago or New York and build suitable tenement houses and give the children playgrounds."[60]

Of all of Sheldon's ideas on urban social problems, only two really stood out as distinctive, and both had to do with crime. One was the advocacy of a Christianized police force; the other was prison reform.

The proposal for a Christian police force was easily the more novel of the two. "Missionary police" was the term Sheldon used: since missionaries in foreign lands seemed able to turn people from their old ways toward Christianity, why should not a missionary police force be able to turn wrongdoers from their evil ways toward activist Christianity?

Sheldon's ideas about missionary police officers probably originated in his antiliquor agitation in the early 1890s, not long after he had arrived in Topeka. A real believer in the doctrine of "hate the sin but love the sinner," he ministered to the men who had ended up in jail as a result of his cleanup campaigns, supplying them with books and newspapers and, where necessary, even money, and seeing that their families were cared for. He genuinely believed, probably with good cause, that he had reformed the lives of at least some of those whom he encountered, and at some point he came to believe that such loving medicine for criminals should be administered prophylactically rather than therapeutically. Thus he began to write and preach in favor of a whole new basis for police work. The year of his greatest activity in that vein was 1913, during which two of his articles in national periodicals set forth his ideas in detail. One was a piece of fiction entitled "The Missionary Policeman," in which a visitor returning to New York after a long absence discovered, to his astonishment, that the behavior of the police force had changed en-

OUR POLICEMEN AS MISSIONARIES.

Cartoon lampooning Sheldon's suggestion that police officers be missionaries (from the Sydney, Australia, *Evening News,* July 30, 1941). Shawnee County Historical Society.

tirely. Police staff meetings were conducted rather like prayer meetings; police had become distributors of Bibles on their beats and generally friendly teachers whose main duty was to establish good rapport with the citizenry; crime statistics had plummeted; and public officials wondered only why they had waited so long to try such a police system.[61]

The other article set out Sheldon's ideas more clearly in a nonfiction setting. The reason he was proposing a wholly new system was, he said, simply that "the present police system is wrong because it is based on a wrong principle. It will never produce ethical results until it is based on the redemptive idea. How long will it take civilization to learn that nothing is so expensive as evil and that nothing can overcome it so quickly and economically as good?" He thus enumerated the qualifications a police officer (male or female) should have and told why the plan would benefit cities. His officers would be well educated and especially trained for the work; they would have to possess a great passion for helping others. They would have to look for the causes rather than the symptoms of crime, and be ready to counsel those needing help. They would have to befriend all on their beats and be devout in their own religious lives. Their duties would range far beyond that of solving crimes; they would have to instruct people in everything from health to physical fitness to sexual conduct. In return, cities would profit from a reduced crime rate; Sheldon flatly guaranteed that his scheme would cut vice and crime in half.[62]

Sheldon had had at least a modicum of experience in police administration by the time he wrote these articles. In the summer of 1910, after he had already made his ideas on the subject public on numerous occasions, Sheldon was appointed by Mayor R.S. Cofran to a brief term as police commissioner of the city of Topeka. There he did make one important contribution to police reform: he appointed Topeka's first policewomen, Elizabeth Barr and Eva Corning. But ongoing basic reforms proved elusive.

Sheldon also was an early and frequently ardent advocate of prison reform. Like many critics today, he believed that prisons were universities of crime and were adequately serving neither society nor the inmates. His first investigation into prison conditions came during his seminary years, when he took a two-month leave of absence to examine the state prisons in New York and New England to see how they affected inmates.[63] This long-standing interest was rekindled by Sheldon's flamboyant prohibitionist activities in the early 1890s. When he became concerned about conditions in the local jail where those arrested as a result of his saloon-smashing activities were sojourning, he obtained permission to spend a week there as an inmate. He duly made a report to the authorities at the end of the week, and many of the most glaring problems he had found were remedied.[64] Later, in about 1901, he and a *Topeka Daily Capital* reporter spent two weeks in the state penitentiary at Lansing. The governor had received complaints about the way the warden had been running the prison and wanted a report; Sheldon was a natural choice for the investigative team.[65] Although Sheldon kept his findings secret for many years, apparently at the governor's request, he eventually intimated that he had found cruel punishment there and had helped effect its abolition by reporting it to the governor.[66]

Actually, the mild-mannered Sheldon may have been a bit less strident a reformer than he later remembered himself as being. When he was an actor during the Kansas Penitentiary scandal of 1908–1909, the committee on which he served seemed less than ardent in its desire for reform, and he did not vocally dissent from the committee's findings. At that time Kansas had well-developed and profitable prison industries that operated so successfully that Oklahoma had taken to shipping its prisoners to the Kansas State Penitentiary. In August 1908, Kate Barnard, Commissioner of Charities and Corrections of the State of Oklahoma, made an unannounced inspection tour of the prison. In December she issued a scathing report charging the prison officials with feeding the prisoners inadequately and administering corporal punishment, in violation of Kansas law. Governor Edward Hoch and his Oklahoma counterpart Charles Haskell appointed investigating committees; Sheldon was named to the Kansas committee. On January 1, 1909, Sheldon's committee urged the immediate destruction of the two "cribs" at the prison, slat-bottomed boxes in which a naked prisoner, bound hand and foot, would be doused with water. But the two committees failed to agree on other reforms, despite what seems to have been substantial evidence of serious mistreatment of prisoners. The Kansas committee, including Sheldon, reported that the serious charges of mistreatment made by Barnard and the Oklahomans were largely unfounded—but then proceeded to recommend eighteen specific changes at the penitentiary, changes which seemed to back up the Oklahomans' complaints. And reforms indeed ensued from the recommendations.[67] Sheldon's commitment to fair and humane treatment of prisoners seems clear enough, but he wasn't the vocal dissenter he wanted to be.

Racism, Classism, Sexism

If there was any point at which Sheldon was clearly more radical than just about any other figure in the social gospel mainstream, it was in his conviction that all persons were essentially equal and deserved to be treated as such. In an age in which even many progressives harbored class and race prejudice, Sheldon believed that blacks and whites were equals and was one of the first Protestant ministers to welcome blacks into a fashionable mainstream church. He believed in fair treatment for Jews and Catholics, even if he thought their ideas sometimes mistaken. And he was nearly a century ahead of the rest of the country in proclaiming the essential equality of men and women. Although he did indeed seem to cling to some fairly traditional notions about sexual roles and family life, he was a staunch supporter of women's rights who went far beyond the position—frequently taken—that women deserved the right to vote but little more. Sheldon saw no sphere of human activity that should be closed to them.

Sheldon's unusually enlightened attitude on race has already been discussed in the earlier chapter devoted to his work in Tennesseetown in Topeka. His commitment to equality seems to have been sweeping, and his relief work among poor blacks cannot be written off to white patronization. In the sermon stories many of the ethnics and virtually all of the blacks were sympathetic figures. One of the later stories, *Of One Blood*, had a brilliant black hero who unjustly suffered many outrages but who managed to meet all challenges and ended by demonstrating the essential idiocy of prejudice. Conquering prejudice was the theme of the story, and it was played upon from several directions; at one point a Protestant and a Jewish college student fell in love—with the sanction of the author.[68]

Apparently Sheldon's oppposition to racial prejudice stemmed from his childhood; his parents taught toleration of all peoples, opening their prairie home to various ethnic settlers and to American Indians. Sheldon himself said several times that he had never felt prejudice and didn't really know why.[69] As for the prejudice of others, he couldn't understand that either.[70]

Whatever the source of his conviction, Sheldon was decades ahead of his time as a white civil rights advocate. He actively opposed antiblack activity in Topeka and spoke out against the Ku Klux Klan when it appeared there.[71] When the famous Kansas editor William Allen White jumped into the 1924 gubernatorial race as an anti-Klan candidate, Sheldon quickly announced his support.[72]

Anti-Semitism did not escape Sheldon's notice, and he condemned it as roundly as he did racism. Although Sheldon was something of a Christian absolutist and strongly favored missionary activities to try to convert nonchristians, he nevertheless found prejudice against the Jews abhorrent. Reminding his readers that Jesus and his disciples were Jewish, Sheldon wrote in 1939, "The entire passion and purpose of Jesus' life centered about human beings," yet if he were to return today, at the brink of World War II, he would find his own people suffering grievously. The returned Jesus would urge Christians to protest the persecution of Jews, and, Sheldon suspected, he might very well go and confront the leaders of Germany and Italy over their anti-Semitism.[73]

If Sheldon was unusually enlightened for his era in his opposition to prejudice based on race or religion or social status or economic circumstances, he was even more so in his affirmation of equal rights for women. He did have a romanticized view of family life and believed that good home life was one of the bases of the perfect society he sought; thus to some degree he accepted stereotypical sex roles for both men and women. With that important limitation, however, Sheldon believed in full equality for men and women and vocally supported the feminist struggle for equal rights. He urged women to become involved in politics, believing that there they would make a difference for the better.[74] He believed that they should have full equality in the workplace and wished that there were more women in mathematics and the sciences.[75] And his views were applied equally to both sexes; he saw nothing wrong with men's working in such traditionally feminine jobs as domestic service.[76] He believed that most perceived differences between the sexes were largely the result of socialization: "Some people think a woman is by nature more trustful and more inclined to believe in religious truths

One of the innumerable poems written by Sheldon and printed in the weekly church newsletter. Central Congregational Church, Topeka.

than man. I don't believe that myself. I think the reason more women than men are found in churches lies back in the past, in false training of boys and girls in Christian homes."[77] He also was far ahead of his time in demanding that the double standard of conduct for men and women be abolished. In one of the early sermon stories, *John King's Question Class*, a young woman asked the Sheldonesque pastor John King, "If it is excusable in my brother to smoke and drink and swear and do about as he pleases why should not society allow me, his sister, to do the same thing and excuse me?" King's answer: "Your brother is no more excusable for doing those things than you would be, and society has no right to make any distinction between an evil life lived by a man and an evil life lived by a woman. Both should be judged by exactly the same standard."[78]

Political Ethics

Sheldon shared with many other social gospelers the conviction that moral suasion, while important, would not suffice to bring about the Kingdom of God on earth, and that it was necessary to use the coercive powers of government to bring about some social reforms. His position was essentially the same as that of civil rights advocates in the 1960s who, when told that legislation would never make white bigots treat blacks with loving kindness, answered that legislation could change behavior, and changed behavior in time just might lead to changed basic attitudes. Thus Sheldon wholeheartedly urged progressive Christians not only to vote, but to run for public office, support public referenda, and participate generally in politics with dedication and conviction.

Sheldon believed that the great questions of the day were all moral in nature.[79] For Christians to address these great moral questions, they had to become active in politics. To those who said they opposed the mixing of religion and politics, Sheldon replied, "It is the unmistakable teaching of Christ that life is all of one piece and that the first duty of a man is always and everywhere to seek first God's kingdom and righteousness."[80]

At a minimum the Christian should vote for good elected public officials, and Sheldon blasted those who "do not wish to take the trouble to do their part."[81] Only by voting en bloc would it be possible to overthrow the cynical politicians who kept the triumph of moral politics at bay.[82] At least once Sheldon tried to help people understand how to vote; in 1902 he published a pamphlet outlining the structure of Topeka's government and the city's manner of conducting elections, together with a "catechism on good citizenship," consisting of aphorisms on local politics. The pamphlet's central message was to urge Christians to vote, arguing that the twelve thousand church members of Topeka could easily hold power, if only they would take it.[83]

Nor did Sheldon leave his readers wondering about just which "good" candidates they should vote for. In some cases he considered the choice obvious, as when a prohibitionist was running against a wet. But in other cases endorsements were in order. Sheldon was involved for some years with the Good Citizenship Federation, which operated in Topeka at the turn of the century and made straightforward endorsements. In what was then an overwhelmingly Republican state the relevant endorsements were usually for GOP primary candidates; in at least some elections a publication called "The Good Citizen" listed the Federation's slate and was distributed at the Protestant churches.[84]

All this implied that good Protestants should run for public office, and Sheldon certainly encouraged the practice. He preached to that effect frequently, and Christians entering politics constituted a recurrent theme in his fiction. The plots varied: sometimes the Christian candidates would win; sometimes they would lose amid Protestant apathy. But the goodness of their cause was not in doubt.[85] In real life, one might have expected Sheldon himself to run for office, but for reasons he never enunciated he did not. Probably he believed his impact on society would be greater from his influential pulpit than from public office.

Sheldon did have a distinct distaste for partisanship in politics, and the partisan political system may have contributed to his own hesitation to run for office. Sheldon lamented that there was in the land "a partisanship that puts success of the party above every other consideration. There are thousands of men in this country who believe more in their party than in their church. They will give more money and more time and more enthusiasm to their party than they ever give to their church."[86] Partisan politicians on several occasions came in for criticism in Sheldon's fiction.[87] In *In His Steps* one of editor Ed Norman's moves to Christianize his newspaper was the renunciation of conventional partisan politics, the backing of Christian politicians, and the evaluation of issues on the basis of right and wrong, not on that of their partisan connections.[88]

Sheldon apparently followed his own advice here; there is no evidence that he ever endorsed one of the major parties. "In politics I am an independent," he said,[89] and, although he once helped the Republican party by writing a "dry plank" for the gubernatorial campaign of Alf Landon, Landon afterwards remembered Sheldon as "voting for the man more than the party."[90] Topeka voting records from that era have not been preserved, but there is no reason to doubt Sheldon's claim of nonpartisanship. He did dabble at times with the idea of helping to found a Christian political party, especially when confronted with an electoral choice between two evils, the lesser of which gave "not much more satisfaction to my conscience than if I had stolen one dollar bill instead of two."[91] But nothing ever came of the notion of a Christian party. He did believe that it was as useful to vote for a minor party as for a major one, and he once proudly announced that he had voted for John P. St. John of the Prohibition Party in 1884, arguing that "votes cast on principle are never thrown away."[92]

Living the Clean Life

Sheldon's reformism went beyond the social gospel's typical concerns for tackling large-scale social problems; he believed that integral to the solution of social ills was the cleaning up of personal life. Much of this was to be done through exhortation; he always seemed to harbor a naive belief that individuals would readily reform their personal lives if only shown the right way. But he also believed firmly in removing the causes of sin, insofar as that was possible. He apparently never had any misgivings about coercive measures to insure sanitized literature, art, and theater; and enforced prohibition of alcohol was of all causes the single one nearest to his heart. He also, however, believed that coercion might in time become less necessary if people were trained in clean living from childhood, and so he advocated nonsectarian (but clearly Protestant) moral and religious education for children in and outside the public schools.

Literature was an important focus of the crusade for decency. Although Sheldon was not as conservative as some of his religious contemporaries—after all, he wrote novels, an activity some Protestants held to be inherently sinful—he nevertheless had a marked distaste for much of the day's literature, including a good deal of the popular religious fiction. In 1899 he expressed his displeasure about two current novels, Hall Caine's *The Christian* and Henryk Sienkiewicz's *Quo Vadis?* Although most of the reading public regarded these as great inspirational books, Sheldon took exception to the "blood and thunder material" he thought they contained. "I do not think there is any necessity for dragging into religious fiction—or any other, for that matter—details that would bring a blush to a young girl's face."[93] Three years later he argued that there were three valid uses for novels: entertainment, so long as it is clean and wholesome and uplifting; instruction in all kinds of fields, from adventure to travel to history; and inspiration. This latter category Sheldon found "the highest office of fiction."[94] Included in it were the books that depicted wrongs and then suggested a remedy. Inspiration and uplift, he contended, were what really made a book valuable.

Sheldon believed that essentially the same rules applied to theatrical productions. In 1901 he argued in the *Independent* for a "Christian Theater" that would consist of a Christian management and acting troupe presenting wholesome materials; he did not advocate the abolition of the institution itself, noting that "the histrionic passion of the human race seems to be born with it."[95] Thus he rejected the antitheater absolutism of his parents, who wouldn't let their children attend even a Shakespearean drama; Sheldon in fact saw wholesome drama as a tool churches might use to keep their young people away from undesirable secular pastimes.[96]

Nine years later, however, in another article in the same journal, Sheldon had become more pessimistic, lamenting that big profits were the dominant goal throughout the theater. The peg for his story was a visit he had received from a theatrical agent who wanted to mount a lavish production of *In His Steps*. When the agent couldn't guarantee Sheldon that the actors and actresses would all be devout Christians, Sheldon refused to grant his permission. He was not willing to cooperate simply for the big money involved, or even in the hope that it might uplift a few fallen lives. The producers had put profit first, and to Sheldon they simply had things backwards.[97]

When movies came along a few years later, Sheldon had the same criticisms waiting for them that he had had for the theater. In 1930 he complained publicly that he had recently seen a film so offensive that he had left in the middle of it and demanded his money back. He tentatively suggested a boycott of movies until the industry got rid of the sex and criminality he saw in its products. Even by the time he was making his case Kansas had a state film censorship board, but Sheldon concluded that it was not doing its job satisfactorily.[98]

Some popular cultural pursuits roundly condemned by many Protestants of Sheldon's day, such as dancing and listening to popular music, escaped any blanket condemnation from him; he only insisted that they be done in uplifting fashion and that any hint of moral decay in them be avoided. That meant that some whole genres were to be condemned, notably jazz. "What is popularly known as 'jazz' music," Sheldon wrote in 1920, "is physical, mental and moral nervousness set to motion, sometimes mistaken for rhythm." But otherwise popular music, he believed, could be compatible with his vision of living the Christian life, and he encouraged young people to compose and perform inspiring music.[99]

The Great Crusade: Prohibition

Fighting alcohol was the single greatest, most passionate social cause in Sheldon's life. He grew up in a teetotaling household; from the beginning of his first pastorate in Vermont he preached abstinence.[100] By the time he had settled in Topeka, fighting the saloon had become a major preoccupation. He was one of a group of clergy who played a pivotal role in finally winning the adoption of the Eighteenth Amendment, which established national prohibition; he championed the cause throughout the fourteen-year life of Prohibition and continued to urge its reinstatement after repeal in 1933. Only in his last two decades or so, when pacifism became his overriding concern, was prohibition ever second to anything else in his social conscience. He was himself a confirmed abstainer: he once told an audience that he had signed a total abstinence pledge—involving both tobacco and alcohol—at the age of seven and had never violated it.[101]

Kansas was theoretically dry when Sheldon arrived there in 1889, but it was surrounded by wet states, and Kansas law forbade only manufacture and sale of alcohol, not importation and possession of it. Moreover, a large loophole in the law allowed liquor to be sold for medicinal purposes. Thus a ready-made crusade lay waiting for him, and his many activities against drink have been sketched in chapter 2, above. Despite the problems of prohibition, Sheldon always believed that those problems were much preferable to the greater ones that would result from freely available liquor. He argued, for example, that undoubtedly the liquor laws of Nebraska and Missouri, where drink was legal, were violated more frequently than was the prohibitory law of Kansas.[102] During the crusade for national prohibition, Sheldon repeatedly pointed to Kansas as a golden land that enjoyed boundless prosperity and was filled with law-abiding citizens as a result of its relative freedom from alcohol.[103]

The crusade against alcohol was prominently featured in most of Sheldon's books. The typical plot of a Sheldon sermon story had a young minister or dedicated layman who became an ardent social and religious reformer; alcohol was nearly always one of the central items on the hero's reform agenda, and a prohibition campaign was usually pivotal to the plot. In *In His Steps* the little band of reformers undertook to save the denizens of the Rectangle, the slum district of the mythical town of Raymond, from the enemy which was drink. What is arguably the most dramatic scene in the book occurs when Loreen, a fallen young woman who has just been saved by the "What would Jesus do?" reformers, is killed by a "heavy bottle" (clearly a liquor bottle) thrown from a window above a saloon. Sheldon's moral was related as Loreen's soul entered Paradise:

> And yet this is only one woman out of thousands killed by this drink devil. Crowd back, now, ye sinful men and women in this filthy street! Let this august dead form be borne through your stupefied, sobered ranks! She was one of your own children. The Rectangle had stamped the image of the beast on her. Thank him who died for sinners that the other image of a new soul now shines out of her pale clay. Crowd back! Give them room! Let her pass reverently, followed and surrounded by the weeping, awestruck company of Christians. Ye killed her, ye drunken murderers! And yet—and yet—O Christian America, who killed this woman? Stand back! Silence, there! A woman has been killed. Who? Loreen. Child of the streets. Poor, drunken, vile sinner. O Lord God, how long, how long? Yes. The saloon killed her; that is, the Christians of America, who license the saloon. And the Judgment Day only shall declare who was the murderer of Loreen."[104]

Most of the other sermon stories had similarly dramatic plots and subplots dealing with demon rum, and two of Sheldon's books were entirely devoted to the prohibitionist cause. *Who Killed Joe's Baby?*, a short story issued as a pamphlet, told of a reformed drinker who fell off the wagon and accidentally killed his new baby; when he sobered up he hung himself in jail. The story ended with a plea for "all who are implicated" in the liquor trade to repent before the wrath of God should strike them.[105] *The Narrow Gate*, Sheldon's sermon story at Central Church in the fall of 1902, was dedicated to the temperance movement and claimed to be based on real events; the novel contains several footnotes explaining that one part or another of the story was taken from real life. The plot involved an idealistic young college graduate who bought a newspaper in a small town and crusaded for prohibition against strong opposition.[106]

Sheldon perhaps emphasized the importance of abstinence more than most of his colleagues in the social gospel movement, but he was by no means unusual in counting liquor a major social problem of the day. Most of the major social gospel theorists and activists saw temperance, at least, as crucial to the achievement of the social agenda. Even today it is hard to criticize their concern for sobriety, for alcohol was then being consumed in enormous quantities (this was the era of cheap liquor, before stiff excise taxes had come into existence), and drunkenness was common. W.D.P. Bliss, in his definitive *New Encyclopedia of Social Reform* (1908), listed yearly per capita consumption figures for alcoholic beverages, taken from the United States Statistical Abstract, and found that consumption had risen from 4.17 gallons in 1840 to 22.27 gallons in 1906. Although a portion of the increase in total gallonage was due to a shift in consumption from liquor to beer, the net increase in alcohol consumption was real—and substantial.[107] To the social gospelers, alcohol had to be brought to heel. If Sheldon was more emphatic than most on the issue, his ideas were nevertheless not atypical.

Sheldon's view of liquor was simple and practical. "If a single blessing has ever come to humanity from the use of intoxicants as a beverage, the experience of the race has so far failed to register it," he proclaimed.[108] Liquor was a drain on the economy (Sheldon firmly believed that the prosperity of Kansas, compared to the lower economic status of its neighboring states, was due to prohibition in Kansas);[109] it led directly to crime;[110] it had no legitimate medicinal value. Nor did the usually tolerant Sheldon have any use for the argument that the final choice ought to be left to the individual: "The cry for personal liberty is a cry for personal selfishness when it is a cry of rebellion against all laws and restrictions. The man who is in chains to habit is the man who is exercising his personal liberty at the expense of some one's development. . . ."[111]

Sheldon's rhetoric was backed up with vigorous actions against drink. His agitation against the illegal "joints" in Topeka, which was discussed in chapter 2, was only one campaign in a lifelong war. He preached prohibition for decades, both at Central Church and on many speaking tours. Occasionally he would engage in a dramatic

Sheldon and associates dumping illegal liquor, 1914. Kansas State Historical Society.

gesture to make his point, as happened on July 19, 1896, when he combed eleven daily newspapers from Topeka and other cities during a one-week run for articles about crimes that seemed directly attributable to drink, pasted the articles together in a roll, and then unrolled it and demonstrated that the articles, forty-six in all, stretched all the way across the church sanctuary—they made up a column nearly twenty-nine feet long.[112]

Sheldon was last a player on the national prohibition scene in the late 1920s, when he composed a "Total Abstinence Promise" and tirelessly urged every audience he could to sign it en masse. He argued that signing the pledge could be construed as an act of patriotism, since prohibition was the law of the land, and remonstrated against being called an unpatriotic pacifist by persons not patriotic enough to support the law by abstaining from drink.[113] Previous attempts at making prohibition work had focused on urging public officials to arrest and prosecute bootleggers, but Sheldon argued that it was also important to cut the problem off at the true source by trying to reform the drinkers."[114] Certainly the pledge appealed to many of his fellow citizens; although firm numbers are hard to come by, signatures may have reached into the millions.

When an attempt was made to repeal prohibtion in Kansas in 1934, following the repeal of national prohibition, Sheldon stumped against it; the repeal effort was defeated by a wide margin.[115] As one might imagine, Sheldon steadily supported the various prohibitionist organizations, notably the Anti-Saloon League and the Women's Christian Temperance Union, which relied heavily on Protestant churches for their support.

The high point of Sheldon's personal campaign for prohibition came with his participation in the "Flying Squadron" in 1914 and 1915, an episode so important to Sheldon that he devoted a whole chapter of his autobiography to it.[116] Simply put, the Squadron was a group of strong public speakers who whistlestopped through the country for prohibition with great impact. Organized by Governor J. Frank Hanly of Indiana (later a prohibition candidate for President) and Oliver Wayne Stewart of Illinois, the project saw three teams of speakers and musicians crisscross the country on trains, stopping in town after town to hold prohibition rallies and using the proceeds of the evening's collection to buy the tickets to the next stop. The three teams operated serially, so that each town had three totally different programs on successive nights. Sheldon was one of the Squadron's most popular speakers, cracking corny jokes and telling stories from his prairie boyhood (for example, one about killing a big rattlesnake, concluding with the moral, "That snake was not something to be regulated . . . ; it was something to be killed.")[117] before getting down to business and sketching his great vision of a dry America. He advanced many reasons for outlawing liquor, but they all boiled down to one: "Humanity is worth too much to be destroyed."[118] Sheldon was no spring chicken at the time; he was approaching sixty years of age, with a lot of hard living in those years. But for eight months he devoted every ounce of his energy to what he considered the noblest cause of the day. In the process he traveled 65,000 miles and spoke in over 250 towns.[119] And he and the other Squadron members surely made an impact; efforts like theirs had more than a little to do with the ratification of the Eighteenth Amendment by the necessary thirty-six state legislatures just three years later.

Sheldon's campaign against alcohol was never violent, but it should be mentioned that he was a relative rarity among proper members of the clergy in defending, at least part of the time, the sometimes-violent antisaloon agitators, notably Carry Nation, the advocate of what Sheldon called "hatchitation" against the saloons. While his clerical brethren were often embarrassed by her physical destruction of speakeasies, Sheldon at least once invited her to give a talk at Central Church. Like many of his clerical colleagues, he tended at the time to counsel moderation and obedience to law. But he loved Nation's spirit, and in a series of three articles written three decades after the height of her prominence he wrote, "Well, if that is queer or abnormal I wish we had a lot more of it. The abnormal men and women of this world are the ones who are breaking the law in various ways, and those who never hear any voice but that of their own selfish passions." Carry Nation "was a saint on earth compared with a lot of smug, self-satisfied 'good citizens' who are so unacquainted with the voice of God that they wouldn't recognize it if they heard it."[120]

Sheldon's crusading for prohibition was not confined to the United States. The runaway success of *In His Steps* in other English-speaking countries led to a plethora of invitations to stump for the cause abroad, especially in Great Britain. The first of these journeys apparently took place during the summer of 1900; on it Sheldon was stunned to see what seemed to be plentiful saloons and rampant drunkenness, and was amazed that Britons seemed to shrug off his concern. He wrote home that if England were to fall in the next century, it would be because it had drunk itself to death, and that Kansans should be more thankful than ever that they lived in a prohibition state.[121] On the next trip, in 1908, Sheldon saw it all again and wrote of his dismay that the liquor business in Great Britain was still respectable and that children even went into pubs with their parents.[122] Nevertheless, Sheldon also encountered many strong temperance organizations and optimistically, as usual, concluded that the beginning of the end of the drinking era was in sight. To him the future was indeed bright; within twenty-five years, he was certain, the drink industry of the English-speaking world would "be a thing of the past historically; and we will look back with astonishment on a time when we permitted it to exist, even as our children ask us questions concerning the fact of chattel slavery."[123]

A decade later Sheldon was back again, lecturing for prohibition in the waning days of World War I. Again he was astonished at what he saw: a nation in which food, but not liquor, was rationed—even though enough grain to make 750,000 loaves of bread a day was going to brewers, as he reported. Even worse, the resulting alcoholic beverages were being sold freely to American soldiers. "It seems to me as though we might as well stand our boys against a wall and shoot them as for them to be sent home diseased and in shame," he argued.[124] Sheldon doggedly carried on, campaigning in fifty British towns and cities in fewer than fifty days, but the optimism of 1908 was no longer there, especially when he deduced that some Protestant denominations were openly against prohibition and that prominent Anglicans had major holdings in the liquor business.[125]

In between the latter two British trips Sheldon took the longest of his prohibition tours, to Hawaii, other South Sea islands, Australia, and New Zealand. Mrs. Sheldon and their son Merriam accompanied him, and his written account of the trip focused on the adventures of traveling and on being in a foreign land at the outset of a world war, leading one to speculate that the speaking engagements themselves were less than memorable.[126] The visited lands, at any rate, did not go dry. He did, however, come up with another new prohibitionist idea at some point in his travels—a proposal for an ocean liner with "the lid on." He was certain that a major ocean liner free of drink and gambling would find a huge market.[127] Alas, it was another Sheldon idea which never came to pass.

Sheldon detested the use of tobacco nearly as much as he did that of alcohol; in 1900, the Christian daily newspaper version of the *Topeka Daily Capital* was as free of advertising for tobacco as of that for liquor. Nevertheless, his love of people overcame his prohibitionism at crucial times. Thus he never really condemned his son, Merriam, when the younger Sheldon took up both smoking and drinking. Indeed, Merriam's own son recalled in 1982, Charles Sheldon secretly abetted Merriam's smoking habit: "He would often send dad a pipe which he would order using a pseudonym."[128]

One last note on intoxicating substances needs to be inserted before we leave the topic. Even though Sheldon never wavered in condemning inebriation, he himself did at least once undergo the transition to an altered state of consciousness through chemical means. And, although he found the experience entirely positive and a boost to his creativity, he apparently never generalized from his experience what many others have: that there are benefits as well as hazards in the uses of psychoactive substances. As he told the story,

> A few years ago when in a hospital recovering from an operation, an assistant gave me a dose of codein, an extract of opium. It had the same effect on me that hashish has on the Andaman natives who take hashish to drown their troubles. And I had the most remarkable dream

that I have ever had. When I recovered and was able to write again, I put that dream down on paper and I have submitted it to six different magazines only to have it rejected by the editors who say the public is not interested. But when I have read that dream to audiences I have never had a more interested hearing. The people come after the meeting and tell me it is the most interesting thing I have ever written.[129]

Sheldon was so enchanted by his story created under a narcotic influence that he published it himself as a pamphlet entitled *For Love of Country*. It is an antiwar vignette in which a soldier becomes so crazed by violence that he finally fires on his own family—just before being killed himself. Sheldon's third-person introduction related, "This parable of war came to Mr. Sheldon as a whole while he was in the hospital two years ago. It was a sort of dream vision, where every detail was clear as day in a series of pictures that he saw, as he wrote, as if they were painted on a circular wall."[130]

So at least once the prohibitionist tasted something of the forbidden fruit—apparently without quite grasping the implications of that fact. Sheldon accepted this experience with an altered state of consciousness but was apparently never interested in pursuing that path further.

Religion in Education

Sheldon recognized that patterns of behavior are instilled very largely in childhood, and he always emphasized the necessity of teaching right conduct to children. From the kindergarten to the Tennesseetown projects to the reading of sermon stories, Sheldon focused a major part of his ministry on the young. But he recognized that the church was not the only influential organization in the lives of children and youth, and in his campaign to teach his ethical ideas he came to advocate injecting religious training into public education.

The schools had failed, Sheldon eventually concluded, because they kept turning out selfish persons with bad habits.[131] He lamented that schoolchildren could study the careers of "killers" such as Caesar, Alexander, and Napoleon, while "the lessons of good will, and the beatitudes, and the golden rule are excluded from the class room because of religious fanaticism or narrow definitions of education."[132] The scandalous imbalance was plain to see, he contended. "Paganism" could be taught while the greatest religious and ethical system the world had ever seen could not.[133]

Sheldon believed that schools needed to teach such things as clean living, humility of spirit, independent thinking, and the importance of working for the betterment of the world.[134] Such teaching could be done at all levels; Sheldon once even envisioned a National Christian University whose prime goal would be the teaching of human conduct.[135]

Like many others in the social gospel movement, Sheldon saw the public schools as essentially Protestant institutions in which Protestant values should logically be taught. At the very least, he considered it essential that students should learn about the Bible in the schools; he believed that all should read such things as the major biblical biographies, the history, poetry, and literature of the Hebrew scriptures, and the life of Jesus, as long as care was taken to avoid passages which might arouse sectarian controversy.[136] Many would find that prescription impossible, but Sheldon, in what was his life's most ambitious editorial project, tried to show how it could be done. For nearly twenty years he spent odd moments editing a condensed and rearranged Bible that was finally published, late in his life, as *The Everyday Bible*.[137] Although he thought the book would be useful to all kinds of Bible students, he expressly desired that his Bible become a text in high schools and colleges.[138] Indeed, his abridged Bible was used for a time in some public schools, including some in Kansas.

He recognized the constitutional problem involved in teaching religion in the public schools, but dismissed it abruptly: "While it may be good statesmanship to separate Church and State, it is poor education to separate a human being from religion." The possibility of bias on the part of teachers didn't bother him, since he could not see how sectarianism had anything to do with the Ten Commandments or the Beatitudes or, for that matter, the life of Jesus. Would it be possible to separate a religion of conduct from a religion of faith, or to teach biblical approaches to ethics while leaving out super-naturalism? Sheldon's answer was to leave the supernaturalism in as part of the text, part of the history lesson, but not to try to confirm or deny it. In any event, he believed that he had solved the constitutional problem: Theology, and doctrine, and creeds might be excluded, "But if religion is love to God and man, it can be taught anywhere and it ought to be taught in our schools. If it is not taught, our whole educational pyramid will continue to wobble on its pinnacle instead of resting firmly on its base."[139]

Pacifism: the Last, Great Crusade

Sheldon was a pacifist as far back as his thought can be traced, and in 1900 one of his relatively early fictional characters, President Royce of Hope College, was depicted delivering a mighty jeremiad against the horrible madness that is warfare and urging his listeners to work actively for a world without it. The speech was pure Sheldon, loaded with the statistics about the cost and destructiveness of warfare and preparation for it that Sheldon liked to engage to make his point.[140]

Although Sheldon was early on the side of peace, in his retirement years it became his central focus, and between the world wars he had no stronger dedication than to working and speaking out, in all kinds of situations, against war and armaments. Some of Sheldon's most eloquent and impassioned prose emerged from that period. But he was no longer young; he had largely passed from the role of a social activist to that of a beloved but not particularly dangerous old man. He was pleasantly tolerated—even by audiences containing many staunch advocates of militarism—and his advice unheeded. John Ripley later recalled that his inability to have any clout for peace "really got him down. That little voice, which had been such a big voice at one time, just wasn't heard."[141] In 1981, Dr. Karl Menninger, then in his late eighties, reflected on Sheldon's situation and lamented that he himself was suffering from the same inability to have much impact in his latter years:

One of the compensations of old age is that you can do anything you want to do; you're so old that it's unimportant. I think I could announce that I was an anarchist or a communist or anything else and who cares? People would say, he's so old, he'll be dead in a little while, but it's a funny feeling to the individual because suddenly it doesn't matter what you say you are. . . ."[142]

However quixotic Sheldon's attempts to galvanize support for pacifism may have been during the years when he professed it most vocally, it was a lifelong concern of his and merits some exposition here. His critique of war was a familiar one: "War is the most wicked, wasteful, stupid, cowardly and unchristian activity of the human race. . . ."[143] "There is nothing bigger to do than to put an end to armed conflict. War is ridiculous as well as wicked."[144] Of course he believed that Jesus would be entirely on his side; in one of his many sketches of what he thought Jesus would do if he returned today he wrote, "I believe the first thing Christ would do would be to call the whole· world to repentance for its militarism," denouncing munitions makers, stockholders in war-related companies, and activities that promote the military spirit.[145] Bringing the world to Jesus would have the effect of promoting world peace;[146] thus did two of Sheldon's greatest causes, pacifism and missionary work, dovetail neatly.

Although Sheldon believed in universal disarmament, he did not believe that formal disarmament negotiations were very productive, and urged unilateral American disarmament. He seemed to believe that the nation could trust the common sense of world opinion to protect it, and that fears of being "exploited and colonized and appropriated by other nations" were groundless.[147] In 1935 he went so far as to predict that Japan would never attack the United States: "Japan has no intention of attacking us. The very idea is absurd."[148] There seems to be no record that he recanted after Pearl Harbor.

Like many other pacifists before and since, Sheldon was aghast at the amount of money spent on warfare. In 1926 he was staggered to learn that over the past forty years the U.S. Navy alone had cost the country 9 billion dollars, even as church people in Topeka were struggling to raise money for a hospital.[149]

Sheldon believed that even the use of military symbols was wrong. After watching the inauguration of the governor of Kansas in 1932 he wondered why, in a state populated with persons who were not bloodthirsty and whose new governor was a professed Christian, the inaugural parade was filled with cannons and uniforms. Why did the music have to come from military bands? Why did there have to be a war-glorifying parade? Why was military pomp necessary to start a new administration in a state which mainly raised food?[150]

Like most other pacifists, Sheldon found internationalism a vital component of his vision. "Life is made new in Christ by a wider horizon," he wrote in 1909. "A man begins to feel that he is a native and citizen of the world. All men become his brothers. His own country is not bounded by his own president, or king, or parliament, but he has a vital and living interest in every other people and government."[151] And just as nations had to forget their differences in order to achieve peace, so should the various religions abandon their long-time animosities. Sheldon believed that an ecumenical peace movement would be enormously powerful, and even at eighty-six years of age, when the Second World War was well under way, he was toiling to get Catholics, Jews, and Protestants to join their voices in protest against war.[152] In 1921 and 1922, as editor of the *Christian Herald*, he used his national pulpit to lobby for peace and personally presented the resulting petition to President Harding.[153] Even in wartime his optimism never flagged; he always seemed to believe that pacifist sentiment was growing and would soon triumph.[154]

Sheldon promoted a number of specific and limited plans that he believed would help bring about world peace. It occurred to him that if the nation had a secretary of war, it surely needed a secretary of peace, and in 1937 he encouraged the churches to petition the president for such an office to promote world citizenship and good will.[155]

In the early 1930s Sheldon campaigned for peace through the use of posters and billboards. Inspired by the use of billboards in China for propagandizing, Sheldon oversaw, at the end of 1931, the erection of ten billboards for peace along the highway between Topeka and Kansas City. Each billboard was different; the first read, "War is wicked, wasteful, stupid, and unnecessary. Fifty nations have by treaty outlawed war. Why not disarm?" The handpainted twelve- by twenty-five-foot signs cost fifteen dollars each; they were funded by such groups as the Topeka Rotary Club, of which Sheldon was an honorary member, and an unspecified women's club, probably the Women's Society at Central Church.[156] One billboard was even funded by U.S. Senator Arthur Capper, the Topeka publishing magnate.[157] Once that campaign was well established, Sheldon moved to install peace posters alongside army and navy recruiting signs. His poster in this case simply reproduced the first two articles of the Kellogg peace treaty ending World War I, to which the United States and sixty-one other nations were signatories—articles that solemnly asserted that the signing nations would never again resort to war to solve disputes.

The two world wars were as disheartening to Sheldon as they were to any other pacifist, but he made the best of a bad situation. One Central Church member wrote, "The impact of the first World War on Central church was a shock. After years of peace, and hearing Dr. Sheldon preach love and brotherhood, Central sent her boys to learn the disciplines of army life, and to fight."[158] Young men from the church joined the various military services; the largest contingent, which included Sheldon's son Merriam, joined the Washburn Ambulance Company, which Sheldon apparently found the best available option since persons in that unit would be working to relieve suffering. Sheldon presided at a farewell dinner for the troops, urging them to stay true to their homes and church and to do the best they could to be constructive rather than destructive.[159] In his most notable sermon on the war, Sheldon sounded like a "just war" proponent in cautioning all parties to avoid personal bitterness, avoid the desire utterly to annihilate the enemy, avoid hate. The goal of war must be the abolition of all war, he contended; Christians must hold to a vision of a world without military forces. Moreover, they must hope for a future world government and remember that "the capacity of the different nations for loving is as large potentially as their capacity for hating, and far more lasting; for hate exhausts, while love recreates, and endures long after hate has ceased to be even a hideous memory." Finally, Sheldon, ever the optimist, hoped that after the war Christianity's most glorious era would begin.[160] He supported Woodrow Wilson's vision of the League of Nations but cautioned that any such union dare not forget that it would fail if it did not depend on divine help.[161]

Nor did his optimism desert him during the next war. He believed that progress toward peace had been derailed only temporarily: "When a mad dog is loose in the world, a just and equitable peace cannot come until his un-Christian force is put down," he was quoted as saying.[162] Even though he realized that the Second World War was the world's most brutal conflict ever, he steadfastly believed it would be the last big one.[163] And in the midst of the war, in 1943, at the age of eighty-six, Sheldon proposed a four-point peace plan that would include the foregoing of the practice of a winner's taking revenge, the complete abolition of imperialism, equitable distribution of the world's raw materials and natural resources, and a grassroots, world-wide encouragement of antiwar sentiment.[164] As he concluded in a dark moment of the war, "We shall win the war against Japan and Germany. But it will depend on our own inner consecration to a real Christian life if we win a world free from war for our children and theirs."[165]

7. The Religious Reformer

S heldon the social reformer was also Sheldon the religious reformer. Given his great love for the church, he naturally wanted it to be the best institution it could be. Thus he plowed new ground in pastoral counseling, liturgical reform, and the role of theology in church life. Most importantly, his was a powerful voice for church union. Sheldon realized that the creation of a united Protestant church would be difficult but, ever the optimist, could still say at the age of eighty-two, "I hope I live long enough to see a United Church of the United States."[1]

Urging a United Church

Sheldon did not invent the idea of a united Protestant church; he was rather an early advocate of an idea that by about the 1880s, the time when Sheldon was honing his ecclesiastical and social theories at Andover Seminary, had gained something of a following in certain Protestant circles. By that time there were several church-unity organizations operating, the most influential of which were the Evangelical Alliance and the Convention of Christian Workers. Another similar group, the Brotherhood of Christian Unity, in the 1890s sponsored a magazine called *Christian Unity*, which promoted the idea to a national audience.[2]

Sheldon was an advocate of unity, then, well before he arrived in Topeka. The theme was one he preached on many times and otherwise promoted in various forums in his first few years there. For example, when he was the guest speaker one day in 1892 at a colloquium sponsored by the department of history and sociology at the University of Kansas in nearby Lawrence, he bemoaned the division of Protestantism and described to his academic audience a town in Kansas with a population of fifteen hundred and with thirteen Protestant churches, each of them tiny and therefore without much moral influence.[3] A few months later, in March 1893, he preached a sermon at Central Church entitled "A Plea for the Unity of Christendom," in which he pointed out that there were over fifty denominations represented in Topeka, separated by various kinds of jealousy. "We have in our own immediate neighborhood," he said, "five distinct churches for a population that is insufficient to support more than two churches with any degree of needed financial power, and the result is a division of strength instead of a division of labor." Knocking on nineteen doors one day, he reported, he had found adherents of ten different denominations. He could conclude that "the only reason why there are 150 churches today instead of one is because of pride, selfishness, narrowness, and wickedness. . . . There is no good reason today why the Congregational, Presbyterian, Methodist, Baptist, Lutheran, Episcopal and Christian churches should not be one church in name and reality." The basis of such a union would be simple: it would be "the creed of Christ. And what was that? *Supreme love for God and supreme love for man.*" And what could a united church do? Such a body, "united in its condemnation of unlawful and selfish getting and holding of God's money, would produce a greater revolution in society and bring about needed reforms in this direction far more speedily and powerfully than any are now being brought about by political agitation."[4]

The argument thus advanced early in his career was basically the one Sheldon stuck with for life. He believed, as always, that his ideas on the matter represented the will of Jesus, who, if he were to return, would "without doubt" call upon the denominations to form "one great United Church of the United States."[5] Jesus, after all, prayed that they would all be one, but his prayer was being mocked by the manifest divisions among the churches.[6] Sheldon found it scandalous that he was not allowed to take communion with his Episcopal brethren and that on one of his triumphant speaking tours in Great Britain he was denied the opportunity to preach in an Anglican cathedral for lack of proper denominational credentials.[7] After once being told by a fellow minister that he could not participate in a communion service he was attending, Sheldon lamented that, despite the good fellowship he and his friend had enjoyed, "we could not sit together at the Lord's table, owing to a rule made by man, not by the Master. I wonder if Jesus himself would be allowed to sit at the communion table if He were here again?"[8]

Sheldon's vision was a practical one in that he always made his case in terms of the impact a united church could have on society. Prohibition was always prominent on his list of things a unified Protestantism could accomplish. He believed that a centralized, coordinated missionary administration would greatly increase the effectiveness of that enterprise. A united church could underwrite a Christian daily newspaper. It could reform American politics.[9] And Sheldon went so far as to argue that it could bring about the end of all wars and create a true universal human fellowship.[10] He was sure that the clout of his united church would be enormous: the government, for example, could not ignore any church that represented 30 million votes.[11]

Sheldon's proposed union was one of commitment, not of doctrine. He well recognized that the churches would never unite on a doctrinal basis. So Sheldon simply proposed bypassing creedal and theological differences by ignoring them and instead making service the basis of union. The two great commandments—love of God and love of neighbor—would be creed enough.[12]

The process of getting from point A to point B, of actually achieving church union, was never much of a concern to Sheldon. He supported such ecumenical ventures as the Federal Council of Churches, but probably would not have had the patience to endure the lengthy negotiations which have proved to be sine qua non to ecclesiastical mergers. He was always willing, however, to do things in his own life and work to promote his vision. He recognized the importance of downplaying denominational distinctiveness and invariably referred to his own institution as "Central church," never using "Congregational."[13] When chances for ecumenical projects in the neighborhood came along, he jumped at them. In 1901, for example, in a lecture at Cobb Divinity School in Lewiston, Maine, he said,

> One of the most useful parts of my own parish work has consisted in the work which I have been able to do with the brother who is in the adjoining church of the Presbyterian denomination. We have, during different years, made our parish calls together, beginning at the limits of our two parishes, which lie together, and calling in person on every family within the boundaries of the two parishes. . . . The sight of two brethren of differing denominations, going together through their parishes, inviting every man, woman, and child to come to service or to belong to some part of God's work, is a sight which will do more in a short time to break down denominational lines, and build up a true federation of Christ's disciples, than possibly any other thing. If Christendom does not come together in practical ways for the building up of God's kingdom, it cannot expect to have success in individual churches in building up Christ's work.[14]

Although Sheldon usually described his ideal "United Church of the United States" simply as Christian, it is fairly clear that he envisioned a union of the major Protestant denominations. However, on a few occasions he specifically noted that the concept of uniting in service, not necessarily in doctrine or even in organization, could embrace the Catholics and, for that matter, even nonchristians. At least once, during World War II, he proposed that Protestants, Catholics, and Jews all unite—not as a single religious body, but as a unified campaign to abolish war forever.[15]

As one might expect, the theme of church union was not confined to Sheldon's nonfiction writings and public speaking. Several short stories and one of the sermon stories addressed the topic as well. The sermon story on ecumenism was entitled *The Miracle at Markham: How Twelve Churches Became One*. The story told of Markham, Ohio, where, for 2800 souls, there were nineteen churches, most of them in debt, unable to pay their ministers decent salaries, and utterly unable to fight such local evils as saloons and political corruption. When a fire destroyed one of the church buildings, two congregations began to worship together—and ecumenism became a real possibility. Finally, after many twists and turns of plot, the churches ended up cooperating—and did a great job of cleaning up the town.[16]

Untheological Christianity

As he contemplated scandalously divided Christendom, Sheldon came more and more to blame doctrine for most of the division, and the basic foundation of his proposed united church came to be what Sheldon called "untheological Christianity." As usual, he based his argument on his perception of Jesus, who, he believed, had been the focus of more theological discussion and more arguments than all other religious leaders combined—yet who had not been a theologian and indeed, in Sheldon's view, had not formulated any theological system.[17] People over the centuries, he contended, took the simple directives of Jesus and wove them into an incredibly intricate metaphysical tangle. From such convolutions had come the myriad sects and denominations; thus had emerged "a system of forms and ceremonies about the thing called Christianity that are as far removed from the teaching of Jesus as He was removed from the scribes and Pharisees of His own time." So why had Christianity wandered so far from the basic thrust of the teachings of Jesus? Because, Sheldon averred, "It is, indeed, easier to give assent to the Westminster Confession than to love one's enemies. It is not so hard to believe in the inerrancy of the Scriptures as it is to practice the brotherhood of man."[18]

Shortly before he died Sheldon told an interviewer, "I have never been able to distil a single drop of human kindness or love out of theological alembics and I have ceased to waste any of my time in breaking retorts and spilling acids over chemical theology."[19] As one of his parishioners summed up Sheldon's teaching on the matter: "He said, . . . thou shalt love the Lord thy God with all thy soul and with all thy might and thy neighbor as thyself. And he said if you keep those two commandments, you'll be so busy you won't have time to think about theology."[20]

The Role of the Minister

Sheldon was a conscientious minister who toiled, as many ministers do, endlessly for modest pay. It is thus not surprising that he had some ideas about the reform of the profession, particularly in the direction of easing the load. But he found specific solutions difficult to come by. In an article in the *Atlantic Monthly* in 1917, he outlined the minister's task in ten separate areas—from preaching to calling to civic projects—any one of which constituted a responsibility larger than, say, a corporate manager handled, and at a small fraction of the manager's pay. Yet he ended the article without being able to identify a single workable solution to the problem.[21] In one piece of fiction Sheldon toyed with the idea of a ministers' strike,[22] but it is inconceivable that he ever would have entertained that option seriously in real life.

Beyond the work load, Sheldon saw other unfortunate limitations on the role of the minister. In 1900 he listed some, among them formality (he abhorred, for example, the term "reverend"),[23] the felt obligation to follow long-established forms of worship, and the fear of offending someone in the congregation.[24] On the other hand, he could see the hard work as redemptive and, beyond that, managed to maintain some pastoral safety valves, such as humor and letter writing.

Whatever his ideas about the need to change the structure of the ministry and ease the minister's burdens, Sheldon was hopelessly addicted to the job all his life. In 1929, after he had been retired from the pastorate but still active in writing and editing for a decade, he wrote a friend that he still longed for the pulpit, that he would prefer a live audience of one or two to the printed audience of 200,000 he had at the *Christian Herald*.[25]

Liturgical Reform

Sheldon often remarked on the liturgical blandness of mainstream Protestantism and believed that reform of worship sevices was an important step toward revitalization of the churches. He frequently advocated various specific kinds of reform, ranging from simply rearranging the order of worship to chucking the entire service and observing an hour of silence.

Through most of his career Sheldon retained the bedrock Protestant belief that the sermon was the essential ingredient of a worship service, and he advocated strengthening its status by moving it to the beginning of the service. If a sermon is what stirs up emotion and conviction, he asked, why not start with it? Thus he proposed an order of worship that opened with a hymn and then went directly to the sermon. Only afterwards would follow the other elements, such as prayers, responsive readings, announcements, and more hymns.[26] These "preliminaries," Sheldon argued on several occasions, deadened the congregation, sometimes so much that "the angel Gabriel himself could not wake up the audience or do it any good by the time the sermon is reached."[27]

But that didn't mean that even rearranged worship services had to be the norm. Eventually Sheldon came to believe that preaching wasn't always necessary—by 1943 he was saying that if he were starting over he wouldn't preach more than once a month.[28] Always a believer in prayer, both corporate and individual, he suggested that the weeknight prayer meeting occasionally be moved to Sunday morning.[29] Some Sundays could be filled entirely with music. Others could be set aside as times for parishioners to ask the pastor questions. Some Sundays could be turned over to lay groups, such as the women's society and the youth group. And sometimes Sheldon advocated holding a Friends' meeting: an hour of silence that the congregation could use for private meditation.[30]

One reform that Sheldon advocated in a 1918 sermon story, although apparently never in his nonfiction writings, was an outdoor service. In *Howard Chase, Red Hill, Kansas*, the title character, a young preacher fresh from the seminary, found his church overflowing and calculated that by having an occasional outdoor service he could draw an additional one to two hundred farmers who would drive in from the country and worship—in their cars! Thus Sheldon anticipated drive-in churches in an era in which cars were still a novelty.[31]

Much of Sheldon's writing about worship reform came after his retirement, and there is little evidence that he tried a great deal of innovation as an active pastor. An observer at Central Church in 1899 saw little difference between worship there and in other Congregational churches, except that Central was "relieved of much of the formality that other churches have. . . . There is no set order in which prayers are offered, songs are sung or sermons preached. Whatever seems appropriate, is done."[32] Sheldon did, however, actually try the Quaker model on his congregation, occasionally announcing that there would be a service in which silence would prevail until someone felt moved to speak. In later life he came to regard those services as the finest he could remember.[33]

Reservations about Revivals

Sheldon lived in the heyday of urban revivalism, the world of Dwight L. Moody and, a bit later, Billy Sunday. Since Sheldon believed fervently in the conversion experience, he had no inherent problem with revivals; indeed, he wrote a short fictional work in which a middle-aged man had his whole life turned around because he finally, grudgingly, attended a revival going on in town.[34] However, he found the most popular revivalists mainly showmen: "If ministers, evangelists, radio commentators, editors would strive as hard to please God as they do to please worldly people, religion would fare far better than it does. Religion can not make strides among men until their leaders get behind it and stay behind it regardless of whether the crowds applaud or not."[35]

Sheldon rarely spoke negatively of any individual, but he apparently thought so little of Billy Sunday that he was moved to put his reservations in writing, although this manuscript appears never to have been published. In part, his objections to Sunday were that the preacher

> insists on a literal obedience to old methods of conversion and breaks every tradition of the way Jesus approached the multitude to convert it. He uses language, business methods, and vulgar mannerisms that Jesus never used and cannot be pictured as using. . . . It is impossible to imagine Jesus trying to convert the world by the spectacular, noisy, vulgar financial methods of Mr. Sunday. . . . I do not believe the methods used by Jesus were inferior to those of the modern professional evangelist. . . . But I do not understand the Christianity or the definition of it which simply hustles my body out into an aisle with a lot of other people before my soul has in its deep quietness assented to the call of the Spirit to live the real life of the Christian. And I cannot reconcile the hullabaloo of modern evangelism with its vulgar methods which *do* attact the crowd—with any definition or picture I have ever had of the way in which Jesus approached either the multitude or the individual. . . . It is not the Christianity of Christ. It is not the Christianity which will sometime be acknowledged by the world and rule it.[36]

Funeral Reform

Nothing about church life dissatisfied Sheldon more than funerals. He went so far as to label them pagan, not Christian, and urged a thoroughgoing reform of funeral practices. Sheldon devoutly believed that for the Christian death was simply an entry into a better life, and to make a fuss over it, to be gloomy about it, was not at all to the point.

Sheldon first became appalled at funeral practices during his first pastorate in Vermont. There, he reported, the services were held in farmhouses filled with relatives and friends; eventually he realized that funerals were, as much as anything, social occasions where there would be an opportunity to talk farming and exchange neighborhood gossip.[37] Sheldon chafed at the prevailing expectation that he preach a long funeral sermon and then another at the grave. And when he ventured to preach an upbeat sermon stressing the joy of immortality he found his ideas roundly condemned.

Even though at Central Church Sheldon managed to reform some of the worst traditional practices, such as a lengthy second funeral at the graveside, he still found things which offended him:

> Why should funeral services be so public? Why should the coffin stand open in church or home for people to pass by and look, the members of the family last of all? Why should the minister be expected to preach a long eulogy and prolong the agony of those who knew and loved and understood the departed one better than anyone else? . . .
>
> Why should not a private service be held, and then at the proper time a public memorial service at which proper and affectionate tribute could be paid, with triumphant music and exultant faith in a life to come? For after all, it is as universal to die as it is to be born, and the custom of making funerals public seems to me to be as much out of order as it would be to have a public service over a birth.[38]

The high cost of dying also astounded Sheldon. The expenses of a terminal illness, even a brief one, and burial could take a year's salary, he noted, and often that was money the survivors desperately needed.[39] To minimize such expenses, Sheldon led Central Church to purchase a large cemetery plot that its members could use without charge, and started as well a separate fund to help cover other funeral expenses.

As for himself, Sheldon proposed that his own funeral adhere to the guidelines he laid down: he wanted a simple ceremony in a positive vein, without much fuss. And if people smiled, or even laughed, at his funeral—that would be more than welcome.[40]

Preaching

Sheldon cut his homiletical teeth in an age of great pulpit oratory, and he found the model wanting. He felt the sermon should be a simple, direct communication between the preacher and the parishioner, without rhetorical frills. He was quite flattered when Luther Burbank, after listening to Sheldon speak in California early in the twentieth century, wrote to the pastor complimenting him on his pulpit style and noting, "I have often wondered why one needed to bellow, paw the earth, pierce the air with shrieks, and raise the devil in order to praise the Lord."[41] Early in Sheldon's career he expressed to an audience at the University of Kansas his conviction that a sermon was simply anything that made the listeners better persons.[42] Brevity, however, he saw as essential. Twenty minutes was plenty long: "No man need take longer than that to tell all he knows."[43] As for subject matter, "Never anything small" was his watchword: "We ought never to dare to preach anything less every time than the whole of man's relations to God and to himself."[44]

A Protestant Confessional

One of Sheldon's more innovative reforms was his development and advocacy of a Protestant confessional. The idea avowedly was based on the familiar Catholic model; in Europe he saw Catholics enter churches for confession all glum and downcast, and emerge cheerful. Confession, he concluded, was a positive force. Whether priests and ministers actually offered penitants any material help was beside the point; what mattered was that their counsel and listening lent psychological support.[45] Sheldon once contended that there were three main sources of influence in the Catholic Church: its unity, its dogma, and its practice of confession, none of which Protestants had. Protestant churches might well find that a confessional would be more important to their members than was the pulpit.[46] Although some stalwart Protestants criticized Sheldon, who seemed to be endorsing one of the most distinctive, and therefore reprehensible, practices of the Roman enemy, he continued to argue that the need to confide and confess was universal.[47]

Actually, Sheldon's confessional was rather different from its Catholic model; in response to criticism, Sheldon said, rather disingenuously, that his concept had "not the remotest similarity" to the Catholic institution.[48] Indeed, in practice Sheldon's version was essentially what today would be called pastoral counseling. It was face-to-face, not anonymous, with the minister and parishioner sitting together in the minister's study. And it never amounted to more than a discussion; there was never any attempt to provide absolution. In any event, Sheldon put the idea into practice for many years at Central Church. He called it the "Open Door," and in retirement said that it was in some ways the most interesting and satisfying experiment of his entire ministry. He therefore urged pastors everywhere to adopt the Open Door to help and comfort parishioners in the hour of their greatest need.[49]

Premarital Counseling

Sheldon's interest in counseling also led him to place an early emphasis on preparation for marriage. Not only did he come to require those whom he was to marry to meet with him to discuss the transition they were about to undertake, but he insisted that they also see a physician and get a certificate of physical and mental health. He became so convinced of the correctness of this latter course that when his strict standards drove many couples elsewhere for weddings, he began to agitate for a state law requiring certification of fitness for marriage.[50] Ultimately efforts like his led to laws requiring testing for syphilis before marriage, although in Kansas the law never covered any other physical or mental conditions, and thus was not nearly as comprehensive as Sheldon wanted it to be. A beneficial side effect, as Sheldon saw it, was that those who knew they would need certification of freedom from disease in order to marry would clean up their lives early on, so they could be sure of passing the test when the time came.[51]

Conventional Ideas

Despite Sheldon's broad interests in ecclesiastical reform, he was in many areas a conventional Protestant. He supported many Protestant traditions, including the centrality of prayer, Sunday observance, the importance of the church as an institution, missions, and conversion to the Christian life. Thus a brief survey should be offered of some of the major areas in which Sheldon supported the Protestant status quo.

Nowhere was Sheldon more devout than in his belief in prayer. He prayed a great deal himself and maintained that those who prayed the most best knew prayer's power.[52] He learned the habit of regular prayer as a child and never departed from it. He always turned to it in need. He once wrote that he had prayed long and hard prior to the delivery of his first sermon and had received so much help from the prayer that from that day onward he never entered any pulpit without first withdrawing into "the secret chamber of communion with the Most High."[53] Worship services at Central Church always had several prayers, and there were separate prayer meetings as well. Sheldon encouraged both silent and spoken prayer, and tried to make sure his parishioners learned to pray in public as well as they did to speak in public.[54]

He was nearly as devout in Sunday observance. Like many other social gospelers, he for years fought the rising tide of Sunday labor. Several of the fictional preachers in his novels delivered jeremiads against Sunday work, and Sheldon himself joined the fray most famously in 1900 by refusing to let the Sheldon edition of the *Topeka Daily Capital* be printed or distributed on Sunday. When *In His Steps* was syndicated to newspapers in 1900, many of them printed the novel on Sunday—and some critics accused him of being "a reformer for revenue only."[55] He was so stung by that libel that he told J.C. Kilner of the Advance Publishing Company, who had made some initial syndication deals before the book was realized to have passed into the public domain, that any future sales must stipulate that no Sunday papers be allowed to use the property.[56] Companies that demanded Sunday labor from their employees were "guilty of the crime of reestablishing slavery."[57] He determined that in Topeka fifteen hundred people had to work "more or less all day Sunday," even though only three hundred of them could have done the truly necessary work such as police and fire protection, delivery of utilities, and hotel and medical work.

Yet despite the firmness of his convictions on Sabbath-keeping, Sheldon as usual deferred to the informed conscientious decision of the believer. When a young working woman wrote Sheldon that she lived in a dank tenement, worked in an equally repugnant environment, and had a strong urge to do something very different—to go to a movie, perhaps, or take a ride on an excursion boat—on Sunday, Sheldon supported her. "I do not know of any set rules for keeping Sunday that apply to all persons alike," he replied to her. "What might be breaking Sunday for one might be keeping it for you." He concluded that she should ask herself "what would Jesus do?" and then proceed.[58]

Sheldon was utterly orthodox in his defense of the church as a great social institution. He once composed an astonishing list of the accomplishments of the church:

> The abolition of slavery; the emancipation of women; the value put on childhood; the education of the masses; the evolution of republics; the movement against intoxicating drink; the organization of missionary societies; the organization of the Young Men's and Young Women's Christian Associations; the rise of young people's societies; the organization of social centers to fight disease; the establishment of hospitals and asylums for the sick and dependent people by the state; the use of cooperative institutions in business; trade-unions; organizations to educate the people against war; Sunday Schools; Bible study classes; the printing press; reform associations to produce a cleaner dramatic life; the gathering of the people in mass conventions to discuss the questions of common interest.[59]

When W.D.P. Bliss attacked the church as an institution in the pages of the *Independent* in 1906, Sheldon sprang to the defense. Bliss found the church unable to provide economic help to persons in the ways that secular organizations, especially unions, could. He saw the churches providing charity when people needed justice, fair play, opportunity, and organization. Indeed, Bliss said that the churches really didn't even do very well at promoting the personal virtues, since wealthy church members were not necessarily more virtuous than the unchurched poor. Sheldon replied, "I have not yet found anything outside the Church which contains the spiritual and Christian leaven necessary to organize men and women together for social service. . . . I have found more selfishness and more hypocrisy and more narrowness in organizations outside the Church than within it."[60]

As we have seen, Sheldon did not particularly champion a set of theological beliefs, but, of course, while he was indeed not one to quibble over points of doctrine, he had a great many theological convictions that were not far from the liberal mainstream in his day. He was no fundamentalist, but he felt that he could easily reconcile his modern ideas with classical Protestantism. "Evolution? I believe in it. It dignifies the work of God. I believe in radio and the miracles, in airplanes and the divinity of Christ. I believe in all those wonderful things."[61]

Having had his own "Damascus Road" experience as a boy in Dakota Territory, Sheldon certainly believed in conversion of life, in being—to use the modern terminology—born again. But he believed that conversion was, as he put it in the first sermon story, not "a matter of emotion, but of will," and thus perhaps not so much a conversion as a decision.[62] Probably his best description of what he thought a converted person experienced is found in *His Brother's Keeper*, an early sermon story. There the character Stuart Duncan experienced something "so remarkable that it seized on him and held him in a loving and joyful grasp, making him feel that all other matters were as nothing compared with this." Now Duncan

> felt as if a new passion had caught him up and held him; a new life swayed his whole being; he was calm, and yet he felt thrilled with this new existence. There were no yesterdays any more. Everything was to-day and to-morrow. Jesus was the one great central, throbbing, pulsing, moving impulse with him. He was a new man.[63]

And conversion, of course, meant following Jesus in daily life. Stuart Duncan thus described his experience to a friend in the novel: "I can't explain it, Eric, but Christ seems the most real of all realities in my life. I can put it this way: henceforth I do not feel able or willing to do anything without first asking, 'Would Christ approve this?' Would he say, 'Do it'?"[64]

Sheldon was also an ardent exponent of missionary work. Even though he was tolerant of others, he believed in the finality of Christianity and argued throughout his life for the evangelization of the world—including his own nominally Christian country, which, since Applied Christianity had not yet triumphed, was still filled with paganism.[65] When an admirer met Sheldon in 1945 and began to ask about *In His Steps*, Sheldon diverted the conversation: "'I am more interested in this,' said Charles Sheldon, pointing to rows of portraits along the wall. 'When I was pastor in the early days, these missionaries went out from this church, more missionaries than from any other church in America, and their work is permanent. Wonderful things have they accomplished through the years for the Lord.'"[66]

Finally, Sheldon believed in the Protestant tradition of living the good, wholesome, devoted life. "Be kind. Be true. Be pure. Love little children. Love hard work. Reverence your body. Worship God. Cultivate clean humor. Hate all shams and falsehoods. Be friends with all the good in history. Begin the day with a song and end it with a prayer," was his prescription.[67]

Perhaps because he never could quite conquer his own appetite, Sheldon believed that diet was important, in quality as well as quantity. He wrote in 1906 that he became a vegetarian even before he had read *The Jungle* and that after he had succeeded in stopping the saloon he would make his next cause the stopping of overeating. For many years, apparently, he got along with nothing closer to meat than milk or eggs, and felt the healthier for it. "The Beef Trust can get nothing out of me," he bragged.[68]

A part of the good life that Sheldon found particularly essential was a traditional family life. Like critics in any age, Sheldon saw myriad problems in society, from crime to war to low church attendance, and often argued that one of the principal reasons for the prevalence of decadence was the breakdown of the oldest and most important human institution, the home.[69] He lamented the fact that families were not together on most evenings—in 1939 he counted 127 different clubs in Topeka which held weekly meetings, taking one or more members of the family away from home, and he knew that he could walk by a pool hall in the evening and see it filled with boys—and said that often it was wrong to speak of a breakdown in home life, because it had never been built up in the first place.[70] Over and over Sheldon urged solid home life on a religious foundation, with discipline, sharing of work, mutual love and respect, and daily worship.[71] Only on such a basis could we expect to see a wholesome new generation of world-savers emerge.

Life was at its best, Sheldon believed, when it was family-centered and free of frivolity. If people would only start at the personal and family level to clean up their lives—not only by emphasizing family values, but by avoiding pointless spending on silly amusements—the churches would be strengthened and the world, in turn, made better.[72]

8. St. Charles of Topeka

S heldon's popularity and renown reached their pinnacle in 1900 with the publication of the Sheldon edition of the *Topeka Daily Capital* and the ongoing sales of *In His Steps*. He could have written his own ticket as a clergyman or journalist anywhere in the English-speaking world, given that he was, at least for a time, the most prominent and popular figure in American religious life, one whom people regarded, as a Topeka historian put it, "variously as a flamboyant actor, a dreamer, an exhibitionist, a reformer, a radical Socialist, a dedicated Christian leader, a saint, and a voice crying in the wilderness of sinful humanity."[1] Instead, he continued to labor at Central Church until an early retirement in 1912, returned for a last stand in 1915, and finally retired permanently in 1919. He continued to make extensive speaking tours and for years was in great demand on the platform; he also continued his prolific output of articles for popular religious publications. But his concern for his flock remained central to his life.

Despite his popularity, or because of it, Sheldon did his best to keep his life as far from public view as possible. For at least twenty-five years following the publication of *In His Steps* in 1897, Sheldon consistently refused to write or be interviewed about the book, or for that matter about much of anything else. When journalists tried to push him he resisted the more stoutly. When a reporter wired Sheldon that he wanted to travel from the east coast to Topeka to interview Sheldon for a syndicated article, the preacher wired him back, "You need not come. I will not talk to you. I have some rights which even you are bound to respect."[2] Thus many articles written about Sheldon during the period of his greatest popularity contain little or no first-hand information, and several of them dwell on his adamant refusal to be interviewed. He was determined to be a pastor not a celebrity, and, as for his ideas, he was quite content to let his books speak for themselves.[3]

Whatever the gaps in our knowledge of the real Sheldon, it is clear that he stuck for the rest of his life to the watchword he had coined in 1896: what would Jesus do? As he expressed his conviction to Bruce Barton in 1930, "In short, I still believe, as I believed thirty-odd years ago, that the biggest question in the world is this: What would He do in my house, in my job, in my town?"[4] In article after article, and in several of his later books, he addressed that question. Some of the books were fantasies on the theme; both *He Is Here* and *In His Steps To-day* depicted Sheldon's Jesus in all kinds of settings, from the coal fields to the railroads to the U.S. Congress.[5] But beyond such works of his imagination, Sheldon found a few bedrock things he was absolutely certain Jesus would do: he would call for a "Christian Union against war, and against social differences"; he would mount "a world-wide campaign against the drink evil"; and he would "call for the preservation of the home life of all the people."[6] Sheldon, for his part, would imitate Jesus to the best of his ability.

Life at Central Church

Central Church prospered under its famous pastor. A steady stream of guests was always present, of course; Sheldon's fame was such that people came to visit his church and see and hear him even after he retired. Membership grew steadily, although not spectacularly: Sheldon did not try to use his fame to attract ever-bigger crowds and probably would not have had much use for the contemporary church-growth movement. He urged discipleship and consecrated service and giving, but never was very good at raising the budget. Figures from 1926, a few years after Sheldon's retirement, show that membership had grown to 2086 percent of the number of charter members (1189, as opposed to 57), but the budget was only 1238 percent of the first year's figure ($26,000, up from $2100).[7]

Sheldon was always a diligent pastor who, despite his heavy

schedule of writing, managed to put endless hours into parish work. He always seemed to find time, for example, to write notes and letters to large numbers of the flock. He did think a pastor's burdens excessive, and, even though his nature would not permit him to lighten his own load, he frequently complained in print that the work load was crushing. As he remonstrated in 1911, "I find it absolutely impossible to do the detailed work required by the pastor in the modern church and at the same time do work outside which seems almost as imperative in its demands as the local church. . . . When I came here 23 years ago, I had a church of 57 members. I have a church of 750 members now and I am only one man just as I was then."[8] In fact he had assistant pastors from time to time, but there is no doubt he carried a heroic load.

On several occasions Sheldon outlined his "typical" work day: Up at 6 or 7 A.M., he received phone calls from breakfast on, two or three dozen a day. For most of his life his mail ran from dozens to hundreds of letters a day, many of which he answered. Callers dropped in all day at his study, leaving him only fragments of time for his sermon preparation and other writing projects. He was always a vigorous parish caller, and for years had a great many speaking engagements. Of course the usual run of church meetings, weddings, and funerals occupied their share of his time.[9] In retirement he recalled that on a single day he had once performed four weddings and three funerals.[10] That he managed to write hundreds of articles and dozens of books is, under the circumstances, a testimony to extraordinary devotion, to say the least. It may also help to explain why there is so little information about a private, inner life of Sheldon: with that kind of work load, what else was there time for?

Sheldon's pay was never commensurate with his labors. For many years his salary remained at $1200. By 1910 it had reached $2500, which may have been the peak. The 1919 budget had it at $3500, but Sheldon didn't complete that year.[11] In any event, his pay never fairly compensated him for his work. Once in the early years the church fell two months—$200—behind in paying him, and on a Sunday morning he mounted the pulpit and announced that he would not—as a matter of principle, not of money—preach until the arrears had been paid. By the next Sunday the accounts had been squared.[12]

Sheldon did receive some money from other sources, especially from book royalties. Gilson Willets wrote in 1900 that Sheldon was then receiving $400 to $500 per month in book royalties, a sum so large that Sheldon was amazed by it.[13] However, he disposed of some of his auxiliary income: wedding honoraria, for example, often went to charity.[14]

Mrs. Sheldon was the daughter of wealthy parents, and eventually her family's fortune underwrote the Sheldon finances. Apparently her father, regarding Charles as "unrealistic" in his handling of money, willed his estate solely to Mary Sheldon, who thereafter controlled it rather tightly.[15] Charles Sheldon's closest associates confirmed Everet Merriam's judgment; all the testimony we have indicates that Sheldon placed no value on money.[16] When he was offered the presidency of Washburn College, he responded that "the thought of entering a place where most of my time must be spent raising money appalled me."[17] John Ripley recalled in 1977 that Sheldon's estate was quite small.[18]

As we have noted, Sheldon was no spellbinder as an orator, although he was widely regarded as a superb pulpit communicator. As early as 1900 he was advising his fellow ministers to preach plainly, straightforwardly, without flourishes.[19] Except for an occasional "illustrated sermon" in his earlier years, in which he might use a prop such as a chemistry set, he simply spoke to his congregation as if he were talking with each one individually. For his lack of style one of his parishioners who was a professional public speaker labeled Sheldon "a rotten speaker" whom people came to hear because he was the famous Dr. Sheldon, not because he deserved his enormous audience.[20] But just about everyone else found his style effective. He was easy to understand and so much at ease in his role that he was known for his ability to give an interesting talk when asked without notice. As one parishioner put it, "Each sermon I left with the feeling I had had a personal interview with him."[21]

There was no part of Sheldon's pastoral life that he found more

COMMUNION HYMN.

No. 440, Pilgrim Hymnal.

O church of God, through all the years
Thy saints have toiled for thee,
Thy servants and thy witnesses
Have longed thy power to see;
The ages mark thy influence,
The freedom of thy truth,—
O church of God, we pledge to thee
The ardor of our youth.

O church of God, thy living stream
Flows onward to the sea
Of mighty deeds in swelling tides,
That owe their power to thee;
The richness of thy heritage
Has made our hearts to glow
With thankfulness to him who leads
Our pilgrimage below.

O church of God, our prayer today
From hearts that throb with love,
Ascends to Him who for our sake
To earth came from above;
O make us loyal to the church
He loved, for which he died,
And cleanse us with the stream that flowed
From out his bleeding side.

O church of God, thy triumph sure
Awaits thee at the last,
When all thy battles have been fought
And all thy tempests past;
Then up the everlasting dome
Of heaven our song shall ring,
"All hail to Thee!   All hail to Thee!
O Christ, triumphant King!"   Amen.

Dedicated to the members of Central Church with the love of their pastor

Charles M. Sheldon

One of the many hymns written by Sheldon and sung at worship services at Central Church. Central Congregational Church (UCC), Topeka.

rewarding than his work with children and youth. He was convinced that teenagers had a fundamental religious hunger that needed cultivation and encouragement, and when some adults would fret aloud about the wildness of the young, Sheldon would remind them that such concern about the younger generation has been common at least since the time of the prophet Isaiah, that "the fact is that every age has the same mixture of good and evil."[22] If anything, he saw more hope in youth than in their elders; he often pointed out that it was the young people of Central Church who undertook the redemption of Tennesseetown, a project that the adults shunned because of their racial prejudice.[23]

Sheldon's Sunday evening services, where the sermon stories were read, were always youth oriented. He also oversaw several separate organizations that kept the young people involved in church life, ranging from such standard activities as a vigorous Sunday school and a large Christian Endeavor group to innovative ones such as "The Young People's Good Citizenship Federation of Topeka," which published its own monthly paper, *The Good Citizen*, and campaigned for enforcement of laws regarding temperance, gambling, cigar and tobacco sales, and Sunday observance.[24]

By far the longest lasting of the youth organizations was the Altruist Club. Organized by Sheldon in 1904 or 1905, the original members were high school and college girls and women who helped out in the Tennesseetown kindergarten. Later their role was expanded to assisting Sheldon whenever he needed extra help for a special project.[25] After some years the club quit accepting new members, but it continued its task of special attention to Sheldon's favorite projects—rather like the Jesuits' provision of special assistance to the Pope—and at this writing still exists as an organization of older women who play an important role in preserving Sheldon's memory in Topeka.

Sheldon's strong work with youth and his ardent support of missionary activities inevitably led to the emergence of a remarkable number of missionaries who went out from Central Church. Sheldon always considered that record one of the crowning glories of his pastorate. Various lists and fragmentary records which have been preserved at Central Church indicate that at least thirty persons (mostly young, but somewhat older in two or three cases) ended up entering church missions or the YMCA foreign service during Sheldon's pastorate or soon thereafter. Their fields of service included China, Mexico, Turkey, Bulgaria, Burma, Japan, Iran, Angola, Micronesia, Thailand, India, and Arizona (in missions to the Navajo, and possibly also the Hopi).[26] Sheldon claimed that Central Church produced "more missionaries than any other church in America," and one would be hard pressed to dispute his claim.[27] Sheldon himself got into the act occasionally, as when, he claimed, he baptized the first two members of the Hopi tribe ever to convert to Christianity.[28]

But Central Church never became so preoccupied with its far-flung missions that it forgot to minister to its own people. Several unusual programs flourished under Sheldon's leadership. Mention was made in the last chapter of the Central Church plot in Mt. Hope cemetery, where church members could be buried free of charge, as well as of the fund established to help defray other funeral expenses. A separate emergency fund was also established shortly after the turn of the century; loans, and occasionally outright grants, were made from it to persons in need. Most of the disbursements from the fund went to persons who had suffered misfortunes, but the record indicates that in some cases it became a source of small business loans, as when a contractor borrowed money to finish a small building project, or when the publisher of a small weekly newspaper used fund money to get through tough periods.[29]

One of Sheldon's more innovative programs at Central Church was his "Open Door." As detailed in the previous chapter, this Protestant equivalent of the Catholic confessional led the way toward the pastoral counseling that is standard everywhere today. Sheldon meanwhile always kept his eyes open for innovative ways to spread his social gospel. In 1901 he gave what is believed to have been the first address via long distance telephone when he spoke from Topeka to a men's group at the Prospect Avenue Congregational Church in Kansas City. Seventy-five receivers were provided for the Kansas City men, who reported good quality voice transmission, even though they found holding the phones to their ears a bit tiresome.[30]

Sheldon stayed at Central Church, despite an enormous work load and a pitiful salary, because he wanted to, not for lack of alternatives. Especially during the height of his fame at the turn of the century he could have had his choice of jobs in churches throughout the country. Several writers of sketches of Sheldon at the time told of the many offers he received, but few details are available. Even his closest friends were not told much about such offers. In his autobiography he wrote, simply, "One had better stay in an environment to which he is accustomed and with people who are familiar with his peculiarities than attempt what would be in reality more of an experiment than a program."[31] He similarly never went after the most lucrative speaking offers, but instead went for low or nonexistent fees to the places he preferred, such as Christian Endeavor groups.[32] Similarly after the Sheldon edition of the *Topeka Capital* caused a nationwide sensation, he was offered as much as $15,000 a year to write for the popular press, but he declined all such offers.[33]

Sheldon the Person

Visitors to Topeka who described Sheldon usually focused on physical features such as "his flashing eyes [which] look straight through you."[34] Topekans, however, always began their descriptions by noting his upright character and his boundless warmth toward his fellow humans. So effusive were their descriptions, in fact, that Sheldon once complained in a letter to a friend, "The only trouble for me is to live up to the press notices. I hope you and my many friends will allow me a few human faults, so that I may have the pleasure of feeling like other people!"[35] However, his passion for living and his enormous love for everyone he met combined to make him a great local hero. Little kindnesses and courtesies endeared him to nearly everyone, and if he had any enemies after his early, confrontational social-activist years, they stayed well hidden.

Perhaps what drew people to him was his bedrock faith. As a visitor observed in 1900, Sheldon radiated "absolute conviction. The man believed. And he believed with such tremendous earnestness that he exuded the atmosphere of certainty."[36] Yet at the same time he retained a great humility and accessibility.

Sheldon's kindness and concern for those with whom he came into contact naturally led him into financial generosity. He helped many through the church's emergency fund, but he also dipped into his own pocket willingly. That led to controls being imposed by Mrs. Sheldon; Sheldon's grandson and namesake recalled in 1982 that "grandma gave him $5.00 spending money periodically because he would give money to anyone with a sad story." Nevertheless, financial impracticality paid human dividends: everywhere he went he made friends, and he was as likely as not to pick average working people over the socially elite.[37]

Sheldon's fundamental human warmth lived in the memories of those who knew him more than anything else about him. During the interviews I conducted with his parishioners in 1981, tales of little acts of kindness—such as a surprise visit on one's birthday from the famous pastor, who was bearing a small gift,[38] or an earnest note of apology for an almost imperceptible slighting of someone[39]—surfaced repeatedly. Over and over the interviewees said that they simply didn't know a bad thing about him. When one of Sheldon's successors as pastor at Central, Charles Helsley, dubbed him "St. Charles of Topeka" in a memoir, he was simply reflecting the consensus of the congregation. And other anecdotes about his gentle kindness are rife in the secondary Sheldon literature. When people asked permission to quote from his works, he would tell them to use his words as if their own, without any reference to himself.[40] When a woman mailed him a copy of *In His Steps* for an autograph and enclosed twelve cents for return postage, Sheldon returned six cents in a separate letter, because the book postage came to only six cents.[41]

Sheldon's gentle sense of humor was well known in Topeka. He once wrote that a sense of humor "is like oil on a squeaky hinge or a rusty journal. It is the lubricant of daily life. Many things become too serious simply because they are treated too seriously."[42] When asked how he might change *In His Steps* were he able to write it over again, he replied, "I am quite sure I should make it a little less solemn. It is only when we get a little older that we grow more patient and dare to laugh."[43] His humor was not of the uproarious sort, but he loved to write lightly funny doggerel and especially to make puns and plays on words.

Sheldon's personal life was never meticulously organized, and as he grew older his absent-mindedness became more and more pronounced. Once he and Mrs. Sheldon drove out to Dover, a few miles from Topeka, for a speaking engagement and stopped at the edge of Topeka for gas. Mrs. Sheldon got out to use the restroom, and while she was gone he drove off. As Peggy Greene reported the incident, "He did not notice her absence as he drove on. On arrival his hosts said, 'We thought Mrs. Sheldon was coming too.' Sheldon looked puzzled, then said, 'Well, she was.'"[44]

He was also capable of forgetting engagements entirely. Once he had accepted an invitation to speak at Vossvangen, a Norwegian community in Kansas, but simply forgot all about it until ten o'clock on the scheduled evening, when the organizers called him and inquired after his welfare.[45] And such forgetfulness extended to social life as well. Once he was called and invited to dinner; after talking to the putative host for several minutes, he rang off and told his wife not to forget that they were to go out to dinner the next Thursday evening at six-thirty. Mrs. Sheldon asked who it was that had extended the invitation, and Sheldon responded, "Why—why, I don't know. I forgot to ask." On Thursday evening the Sheldons dressed for dinner and waited for someone to call them and ask why they were late, but the call never came. "We are still wondering who we offended," Sheldon told a friend.[46]

In his latter years Sheldon bought a car and took up driving, with less than spectacular results. Perhaps his absent-mindedness was a contributing factor. As John Ripley put it, "He'd be going down the street and thinking of something else and he'd be weaving back and forth."[47] Sheldon's grandson has recalled a scary moment when Sheldon killed the engine of his Pontiac by trying to climb a steep hill in high gear and somehow managed to back down through many sharp turns without disaster.[48] Fortunately for him, he was only ticketed once, for an illegal U-turn, until an accident in March 1945, shortly after he had turned eighty-eight, put an end to his driving career. Sheldon managed to run into another car and then lose control of his own, ending up on the sidewalk. Three persons (not including himself) were hurt in the melee,[49] and the upshot of it was that he lost his driver's license.

Home and Family

Sheldon always believed that solid, wholesome home life was the cornerstone of social progress, and he tried diligently to keep his ties with family and close friends strong. Given the worldwide demand for his speeches and the never-ending local demand for his pastoral services, he must have had trouble supplying the family with consistent attention, but he did better at it than many another busy celebrity. After his retirement he spent more time than ever with the family, and when grandchildren came along they became his immediate favorites. Holidays, especially Christmas, were always occasions for the Sheldon family to spend together—but often not without other company, for Sheldon could not bear to leave out those who otherwise would have been alone for the holiday.[50] Close personal friends were a kind of extended family, Sheldon believed, and he cultivated his friendships vigorously: "I cannot help wondering whether even the reforming of the world is so important that human needs and cravings must be denied. . . . The number of men I know who have or take time for leisurely visits with friends is fast dwindling. After a while I wonder if there will be any left who are not too busy to enjoy living."[51]

By all accounts Charles and Mary Sheldon (he called her "May"; she called him "Charl") had a warm and devoted marriage. Sheldon's Central Church successor Charles Helsley said that an intimate Sheldon friend described the marriage thus: "It was the most beautiful, sweet, lovely relationship that I have known. Their achievement of unity—of oneness of personality—was most unusual."[52] But the two were different, in personality as well as in philosophy. Charles Sheldon was the activist, the heartfelt friend of the social outcast; Mary Sheldon was the scion of a family in Topeka's aristocracy, and she acted that role. "She was rich and he was bright" was Dr. Karl Menninger's capsule characterization of the couple.[53]

Those who in 1981 described their memories of Mary Sheldon often used terms like "stately." As Ralph Glenn put it, she was "well dressed, well spoken, well informed, and well educated."[54] Peggy Greene recalled her as "a very lovely woman but a little bit more reserved."[55]

Mary Sheldon had special talents in the arts. She was a good pianist and had ability in the theater, as both actress and director. She was also a writer of a number of works, including several magazine articles (perhaps the best was a humorous account of a nineteen-year-old girl who volunteered to help out during a Sheldon family crisis and managed to make everything worse)[56] and several pieces of drama. She wrote three substantial plays, entitled "Nothing to Speak of," "Fifty-Fifty," and "Trifles," which were produced at Central Church; she also dramatized several of her husband's works.

For many years Mary Sheldon was not in good health; the worst of her afflictions was arthritis. In about 1937 the Sheldons heard of a bee venom treatment for arthritis that sounded promising, and about 1941 they went to Oakland, California, for the bee-sting treatment. A Topeka newspaper carried an account of her treatment after she had had thirty-six stings and was ready to return home.[57] But apparently the cure was unavailing.

Perhaps the sharpest contrast between the Sheldons came in their treatment of those who might have been regarded as their social inferiors. Charles Sheldon, of course, believed in the equality of all people and especially championed the lot of domestic servants, whose work, he said, was important and who thus deserved respect, good treatment, and good pay. One Central Church member recalled that Mary Sheldon objected to having the servants eat dinner with the family—something Charles Sheldon very much favored.[58] Another recalled an instance in which a young housekeeper ("just an average person like us") had finished her day's work in the hot upstairs of the house and, upon coming downstairs, sat on the front porch to rest. Mary Sheldon sharply told her that she wasn't to sit on the porch, that she would get her a chair for her room.[59] Vivian Rut-

"The Wren," the Sheldon family cabin at the Congregational Assembly Grounds near Frankfort, Michigan. Sheldon is at right; man at left is not identified. Central Congregational Church (UCC), Topeka.

ter recalled that Mary was strict about not overpaying her help, but that Charles would slip the young women an occasional extra dollar on the sly.[60]

Few at Central Church have many memories of the Sheldons' only child, Merriam. Apparently he left Topeka after finishing high school and rarely returned. He did accompany his parents on at least one long trip, a speaking tour of Australia and New Zealand in 1914. According to one account, Merriam was the first American arrested as a spy in World War I. They were in Sydney when the war broke out, and Merriam was observed by the military police taking pictures of the harbor. He was detained for questioning and his film was confiscated.[61] Later he joined several other young men from Central Church in volunteering to serve in an ambulance company in the war.

Merriam was something of a disappointment to his parents. Perhaps he was simply a stereotypical preacher's kid, determined not to

Mary, Merriam, and Charles Sheldon at their cabin in Michigan. Kansas State Historical Society.

look like a goody-goody, rebelling against his saintly father. John Ripley commented, "He tried to do everything he could to prove that he was a he-man and a ladies' man and he'd drink and smoke, and later Sheldon told a friend of ours that he was very upset about his son. . . . His father would go and visit him, and he would drink beer at the table and smoke at the table, right in front of his dad. That irritated his father."[62]

E.B. Merriam built a house for his daughter and son-in-law at 1515 W. 15th, a few blocks from the church, and the Sheldons lived there for many years. After the Merriams died, the Sheldons moved into their house at 1621 College, a stone's throw from the Washburn University campus. There they lived out their lives. The house on College was torn down in 1964 to make way for an addition to

Euclid Methodist Church next door. The house on 15th Street is also gone; it was torn down about the same time to make way for a low-income apartment house. As Edna Burkhardt, in 1981 one of Sheldon's oldest surviving parishioners, conjectured, Sheldon would have approved of his home's having given way to housing for the poor black families who now live there.[63]

The Sheldons spent their summers for many years at a church camp called the Congregational Assembly at Crystal Lake near Frankfort, Michigan. There they built a little cabin sometime between 1905 and perhaps 1915.[64] Sheldon's grandson wrote in 1982, "Our little cottage, which my grandmother named 'The Wren,' still stands. Architects and engineers have looked at it and all agree it can't stand up. Maybe it's an act of God."[65]

It was also in Michigan that Sheldon apparently took up his long-time hobby of rock collecting. He developed an interest in the unusual Petoskey stones which were found only on the northeast shore of Lake Michigan. Later on he began gathering other rocks as well, until he had accumulated an extensive collection. His collection of amber was held in especially high esteem in Topeka.[66] He took to cutting and polishing stones at home, and often carried a small polished stone in his vest pocket. If someone expressed interest in it, Sheldon would give it to the person as a souvenir.

Sheldon long kept up some of his hobbies from earlier years, such as juggling and performing magic tricks. He occasionally tried his hand at making music, working at the harmonica for several years, but mainly found himself playing "some pretty rotten tunes."[67] Later on he took up golf, and his grandson remembered him as "an enthusiastic and good golpher. He beat me in nine holes on the hilly, sand trap-infested Frankfort Golf Course when he was in his 80s and I was about 17."[68] But his favorite sport during his last two or three decades was horseshoes. As he got older he found tennis, an earlier favorite, too strenuous. Golf, although he enjoyed it, he found "too financial." Walking was too solitary, and riding too risky. But "Any man who can throw two pounds and a half of iron forty feet and make ringers every other time is entitled to be a descendant of a Greek king. . . ."[69]

A Temporary Retirement

At the January 25, 1912, annual meeting of Central Church, Sheldon announced that he was retiring after nearly two dozen years of service. In his autobiography Sheldon wrote that he took a leave of absence at that time in order to undertake extended speaking tours, especially on behalf of temperance,[70] and many accounts of Sheldon's career characterize things that way. But that he actually resigned, effective the following June, seems clear enough from church records and from contemporary newspaper accounts, especially since a successor was hired on a permanent basis. The congregation adopted a resolution in accepting the resignation that "Dr. Sheldon should remain in a close relationship with the Church, a suitable title to be given to him later."[71] Poor health may have been involved in Sheldon's decision to retire, but if so it didn't last, because before long he was indeed traveling the world as a much-sought speaker. In March the church called Roy Guild to be the congregation's pastor. Guild had spent part of his childhood in Topeka and at the time was serving as executive secretary of the Men and Religion Forward Movement, a national organization that tried to push marginal church members into more active participation. Guild took a pay cut, from $4000 to $2500, to enter the famous Central pulpit.[72] Two months later the church awarded Sheldon the honorary title of "Minister-at-Large," which he bore with some pride on his platform tours. Guild proved a good administrator (something Sheldon never could have claimed), overseeing a period of growth in membership and budget as well as a flowering of various groups, such as the Women's Society, within the congregation.[73]

Sheldon's most important activity during this retirement was his participation in the Flying Squadron, the road show of orators and musicians stumping for prohibition in 1914 and 1915, which was discussed in chapter 6. Sheldon always believed, probably with justification, that that tour had much to do with the ratification, three years later, of the Eighteenth Amendment. The exhausting enterprise must have been especially satisfying to Sheldon because it came on the heels of a trip he took to Australia and New Zealand, also to push the prohibitionist cause, where his message was not very warmly received.[74]

After three years, in March 1915, Roy Guild resigned to become executive secretary of the Commission on Interdenominational Activities of the Federal Council of Churches. The people of Central missed their beloved founding pastor, who was still living in Topeka, and they managed to prevail on him to return to his former post. With Willis Goldsmith as his assistant—apparently the first full-time assistant pastor he ever had—Sheldon plunged back into his work with his usual vigor. Thus he labored for four and a half years. However, he continued to stump occasionally for prohibition, and took a three-month leave of absence toward the end of 1917 to carry the cause to England under the auspices of the National Temperance Foundation of Great Britain. Realizing that national prohibition in Great Britain was out of the question, Sheldon announced before he left that his purpose was simply that of a teacher who would educate the British people, and particularly the laboring classes of the country, on the evils of drink.[75] As popular as ever in England, he entertained tens of thousands of listeners with the message that prohibition had "made the sight of a drunkard as rare in Kansas as would be the sight of a Hohenzollern in Europe when the war ended."[76] Sheldon also tried to get the British to work out ways of keeping alcohol out of the hands of American soldiers stationed there, all, of course, to little avail.

In the autumn of 1919 Sheldon retired again. He had been ill for six months; he had spent many weeks recovering from an operation, only to crack a rib when he finally ventured out and promptly slipped and fell on a patch of ice.[77] This time he stayed retired, at least from the pastorate, if one doesn't count an interim stint following the resignation of a later successor in 1942 (Sheldon carried out his duties quite capably despite his age; he reached eighty-six during those months).[78] Sheldon naturally overshadowed all of his successors; as one parishioner wrote in 1947, Sheldon's occasional pulpit appearances would be announced well in advance, and on the scheduled Sunday the church would be full as it normally was only on Easter and at Christmas.[79]

When Sheldon finally retired, his parishioners chose what was surely the most appropriate memorial to his career they could have conceived: a large addition to the church building which would enable Central to become a true social-gospel institutional church. Sheldon had long wanted such a facility; perhaps it was because he was more a dreamer than an administrator that under his leadership the church was never able to undertake such an extensive project. Or perhaps it was because Sheldon's concern for persons meant supporting projects of more immediate effects than might be realized through bricks and mortar. Whatever the cause, he was greatly honored by the undertaking. Central Church began preparations for the building in 1922 and began to raise money to meet the $100,000 price in 1923. Ground was broken early in 1924, and the building was dedicated that November.[80] Built on what had by then become the standard model for an institutional church, the large new structure included space for a gymnasium, classrooms, meeting rooms, a theater, a chapel, a library, and other facilities. And indeed the Sheldon Community House has been used by the community ever since. The uses have changed over the years, of course, but at this writing the facility is home not only to diverse Central Church and denominational programs but to such community services as a child care center.

Sheldon did not exactly vegetate in retirement. Only a matter of months after he had announced his final retirement at Central Church, the *Christian Herald*, then the country's foremost Protestant periodical, announced with considerable fanfare in its first issue of 1920 that the famous pastor and novelist would become its new editor-in-chief.[81] That wasn't quite the job it sounds like; the magazine then had a practice of naming figurehead editors who were actually prominent regular contributors, while a professional staff in fact edited the magazine.[82] Thus Sheldon stayed in Topeka during his editorship, but he contributed to the magazine on a weekly basis, sometimes producing a major article or sermon in addition to one or more editorials. The job also brought with it a voluminous correspondence, which Sheldon in 1923 pegged at three hundred letters per week.[83] He kept up that pace for five years, finally slowing down

Central Church shortly after the completion of the Sheldon Community House in the early 1920s. Central Congregational Church (UCC), Topeka.

somewhat in 1925, when he became a contributing editor. His contributions were heavy for many years afterwards, and they continued until his death, the last ones appearing posthumously. Meanwhile, after early 1925 he concentrated on writing more books, including his autobiography and a number of short inspirational works. He also resumed an active public-speaking career, and throughout his latter years stumped the country—and the world—on behalf of world peace. Wherever he went big crowds turned out to hear him.

Sheldon also spent some time, both before and after his retirement from Central Church, on the chautauqua circuit. Despite blistering summer heat, Sheldon always found an audience willing to sit for an hour and a half in a tent to hear him. His favorite chautauqua season was the one he spent teamed with no less a dignitary than William Jennings Bryan.[84]

But all of Sheldon's travel was not as a speaker. Early in 1926 the Sheldons sailed to the Holy Land on a tour sponsored by the *Christian Herald*, and they took a second Mediterranean cruise the following year. Sheldon enormously enjoyed the opportunity actually to walk In His Steps through Palestine. At one point, he was convinced, he actually got to sit on a stone where Jesus had once sat; at Jacob's Well, where, tradition has it, Jesus talked with the woman from Samaria, Sheldon discovered that "that curb has never been changed or rebuilt. So in order to be sure that I had sat on the very stone that Jesus sat on that day I sat on every part of the curb all the way around! I don't know when I have had a greater thrill than that."[85] He also thrilled to preach where Jesus and Paul had preached before him—on the top of Mt. Carmel, on the Mount of Olives, at the Mars Hill in Athens. He also got to retell the story of the feeding of the five thousand on the shores of the Sea of Galilee at sunset.[86]

Whether touring, or speaking, or writing in Topeka, Sheldon remained the reformer to the end. His last article, published in the *Christian Herald* posthumously, was a plea for church people to keep working at "making human beings better. Making them free from hatred, prejudice, greed and selfishness."[87] On the 1926 trip to Palestine he urged his fellow travelers to help improve the impoverished lives of those living in that part of the world and even took time to work on a specific problem: finding a terrible water shortage in Jerusalem, which he attributed to a governmental interest in placing military conquests before providing necessities of life (General Edmund Allenby had conquered Jerusalem just a few years earlier, and a military government still ruled the city), he undertook an extensive correspondence with citizens and government authorities and finally managed to prod the government into seeing that a new water supply was obtained.[88]

The Grand Old Man

Inevitably, even the most strident radical, if s/he lives long enough, comes to seem harmless and tame, and it happened to Sheldon as surely as it does to anyone else. Sheldon was beloved in Topeka, despite his espousal in his latter years of the most radical social and political positions he had ever taken, notably a pacifism that extended even into World War II. He was nonetheless always in demand as a public speaker and was continually sought after to perform baptisms and marriages. Firm of mind and body until the very end, his fame endured, and many prominent persons, when they were in the vicinity of Topeka, would seek him out, still wanting to meet the author of the famous book they had read years ago. When Sheldon traveled, crowds would turn out to see him. As Carmie Wolfe, the young Topeka woman who accompanied the Sheldons on their 1926 trip to Palestine, recalled many years later, "At every port we entered, there was a delegation to meet the ship, with gifts and flowers for the beloved author of 'In His Steps.' In Madeira, a large procession of children, all in white and strewing flowers and singing 'I Want to Be a Sunbeam,' walked before the flower-covered carriage in which Dr. and Mrs. Sheldon rode to the hotel where he was to speak. At many of the ports of call, a copy of a translation of 'In His Steps' was left as a calling card in the Sheldon stateroom."[89]

Sheldon received four honorary doctorates as well: Doctor of Divinity degrees from Temple College, Washburn College, and Brown University, and a Doctor of Letters degree from Yankton College in

South Dakota, his old stomping ground. In Topeka a junior high school, now a Head Start center, was named for him in 1957.

One slightly offbeat honor came in 1936, when officials at Rollins College of Winter Park, Florida, requested a stone from the walls of Central Church to be placed in a "Memorial Walk of Fame" they were building on their campus. Over 450 stones representing the birthplaces or former homes of dignitaries—from Confucius to Marco Polo to Shakespeare to Charles M. Sheldon—were being gathered for the walk. Central Church complied with the request.[90] Sheldon's stone was placed next to that of Joshua, a stone from ancient Jericho.[91]

Sheldon did his best to downplay the honors and tributes he received, preferring that people focus their attention on his message: the challenge of Jesus-like living. His speeches and articles remained acute and evangelical. But he, like millions before him, couldn't escape the box into which he was put by his age. He was, as one reporter put it, "looked upon as a silver-haired saint in the churches."[92] A sad state of affairs for a still-vigorous crusader who could not make himself heard of on behalf of an unpopular cause.

Two Old Friends: Old Age and Death

By the time he was in his mid-sixties Sheldon was writing about old age and death, though the latter would not claim him for over two decades. He told an interviewer in the 1940s, "I long ago made up my mind to regard Old Age as a friend, and cultivate him with cheerful and fearless equanimity. . . . It is not possible to avoid him, but it may be possible to forget him by being preoccupied with an endless variety of occupations."[93] In short, as he wrote in a widely quoted and reprinted pamphlet in 1925, old age should be a "mellow and gracious ripening, rather than a rotting."[94]

As early as 1909, in an era when frank talk about death was taboo, Sheldon was addressing the subject openly and urging upon his hearers his conviction that death was to be welcomed, for it was a passing into eternal life in glory:

The last photograph of Sheldon, taken on February 15, 1946, eleven days before his death at eighty-eight. Central Congregational Church (UCC), Topeka.

It is not death but life I greet
  When he who loves me calls me home;
The voice I hear is very sweet:
  "My weary child, no longer roam."[95]

Sheldon's devoted disciples in Topeka appreciated his frankness in talking about the unspeakable. As Karl Menninger recalled one of Sheldon's matter-of-fact sermons on death, "I was impressed with the fact that he was telling me a jewel of a truth. . . . It seemed to me that here was a very wonderful minister who would actually advocate we not be so jittery and skittery about discussing death. He was way ahead of his time."[96]

Sheldon was also convinced that he would be reunited with his old friends and loved ones in heaven, and beyond that he often spoke of great anticipation of meeting people whose acquaintance had been impossible in earthly life. His typical list of people to talk to within the pearly gates included such luminaries as Lincoln, Bunyan, Paul, Peter, and Augustine; occasionally he could expand on the subject at some length and aver his intention of sitting down with Phillips Brooks, Henry Ward Beecher, Wesley, Browning, Whittier, Socrates, Thomas Kempis, Moses, and a myriad of others, including the "countless number of saints who suffered martyrdom for their faith, and the host of those who are worth knowing because they have lived worthily."[97] (No matter that some on his list weren't Christians; Sheldon, remember, cut his theological teeth on the Andover heresy, which gave *everyone* a shot at salvation.) And beyond that there was the thrill of entering the unknown: "I can say with my old friend Lyman Abbott: 'When the time comes for my embarkation and the ropes are cast off and I put out to sea, I think I shall still be standing in the bow and still looking forward with eager curiosity and glad hopefulness to the new world to which the unknown voyage will bring me.'"[98]

In keeping with his optimistic appraisal of death, Sheldon frequently proclaimed his desire for an upbeat funeral. As he said, he wanted "no dirge, but a paean of victory."[99] On several occasions he outlined his desires pretty clearly:

> I hope I am not expressing any unchristian desire when I say that when my own time comes to put on immortality, I hope a few of the

people whom I have loved, and who, I hope, have loved me, will see that my body is placed in the spot provided, sing a hymn of exultation over the life that is to be, give the money that a costly funeral would exact to some human need, and then go home gently and take up their day's work. I have said what I feel.[100]

Sheldon's death followed an accident that probably weakened him. Early in 1946 he attended a performance of Nan Herron's *Historical Pageant of Kansas*, which was presented at the Women's Club of Topeka. It was a long show, lasting between four and five hours. Sheldon was stiff when he got up from sitting so long and proceeded to fall all the way down a long flight of steps at the entrance to the building. "It was a wonder he was not killed," Charles Helsley remarked of the spill. But a few weeks later, on February 18, according to Helsley, Sheldon suffered a stroke while sitting in a rocking chair and talking with a friend about the burning of the mortgage on Central Church's Sheldon Community House, an event scheduled for his birthday a few days thence.[101] (The topic was a happy one for Sheldon, for, as he had told friends, he hated the thought of explaining to heavenly officials why there was a debt on a building with his name on it.) After his collapse, he was taken to Stormont Hospital.

There is another, slightly different, account of the fatal stroke. Mae Fisk, who was working in the Sheldon household at the time, recalled,

> One day Dr. Sheldon went out of the house, I believe to get the milk. He came back in through the kitchen and didn't say anything to Mrs. Sheldon as he went by, which she thought was unusual. He went into the den and fell. Mrs. Sheldon was washing her hair at the time, and when she called me I was washing mine. I put a towel around my head and drove out there. She had a towel around her head, too. We agreed that he should go to the hospital.
>
> We took him to the hospital. He was in the hospital about a week or so. On the last day, Dr. Helsley came out to the hospital and then left, saying he would come back that evening. I said that might be too late, but Helsley didn't think so and left; he had work to do at the church, because it was a Sunday. Before he got back that evening, Dr. Sheldon had died.
>
> He was propped up in bed, sitting against a backrest. I was standing at the foot of the bed. He sat up, straight up in bed, and raised up

his hands in front of him, and gave a cry like the bleat of a sheep. Then it wasn't long until he was gone."[102]

The date was February 24, 1946.

A Joyous Funeral

On February 26, his eighty-ninth birthday, Sheldon received the joyous funeral he had requested. It might not have been as simple as he would have wanted, but simplicity is hard to achieve when a whole city turns out to jam a large church sanctuary for a service. Helsley opened with one of Sheldon's written prayers, read from Sheldon's essay on old age and death—"Two Old Friends"—and recounted a life which he characterized as "not only a symbol of love, but a miracle of love as well." He told of Sheldon's idealism, his hatred of evil, and his devout life spent walking In His Steps. And then, to the astonishment of the assembled congregation, the service concluded with a performance of the Hallelujah Chorus. A happy ending, as Sheldon wanted it.[103]

From the time word of his death was received until after the funeral service, the flags atop the state capitol and the Topeka city hall flew at half mast—apparently the first time such an honor had ever been accorded a private citizen.[104] Burial took place as planned in Mt. Hope cemetery, near the plot bought years earlier as the final resting place of poorer Central Church members.

Fame is transient; a new generation of Topekans has grown up for whom Sheldon is mainly the name of a school building (once a junior high, now a Head Start center) or the subject of an occasional retrospective piece in the *Capital-Journal*.

For historians, written material has been preserved at Central Church, the Kansas State Historical Society, and the Topeka Public Library. The physical monuments are few; the two houses in which Sheldon lived the majority of his life have long since been torn down. His name is preserved in the Head Start center and in the Sheldon Community House at Central Church.

The best monument, however, is the little brown study that was built in his back yard as a place for him to write during retirement. When the house was torn down in the 1960s, Topekans rallied to save the study. Today it sits in Ward-Meade Park as a part of Prairie Crossings, the park's turn-of-the-century town. It was preserved through the efforts of the surviving Altruists, carrying on their old pledge to help their good pastor, walking faithfully in his steps.

Appendix

British, American, and Canadian Publishers of *In His Steps*

C=listed by Emma Crabb, 1967
D=listed by Gene DeGruson, 1970
*=in print at this writing[1]

CD	Advance Publishing Co., Chicago, 1897
CD	Allenson, H.R., London, 1898
CD	Altemus, Henry, Co., Philadelphia, 1899
	American Baptist Publishing Society, Philadelphia, 1898
	Baker Book House, Grand Rapids, Mich., 1978
*	Barbour and Co., Westwood, N.J., 1982
CD	Books, Inc., New York, n.d.
CD	Bowden, J., London, 1899
CD*	Broadman Press, Nashville, Tenn. n.d.
*	Brownlow Publishing Co., Fort Worth, Tex. 1982
CD	Burt, A.L., Co., New York, 1910
CD	Caldwell, H.M., Co., New York and Boston, 1899
*	Casa Bautista Publications, El Paso, Tex. 1981 (*En Sus Pasos*—Spanish translation)
CD	Christian Herald Bible House, New York, 1919
CD	Chatterdon, A.L., and Co., New York, n.d.
	Commission Press, Inc., Charlotte, N.C., n.d.
CD	Cook, David C., Publishing Co., Elgin, Ill., 1899
CD	Dickerman, G.S., New York, n.d.
D	Dodson, place and date unknown
D	Donohue, M.A., and Co., Chicago, 1900[2]
	Doubleday, Nelson, Garden City, Long Island, 1952
CD	Federal Publishing Co., Garden City, Long Island, 1925
*	Good News Publishers, Westchester, Ill., 1962
CD	Grosset and Dunlap, New York, 1900
CD	Guideposts Association, Inc., Carmel, N.Y., 1962
D	Holt, Rinehart, and Winston, New York, 1937

CD	Horton, J. B., London, n.d., under the title, *In His Steps, or, The Rescue of Loreen*
CD	Hurst and Co., New York, n.d.
CD	Judson Press, Philadelphia, n.d.
*	Keats Publishing Co., New Canaan, Conn., 1982
CD	Kelly, C. H., London, 1899
CD	Ketcham, Wilbur B., New York, 1899
CD	Laird and Lee, Chicago, 1900
CD	Lupton, F. M., Publishing Co., New York, n.d.
CD	McKay, David, Co., Inc., New York, 1946
D	McLeod, George J., Ltd., Toronto, 1961
CD	Mershon Co., New York, n.d.
CD	Moody Press, Chicago, n.d.
CD	Munro's Sons, George, New York, 1899
CD	National Temperance Society, New York, n.d.
CD	Newnes, G., London, 1899, under the title, *What Would Jesus Do? In His Steps*
CD	Nimmo, Hay and Mitchell, Edinburgh, 1899
CD	Odyssey Press, New York, 1966
CD	Ogilvie, J.S., Publishing Co., New York, n.d.
CD	Partridge, S.W., London, 1898, under the title, *Our Exemplar: or, What Would Jesus Do?*
CD	Permabooks, New York, 1949
CD	Pettigrew and Stephens, Glasgow, 1898
*	Putnam Publishing Group, New York, 1982
CD	Pyramid, New York, 1960
CD	Revell, Fleming H., Co., Chicago, 1899
CD	Routledge, George, and Sons, London, 1899
CD	Scott, Walter, London, 1898
CD	Sears, J.H., and Co., Inc., New York, 1927
D*	Shawnee County Historical Society, Topeka, Kans. 1967 [3]
CD	Simpkin, Marshall and Co., London, 1899
CD	Street and Smith, New York, 1899
C	Street-Andrews, n.p., n.d.
CD	Sunday School Union, London, 1898
D	Sunshine Press, Litchfield, Illinois, 1948
CD	Sword of the Lord Publishing Co., Wheaton, Illinois, 1954
CD	Thompson, Charles C., Co., Chicago, n.d.
D	Universal Book and Bible House, Philadelphia, 1937
CD	Walter, Henry E., Worthing and London, 1948
CD	Ward, Lock and Co., London, 1899

C   Warne, Frederick, and Co., London, 1899
CD   Western News, n.p., 1899
CD   Western Printing and Lithography, n.p., n.d.
CD   Winston, John C., Co., Philadelphia and Chicago, 1937
*   Whitaker House, Springdale, Penn., 1980
CD   Whittaker, Thomas, New York, n.d.
CD*   Zondervan Publishing House, Grand Rapids, Mich., 1967

Abbreviations

Autobiography—Charles M. Sheldon, *Charles M. Sheldon: His Life Story* (New York: George H. Doran Co., 1925)

CC—Christian Century

CH—Christian Herald

CMS—Charles M. Sheldon

KCS—Kansas City Star

KCT—Kansas City Times

KSHS—Kansas State Historical Society, Topeka

Sheldon Room—Sheldon Memorial Room archives, Central Congregational Church (UCC), Topeka

TCJ—Topeka Capital Journal

TDC—Topeka Daily Capital

TDSJ, TSJ—Topeka (Daily) State Journal

All citations of *In His Steps* refer to the Shawnee County Historical Society's 70th Anniversary Commemorative Edition (*Shawnee County Historical Society Bulletin* no. 44, [Winter, 1967]). This edition is a photoreproduction of the earliest printed text of the story, its serial publication in the *Advance* (Chicago).

Notes

Introduction

1. In the course of my research I have gathered much more information than fits within the scope of this book. A copy of my first-draft manuscript, which contains many details dropped from the final product, has been deposited at the Kansas State Historical Society in Topeka.
2. Letter from John Ripley to Hector Cordova, Aug. 27, 1966, cited in Hector Leroy Cordova, "The Formation of the Social Gospel of Charles Monroe Sheldon, 1886–1919," (M.A. thesis, San Jose State College, 1967), 11.
3. Quoted in John Pond Fritts, "The Author of 'In His Steps,'" *Critic* 34:864 (June 1899), 540.

1. The Early Years

1. Charles Martyn, *The William Ward Genealogy* (New York: Artemus Ward, 1925).
2. Sarah Sheldon, "A Bit of Family History," ms. in Sheldon Room.
3. CMS, "The Man Who Taught Me Most," undated clipping, probably from the *Christian Herald*, in Sheldon Room.
4. "Necrology," *Congregational Year-Book* (1913), 31–2.
5. *The Kansas Congregational Conference, Fifty-Ninth Annual Session*, 1913 KSHS.
6. CMS, "A Preacher: Old Style," *CH* 53:16 (Apr. 19, 1930), 10.
7. CMS, "Making Your Words Count," *Rotarian* 55:5 (Nov. 1939), 20.
8. CMS, "Let Us Open the Meeting," *CH* 50 (Sept. 17, 1927), 795.
9. CMS, "What Is the Matter with Kansas?" *Magic Mirror* 1 (Nov. 1939), 5.
10. CMS, "Life Is My Teacher," part 1, *Household Magazine* 36:11 (Nov. 1936), 5.
11. Information supplied by Shirley Rider of the Sheldon Family Association, Inc.

12. CMS, "Life Is My Teacher," part 4, *Household Magazine* 37:2 (Feb. 1937), 61.
13. CMS, "Dr. Charles M. Sheldon Saw Custer's Cavalry on Last Ride to Indian War," *TDC*, June 25, 1922, 12c.
14. Ibid. See also Charles Helsley, "Charles M. Sheldon," ms. in Sheldon Room. Helsley, the Central Church pastor at the time of Sheldon's death, collected several such stories directly from Sheldon.
15. Autobiography, 29.
16. See Autobiography, ch. 1, and "Meet the Farmer," in *Dr. Sheldon's Scrap Book* (New York: Christian Herald Association, 1942), 86–91, for many more homesteading tales.
17. CMS, "Meet the Farmer," 90.
18. Peggy Greene, "As Peggy of the Flint Hills Sees It," *TDC*, Feb. 9, 1943, 4.
19. Cecil Howes, "Dr. Charles M. Sheldon Tells of the Best Years of His Life," *KCS*, July 29, 1945.
20. Quoted in Glenn Clark, *The Man Who Walked In His Steps* (St. Paul, Minn.: Macalester Park Publishing Co., 1946), 25.
21. Autobiography, 23.
22. CMS, "Is Life Worth Living?" *CC* 45:27 (July 5, 1928), 852.
23. CMS, "My Damascus Road," *CH* 69 (Apr. 1946), 20, 74. In this article Sheldon puts his age at the time at sixteen; but in his autobiography he places the event in his last winter on the farm before leaving for prep school, which would have made him about nineteen then, since he left in 1877, shortly after his twentieth birthday.
24. "Dr. Sheldon at Eighty-Six Has New Ideas on Religion, and Never Reads of War before Breakfast," *TSJ*, Feb. 25, 1943.
25. CMS, "Life Is My Teacher," part 1, 5.
26. CMS, "Short Talks about Vocations," *Kansas Authors Club Yearbook* (Topeka, 1944), 30. Sheldon gave essentially this account of his first literary sale often enough that it must be assumed to be correct, although in 1891 he wrote that his first sale had been made to the *Youth's Companion* while he was a junior at Brown University (CMS, "The Student and Humanity," *University Review* 13:2 [Sept. 1891], 1).
27. Unfortunately, most of these earliest Sheldon writings are virtually impossible to locate. Most articles in the magazine were not signed, or were signed with a first name and initial only. The index to *Youth's Companion* lists twenty-three Sheldon articles between 1883 and 1911, a single entry for Robert Cheviot, a pseudonym Sheldon used occasionally, and one entry for a C.H. Sheldon, which may or may not be a typo (the story referred to is in some ways similar to some of Sheldon's). We must presume that these two-dozen items constitute

only a small portion of Sheldon's work printed in the periodical. See Richard Cutts, *Index to The Youth's Companion: 1871–1929* (Metuchen, N.J.: The Scarecrow Press, 1972).

28. CMS, "The Christian Life an Unselfish Life," ms. sermon from Waterbury, Vt., Nov. 6, 1887; in Sheldon Room. See also CMS, "The Man Who Taught Me Most," and "Life Is My Teacher," part 1, 42.

29. Charles Warren Helsley, "St. Charles of Topeka," in Henry F. Henrichs, ed., *St. Charles of Topeka* (Litchfield, Ill.: Sunshine Press, 1948), 46–47.

30. George Harrison Durand, *Joseph Ward of Dakota* (Boston: Pilgrim Press, 1913), 101–2.

31. "The Capital's Gallery of Some Familiar Faces," *TDC*, June 29, 1906, 7. This article states that Stewart Sheldon helped organize "over 100 churches" and 214 Sunday schools, mainly in Dakota.

32. CMS, "If I Could Take My College Course Over Again," *CH* 55:10 (Oct. 1932), 11.

33. Autobiography, 43–44.

34. Glenn Clark, *The Man Who Walked In His Steps*, 13–14.

35. L.D. Whittemore, "Charles M. Sheldon," ms. dated 1902, 7. Supplied by his daughter, Margaret Whittemore; now in Sheldon Room.

36. CMS, "Life Is My Teacher," part 2, *Household Magazine* 36:12 (Dec. 1936), 37–38.

37. Whittemore, "Charles M. Sheldon," 11.

38. CMS, "Life Is My Teacher," part 4, 17.

39. Autobiography, 59.

40. Ibid., 56–57.

41. Frank M. Chase, "Charles M. Sheldon, Author, Preacher, Editor," *Dearborn Independent* 22:15 (Feb. 4, 1922), 13.

42. John W. Ripley in "The Strange Story of Charles M. Sheldon's *In His Steps*," *Kansas Historical Quarterly* 34:3 (Autumn 1968), 10.

43. Henry K. Rowe, *History of Andover Theological Seminary* (Newton, Mass.: n. p., 1933), 176. Pp. 163–78 of this work contain a discussion of the upheavals at Andover in the 1880s and subsequent years. Smyth took the Visitors to court over the issue; finally, in 1892 the Visitors, whose membership had undergone change, dropped the case.

44. See Martin E. Marty, "Martin Luther's Reckless Grasp of Grace," *CC* 100 (Oct. 26, 1983), 963–64.

45. H. Shelton Smith, Robert T. Handy, and Lefferts A. Loetscher, eds., *American Christianity* (New York: Charles Scribner's Sons, 1963), vol. 1, 255.

46. The Rev. Thomas P. Field, D.D., *The "Andover Theory" of Future Probation*, pamphlet in Sheldon Room.

47. Untitled Sheldon sermon from Waterbury, dated Jan. 8, 1888; in Sheldon Room.

48. For information about Wheeler's pastorate, see Theodore Graham Lewis, ed., *History of Waterbury, Vermont, 1763–1915* (Waterbury, Vt.: Harry C. Whitehill, 1915), 214–15.

49. See, for example, "An Ideal Town," a Sheldon sermon at Waterbury preached on Sept. 16, 1888; ms. in Sheldon Room.

50. CMS, "Life Is My Teacher," part 3, *Household Magazine* 37:1 (Jan. 1937), 29.

51. Ibid., 29.

52. Autobiography, 71–72.

53. Ibid., 77–78.

54. CMS, "The Problem of the Country Church," *Andover Review* 10:58 (Oct. 1888), 382. The article tells briefly of Sheldon's most important ecclesiastical innovations in Waterbury.

55. Sheldon's "boarding around" episode has been reported in many places. The best accounts are in the Autobiography, 74–75, and in Sheldon's article "Life Is My Teacher," part 3, 29.

56. CMS, from his printed sermon of Jan. 8, 1888; in Sheldon Room.

57. *Plan of Morning Sermon*, Feb. 19, 1888, pamphlet at Waterbury Congregational Church.

58. CMS, "Try the New Thing!" *CH* 68:10 (Oct. 1945), 32.

59. CMS, "Our Pagan Funerals," *CH* 69:2 (Feb. 1946), 58.

60. CMS, "Cheerful Funerals," *CH* 42:12 (Mar. 22, 1919), 332.

61. CMS, "Our Pagan Funerals," 58.

62. CMS, "Life Is My Teacher," part 3, 29.

63. Zula Bennington Greene, "As Peggy of the Flint Hills Sees It," *TDC*, n.d. (ca. Dec., 1938), clipping in Sheldon Room. This account of the meeting of Charles Sheldon and Mary Merriam is based on Mrs. Sheldon's memory of it in 1938.

64. Mary Merriam Sheldon, "The First Chapter of a Romance," in the Autobiography (ch. 11).

65. CMS, "Horizons Seen and Unseen," *CH* 61:10 (Oct. 1938), 41.

66. Peggy Greene, "'In His Steps' Author Lived 'As Jesus Would,'" *TDC*, Mar. 3, 1957.

67. Minutes of Waterbury Congregational Church, Dec. 11, 1888.

2. A Young Man Goes West

1. Russell K. Hickman, "First Congregational Church of Topeka, 1854–1869," *Shawnee County Historical Society Bulletin* 3:1 (Mar. 1949), 3–4.
2. A.G. Kittell, "Early Day Incidents in 'Sheldon's Church,'" *TDC*, Nov. 27, 1938.
3. Ibid. For a more detailed account of Central Church's founding, see A.B. Whiting, "The Beginning of Central Congregational Church," ca. 1904, ms. in Sheldon Room.
4. Cecil Howes, "Dr. Sheldon and Topeka Mark Half a Century 'In His Steps,'" *KCT*, Dec. 12, 1938.
5. CMS, "First Sermon Preached in the Chapel of the Central Congregational Church, Topeka, Kansas, June 23, 1889," pamphlet in Sheldon Room.
6. Quoted in "How to Help Mankind," *TSJ*, Nov. 9, 1891.
7. From an untitled set of notes by Emma Crabb, long-time Central Church historian and Sheldon archivist, in Sheldon Room. The incident here described, incidentally, may have provided the raw material for the very similar incident which opens *In His Steps*.
8. Clarence Gohdes suggests that this adventure was not Sheldon's own idea but rather was inspired by a virtually identical incident in Mrs. Humphrey Ward's novel *Robert Elsmere*. See Gohdes, "*In His Steps*" (book review), *Georgia Review* 8:3 (Fall 1954), 354.
9. CMS, *The Statesmanship of Christ* (Topeka: privately printed, 1890), pamphlet.
10. CMS, "What Will You Do with Him?" *Kingdom* 9:43 (Feb. 5, 1897).
11. CMS, "Practical Sociological Studies," *Andover Review* 14:82 (Oct. 1890), 370.
12. Ibid.
13. Ibid., 371.
14. CMS, "A Newspaper Man for a Week," in *The First Christian Daily Paper and Other Sketches* (New York: Street and Smith, 1900), 30–31.
15. CMS, "Practical Sociological Studies," 373–74; see also "How to Help Mankind."
16. See CMS, "Short Talks on the Kindergarten": installments 1 through 5, *TDC*, Jan. 24 through 28, 1893.
17. "The Bowman Memorial," undated clipping from a Topeka newspaper in kindergarten scrapbook in Sheldon Room.
18. "Kindergarten Work," clipping from Topeka newspaper, Oct. 14, 1897 (?), in kindergarten scrapbook in Sheldon Room.
19. Interview with Dr. Karl Menninger, Aug. 27, 1981.

20. Blanche M. Taylor, "Twentieth Century Utopia—Topeka," *Shawnee County Historical Society Bulletin* 44 (Winter 1967), 7.
21. CMS, untitled manuscript page in Sheldon Room.
22. "Mr. Sheldon's Sermon," *TSJ*, Oct. 5, 1896.
23. CMS, "Sheldon as a Crusader," *Progress* 46:3 (Mar. 1946), 5. See also L. Cady Hodge, "Recollections of Dr. Chas. M. Sheldon," ms. in Sheldon Room.
24. "Dr. Charles M. Sheldon Dies," *KCT*, Feb. 25, 1946.
25. CMS, "Sheldon as a Crusader," 5.
26. Clark, *The Man Who Walked In His Steps*, 36.
27. Interview with Charles Sheldon "Chick" Graves, July 10, 1981.
28. CMS, "Some Experiments Worth Trying in the Ministry," *Andover Review* 16:93 (Sept. 1891), 265–70.
29. In Sheldon's book *John King's Question Class* (Chicago: Advance Publishing Co., 1899), youthful members of a fictional Chicago church have a weekly session with their pastor in which he answers questions they have submitted the week before. In the preface, Sheldon says that the questions used in the book are ones actually asked in a similar format by his own young people.
30. "Mr. Sheldon's Symposium," *TDC*, July 3, 1896.
31. "New Covenant Is Adopted," *TDC*, Nov. 17, 1899.
32. "A New Creed," *TDC*, Nov. 10, 1899.
33. "Author of 'In His Steps,'" *TDC*, Apr. 22, 1899.
34. "What the Preacher Was Like," *Chicago Journal*, Mar. 13, 1900. Accounts of the same service by other correspondents varied somewhat.
35. Gilson Willets, "A Day with Sheldon," *CH*; reprinted in *TDC*, Mar. 9, 1900, 3.
36. William Bos and Clyde Faries, "The Social Gospel: Preaching Reform, 1875–1915," in DeWitte Holland, ed., *Preaching in American History* (Nashville: Abingdon, 1969), 224.
37. Ibid., 227–38.
38. Interview with Lenore Stratton, Aug. 19, 1981.
39. In one account, Sheldon describes this kind of prodigious letter-writing as a form of relaxation. See CMS, "Safety-Valves," in *The First Christian Daily Paper and Other Sketches*, 100–1.
40. CMS, "Sociology from the Preacher's Standpoint," 80.
41. Interview with Marguerite Stuenkel, Aug. 13, 1981.
42. *Seventy-Five Years of Central Congregational Church 1888–1963*, pamphlet in Sheldon Room.
43. "Central Congregational Is Fifty-Four Years Old Today," *TDC*, Apr. 7, 1943.

44. Interview with John W. Ripley, July 8, 1981.

45. Carmie Wolfe, "Charles M. Sheldon—World Citizen," *Shawnee County Historical Society Bulletin* 38 (Dec. 1962), 44.

46. Whittemore, "Charles M. Sheldon."

47. "The Author of 'In His Steps,'" *The Ram's Horn*, ca. 1898, clipping in Sheldon Room.

48. George T. B. Davis, "Charles M. Sheldon, Novelist," *Our Day* 18:3 (Mar. 1899), 75.

49. Whittemore, "Charles M. Sheldon."

50. CMS, "Golden Wedding Anniversary of Father and Mother: The Wedding Journey of Fifty Years," ms. dated Oct. 15, 1902, in Sheldon Room.

51. Letter dated October 28, 1889; Sheldon Room.

52. Cordova, "Formation of the Social Gospel of Sheldon," 65.

53. Letter from Mary Merriam Sheldon to "Woodie" Maus, Nov. 18, 1947; in Sheldon Room.

54. For more information on Everet Brooks Merriam, Mary Merriam Sheldon's father, see *The National Cyclopedia of American Biography* (New York: James T. White Co., 1927), 101.

55. "Executive Found Dead of Wound," *Milwaukee Journal*, Dec. 2, 1964.

56. "Author of 'In His Steps,'" *TDC*, 2.

3. The Tennesseetown Projects

1. CMS, *The Redemption of Freetown* (Boston and Chicago: United Society of Christian Endeavor, 1898).

2. Frye W. Giles, *Thirty Years in Topeka: A Historical Sketch* (Topeka: Capper Special Services, Inc., 1886; reprinted in 1960), 152.

3. Stratton interview.

4. Giles, *Thirty Years*, 153.

5. Menninger interview.

6. Thomas C. Cox, *Blacks in Topeka, Kansas, 1865–1915* (Baton Rouge: Louisiana State Univ. Press, 1982), 52.

7. Whiting, "Beginning of Central Conegregational Church." Early Topeka city directories refer to the church as the "Colored Congregational Church," but contemporary Central Church documents consistently use the name "Tennesseetown."

8. Giles, *Thirty Years*, 153.

9. "The Sheldon Uplift of the Old and Young," *TDC*, Sept. 9, 1906.

10. Cox, *Blacks in Topeka*, 107.

11. "Sheldon Uplift of the Old and Young."
12. Robert A. Swan, Jr., *The Ethnic Heritage of Topeka, Kansas: Immigrant Beginnings* (n.p.: Institute of Comparative Ethnic Studies, 1974), 72.
13. CMS, "A Local Negro Problem," *Kingdom* 8:52 (Apr. 10, 1896), 828.
14. CMS, "Sociology from the Preacher's Standpoint," *Seminary Notes* 1:4 (Dec. 1891), 80.
15. Ibid., 80.
16. 1898 Tennesseetown survey, KSHS. See also Martin Hawver, "1898 'Tennessee Town' Surveyed," *TDC*, Mar. 3, 1973.
17. Leroy A. Halbert, *Across the Way: A History of the Work of Central Church, Topeka, Kansas, in Tennesseetown* (privately printed, 1900), 4.
18. Clark, *The Man Who Walked In His Steps*, 8.
19. "Sheldon Uplift of the Old and Young."
20. Peggy Greene, "Sheldon Kindergarten Recalled," *TDC*, Nov. 17, 1963.
21. John S. Sparks, Jr., "First in Kansas: Original Kindergarten was in 'Tennessee Town,'" *TSJ*, Nov. 17, 1928.
22. Halbert, *Across the Way*, 5.
23. "Kindergarten Notes," undated clipping in kindergarten scrapbook, Sheldon Room.
24. "Kindergarten Work in Tennesseetown," *TDC*, Dec. 16, 1900.
25. *Sheldon Congress of Mothers, 1906–7: Parents Meeting at Sheldon Kindergarten*, pamphlet at KSHS.
26. Halbert, *Across the Way*, 6.
27. "Colored Children Grow Cotton Here," undated clipping from *TDC* in kindergarten scrapbook, Sheldon Room.
28. "Organized the Last Juvenile Flower Club," undated clipping from *TDC* in kindergarten scrapbook, Sheldon Room.
29. "Colored Children Have Cornet Band," undated clipping in kindergarten scrapbook, Sheldon Room.
30. "Governor Hoch and the Colored Kindergartners," undated clipping in kindergarten scrapbook, Sheldon Room.
31. "Honor Frobel's [sic] Birthday," *TDC*, Apr. 22, 1898.
32. "The Sheldon Uplift of the Old and Young."
33. Ibid.
34. Interview with Minus Gentry, July 22, 1981.
35. Halbert, *Across the Way*, 6, 9.
36. Ibid., 9.
37. Ibid.
38. Gentry interview.
39. Halbert, *Across the Way*, 10–14.
40. Ibid., 14–15.
41. Letter from William H. Guild to Timothy Miller, Nov. 7, 1981.

42. Halbert, *Across the Way*, 15–16.
43. Ibid., 19–21.
44. Ibid., 36.
45. Cox, *Blacks in Topeka*, 151–52.
46. Halbert, *Across the Way*, 21–36.
47. Peggy Greene, "Dr. Sheldon and Tennesseetown," *Shawnee County Historical Society Bulletin* no. 58 (Nov. 1981), 119.
48. Emma Crabb, untitled ms. notes in Sheldon Room.
49. CMS, "My Most Unusual Layman," *CH* 64:12 (Dec. 1941), 42.
50. Halbert, *Across the Way*, 37.
51. "Rev. Charles M. Sheldon: His Life, Labors and Aims," unattributed article in CMS et al., *The First Christian Daily Paper and Other Sketches* (New York: Street and Smith, 1900), 116.
52. CMS, "Doctor Sheldon Says Victory Garden Movement Began Here in Tennesseetown Years Ago," Topeka newspaper clipping (n.d., early 1940s), in Sheldon Room.
53. Halbert, *Across the Way*, 33.
54. Ibid., 34.
55. "Dr. Sheldon's Work," *TDC,* Oct. 14, 1899.
56. Halbert, *Across the Way*, 35.
57. "To Be Their Own Affair," *TDC,* Mar. 27, 1901.
58. Untitled ms. in Sheldon Room.
59. Clipping from unspecified Topeka newspaper, Oct. 8, 1903, in Sheldon Room.
60. L.C. Hodge, "Problem of Self-Help," *Civic Pride* 1:3 (May 1904).
61. "Sheldon Uplift of the Old and Young."
62. See, for example, Cox, *Blacks in Topeka*, 147.
63. Clark, *The Man Who Walked In His Steps*, 9.

4. The Astounding Success of In His Steps

1. John W. Ripley, "Last Rites for a Few Myths," *Shawnee County Historical Society Bulletin* 44 (Winter 1967); Ripley, "The Strange Story of Charles M. Sheldon's *In His Steps.*"
2. "Many Join in Tribute to Noted Topeka Minister-Author," *TDC,* May 4, 1935.
3. George T.B. Davis, "Charles M. Sheldon, Novelist," 75–76.
4. See David G. Johnson, "A Study of the Ideas of Charles M. Sheldon" (M.A. thesis, Univ. of Kansas, 1965), 118–19, for a discussion of the appeal of Sheldon's stories.

5. For an extended discussion of the genre, see "The Social-Gospel Novel," ch. 5 of Elmer F. Suderman, "Religion in the American Novel: 1870–1900" (Ph.D. diss., Univ. of Kansas, 1961).

6. Wallace Evan Davies, "Religious Issues in Late Nineteenth-Century American Novels," *Bulletin of the John Rylands Library* 41:2 (Mar. 1959), 358–59.

7. Henry F. May, *Protestant Churches and Industrial America* (New York: Harper, 1949; rpt., New York: Octagon Books, 1963), 207.

8. Washington Gladden, *The Christian League of Connecticut* (New York: The Century Co., 1883).

9. See Charles Howard Hopkins, *The Rise of the Social Gospel in American Protestantism, 1865–1915* (New Haven: Yale Univ. Press, 1940), 140–41 and 145–48, for descriptions of many social gospel novels. Robert T. Handy, *The Social Gospel in America, 1870–1920* (New York: Oxford Univ. Press, 1966), also contains a useful discussion of the genre.

10. William Dean Howells, *A Traveller from Altruria* (New York: Harper and Brothers, 1894), *A Hazard of New Fortunes* (New York: Harper and Brothers, 1890), *Annie Kilburn* (New York: Harper and Brothers, 1889).

11. Hopkins, *Rise of the Social Gospel*, 148.

12. "In His Steps," review by Clarence Gohdes, 354.

13. Mrs. Humphrey Ward, *Robert Elsmere* (London and New York: Macmillan, 1888).

14. W.T. Stead, *If Christ Came to Chicago* (London: "Review of Reviews" Office, 1899), iv. Originally published in 1894.

15. Ibid., 432.

16. See account in ch. 2 of event in Sheldon's experience on which this incident was modeled.

17. "Mr. Sheldon's Sermon," *TSJ*, Oct. 5, 1896, 8.

18. Ripley, "Strange Story," 2.

19. Ripley, "Last Rites," 17.

20. Quoted in ibid.

21. CMS, in an interview published as a foreword to the *Christian Herald* edition of *In His Steps* (1920); cited in Ripley, "Strange Story," 3.

22. CMS, *The History of "In His Steps"* (Topeka: privately printed, 1938), 7.

23. George H. Doran, *Chronicles of Barabbas* (New York: Harcourt, Brace, 1935), 26–27. But Doran's memory itself is a bit suspect; the serial publication of *In His Steps* did not commence until November 1896, and Sheldon almost certainly did not approach the publishers until very late that year or early in 1897. Thus Doran's firm could not have been preoccupied with the approach of the 1896 election.

24. John K. Hutchins, "People Who Read and Write," *New York Times Book Review*, Mar. 10, 1946, 27.
25. Ripley interview.
26. CMS, "The Ethics of Some Publishers," *CC* 50 (Sept. 27, 1933), 1206–8.
27. William L. Stidger, "'In His Steps' Brought No Wealth," *Dearborn Independent* 26 (June 12, 1926), 2.
28. Undated letter from the Rev. F.J. Leibenberg, Stellenbosch, South Africa, to Sheldon; in Sheldon Room.
29. CMS, "Ethics," 1206.
30. Figures supplied by John Ripley, "Strange Story," 15.
31. Autobiography, 104.
32. Fred Barton, "The Parson's Sensational Book," *CH* 82 (March 1959), 40–41.
33. CMS, "Ethics," 1206.
34. Letter from CMS to "Brother Fisk," Jan. 28, 1902; KSHS.
35. CMS, *History*, 11.
36. See, for example, the *Daily Iowa Capital* (Des Moines), Aug. 26, 1899, where the entire book appears at once in a special section.
37. A turn-of-the-century report has it that the *Melbourne Evening Herald*, for example, was publishing the book chapter by chapter. See "The Pulpit: The Man Who Has Reached the Masses," *Century Magazine*, ca. 1900 (undated clipping in Sheldon Room).
38. CMS, "Ethics," 1206.
39. Taylor, "Twentieth Century Utopia—Topeka."
40. Jennie Small Owen, "Kansas Folks Worth Knowing: Dr. Charles M. Sheldon," *Kansas Teacher* 46:2 (Dec. 1937), 31.
41. "The Pulpit: The Man."
42. Autobiography, 100–1.
43. CMS, *History*, 18–19.
44. Ripley, "Last Rites," 25.
45. Frank Luther Mott, *Golden Multitudes: The Story of Best Sellers in the United States* (New York: Macmillan, 1947), 196–97.
46. CMS, "Ethics," 1208, says "969000th"; CMS, Autobiography, 100, says "971000th."
47. CMS, *History*, 15.
48. Ripley interview.
49. Peggy Greene, "Best Seller from the Pulpit, *TDC*, Oct. 29, 1967, 5M. See also Greene's apparent source, James C. Marvin, "A Lively Septuagenarian," *Shawnee County Historical Society Bulletin*, 44 (Winter 1967), ii.
50. Ripley, "Strange Story," 23.

51. Cecil Howes, "New Honors for the Topeka Author of 'In His Steps,'" *KCS*, Apr. 12, 1936, C1; Cecil Howes, "Dr. Sheldon and Topeka Mark Half a Century 'In His Steps,'" *KCT*, Dec. 12, 1938. On the other hand, in the Autobiography (105), written thirteen years earlier, he claimed to own a Russian copy.

52. Clark, *The Man Who Walked In His Steps*, 22.

53. "'In His Steps,' Dr. Sheldon's All-Time Best Selling Novel, Made Radio Drama for KTSJ," *TSJ*, Mar. 25, 1947.

54. John W. Ripley, "George Bond Made Photo Play from Popular 'In His Steps,'" *Capper's Weekly*, Feb. 13, 1968. Ripley credits this opinion to McDonald. Ripley later specified that *In His Steps* was actually only the first *published* novel to be screened; he had learned of an earlier lantern slide play from an unpublished manuscript. (Letter from John Ripley to Tim Miller, Nov. 17, 1984.)

55. CMS, *History*, 9.

56. CMS, "The Story of 'In His Steps,'" *CH* 68 (Nov. 1945), 89–94.

57. CMS, *History*, 21.

58. John W. Ripley, "'In His Steps' on Stage and Screen," *Shawnee County Historical Society Bulletin* 43 (Dec. 1966), 68.

59. "Dr. Sheldon Not Pleased with Film 'In His Steps,'" *TSJ*, Sept. 29, 1936.

60. Gerald D. McDonald, "*In His Steps*—All-Time Best Seller on Nobody's Best Seller List," *Shawnee County Historical Society Bulletin* 44 (Winter 1967), 4–5.

61. Greene, "Best Seller," 5M.

62. An interesting discussion of the appeal of the book along these lines can be found in James H. Smylie, "Sheldon's *In His Steps*: Conscience and Discipleship," *Theology Today* 32:1 (Apr. 1975).

63. Gerald D. McDonald, "*In His Steps*: All-Time Best Seller," 5–6.

64. Eric F. Goldman, "Books that Changed America," *Saturday Review* 36:27 (July 4, 1953), 9, 38.

65. "The Pulpit: the Man."

66. "Our Literary Triumvirate," *TDSJ*, July 26, 1899, 6.

67. "Idea Spreading," *TSJ*, July 5, 1899, 6.

68. Notes on Sheldon by L.D. Whittemore; supplied by Margaret Whittemore.

69. Whittemore, "Charles M. Sheldon," 18. That formulation of Sheldon's advice, incidentally, makes him seem very much like a foreshadower of Joseph Fletcher, who in the 1960s developed the "situation ethics" school of thought, which advocated moral decision-making free of rigid rules, based on the law of Christian love. Fletcher argued that "Love's decisions are made situationally, not prescriptively." See

Fletcher, *Situation Ethics* (Philadelphia: Westminster Press, 1966), 134.

70.   "Mr. Sheldon's Sermon-Stories," *Spectator* 82 (June 3, 1899), 789.

71.   William E. Barton, "What Would Jesus Do?" *Christian Endeavor World* 14 : 33 (May 17, 1900), 674.

72.   "Fashion in Fiction," *Blackwood's Edinburgh Magazine* 166 : 1008 (Oct. 1899), 537 – 38.

73.   Paul S. Boyer, "*In His Steps*: A Reappraisal," *American Quarterly* 23 : 1 (Spring 1971), 61.

74.   Ibid., 62.

75.   Ibid., 69.

76.   Ibid.

77.   Ibid., 71.

78.   Ibid., 78.

79.   See, for example, Wayne Elzey, "'What Would Jesus Do?': *In His Steps* and the Moral Codes of the Middle Class," *Soundings* 58 : 4 (Winter 1975), 483; Peter W. Williams, *Popular Religion in America* (Englewood Cliffs, N.J.: Prentice-Hall, 1980), 140.

80.   James H. Smylie, "Sheldon's *In His Steps*," 42 – 43.

81.   CMS, "The Real Sacrilege," *Christian Endeavor World* 14 : 28 (Apr. 12, 1900), 576.

82.   Autobiography, 110 – 11.

83.   A copy of the London penny edition of *His Brother's Keeper* is in the Sheldon Room.

84.   CMS, *Jesus Is Here!* (New York: Hodder and Stoughton, 1914), 32.

85.   "Christ Will Appear among Men and Live and Work," *KCS*, Apr. 12, 1914.

86.   "Second Sheldon Story Dramatized for Movies," *TDC*, Aug. 16, 1916. Actually, the movie never materialized.

87.   "Mr. Sheldon's 'Sermon-Stories,'" 789.

88.   Glenn Clark, *What Would Jesus Do?* (St. Paul, Minn.: Macalester Park Publishing Co., 1950).

5. The Christian Daily Newspaper

1.   CMS, *Richard Bruce, or The Life That Now Is* (Boston and Chicago: Congregational Sunday-School and Publishing Society, 1892), 288.

2.   James Melvin Lee, *History of American Journalism* (Boston and New York: Houghton Mifflin, 1923), 268.

3.   See ibid., 266 – 69, 331 – 32, for an account of these ventures into religious journalism.

4. John W. Ripley, "Another Look at the Rev. Mr. Charles M. Sheldon's Christian Daily Newspaper," *Kansas Historical Quarterly* 31:1 (Spring 1965), 6–7.

5. For a good history of the post–Civil War religious press, see Frank Luther Mott, *A History of American Magazines*, vol. 4 (Cambridge: Harvard Univ. Press, 1957), 276–305.

6. See, for example, James A. Chamberlin, "If Jesus Were an Editor," *Kingdom* 9:51 (Apr. 2, 1897), 820–21. Chamberlin's ideas about a Christian daily are indistinguishable from Sheldon's.

7. CMS, "A Plea for a Christian Daily Newspaper—I," *Kingdom*, June 28, 1895, 165.

8. Ibid.

9. Homer E. Socolofsky, *Arthur Capper* (Lawrence: Univ. of Kansas Press, 1962), 41, 45–46.

10. *Topeka Mail and Kansas Breeze*, Oct. 18, 1895, 1.

11. "A Preacher's Ideal," *Mail and Breeze*, July 10, 1896. See also another report of Sheldon's question-and-answer session, "Mr. Sheldon's Symposium," *TDC*, July 3, 1896.

12. Report on the Eighteenth International Christian Endeavor Convention, Detroit, July, 1899, 113–18; at KSHS.

13. Ripley, "Another Look", 6.

14. Dave Meier, "Casual Conversation Touched Off One of Journalism's Most Amazing Experiments," *TDC*, May 24, 1953. Some critics denounced the 150% temporary increase in the paper's price, but others defended Sheldon by arguing that the regular ten-cents-a-week price was for those near Topeka, and that a quarter was already the regular price for distant subscribers. See "The Interest Is Increasing," *Christian Endeavor World* 14:21 (Feb. 22, 1900), 450.

15. Richard A. Ek, "The Irony of Sheldon's Newspaper," *Journalism Quarterly* 51:1 (Spring 1974), 23.

16. Ripley, "Another Look," 21–22.

17. "More Help Needed," *TDC*, Feb. 28, 1900, 5.

18. *Christian Endeavor World* 14:19 (Feb. 8, 1900), 410.

19. Quoted in "Opinions of Editors," *TDC*, Jan. 24, 1900, 1.

20. "The Sheldon Edition," editorial, *Emporia Gazette*, Mar. 13, 1900, 2.

21. Ripley, "Another Look," 17.

22. "Editor Sheldon at Work on His Christian Daily," *Mail and Breeze*, Mar. 9, 1900, 1.

23. Gilson Willets, "Pastor Sheldon's Editorial Experiences," *CH* 23 (Mar. 21, 1900), 231.

24. Harold T. Chase, "Mr. Sheldon in the Editor's Chair," *Christian Endeavor World* 14 (Apr. 5, 1900), 567.

25. "When Sheldon Published the Capital the Way He Thought Jesus Would," *TDC*, Feb. 27, 1916.

26. Ray Heady, "Even Ads Came under Editor's Pencil When Charles M. Sheldon Ran a Paper," *KCT*, Feb. 26, 1946.

27. "Declines to Talk," *TDC*, Mar. 20, 1900.

28. Chase, "Mr. Sheldon," 567.

29. John Ripley reported this headline in the Mar. 15, 1900, *New York Herald*: "Suicide Due to Sheldon Edition.—An Intemperate Printer Discharged for Fear of Offending Reverend Editor, Kills Himself." See Ripley, "Another Look," 29.

30. "Many Join in Tribute to Noted Topeka Minister-Author," *TDC*, May 4, 1935.

31. Chase, "Mr. Sheldon," 567.

32. "They Are Legion," *TSJ*, Mar, 15, 1900, 5.

33. "Sheldon Questions," *TSJ*, Mar. 16, 1900, 1.

34. There were two other omissions, both of them more comprehensible: J.K. Hudson's name did not appear, but Sheldon was replacing him as editor for the week, and Hudson did little if anything for the duration. Also missing was the name of Auguste Babize, the *sub rosa* promoter of the Sheldon edition; but he was also working as a correspondent for a Chicago newspaper and Sheldon may well not have known that he was working for the *Capital* as well.

35. Rutherford B. Hayes, "When Topeka Was the Focal Point of All Christendom," *TDC*, Mar. 10, 1940.

36. "Sheldon Edition Broke All Circulation Records," *TDC*, Feb. 27, 1916.

37. "Ended Before Midnight," *TSJ*, Mar. 19, 1900, 1, 6.

38. "Editor Sheldon at Work," 1.

39. Reported in letter from Stuart Reid, London, to John Ripley, June 15, 1964; at KSHS.

40. "Sheldon Paper in London," *TDC*, Apr. 1, 1900, 1.

41. Figures from *American Newspaper Annual*, 1899; cited in Ripley, "Another Look," 13.

42. "362,684," *TDC*, Mar. 25, 1900, 1.

43. "Jesus Is His Model," *Chicago Sunday Inter Ocean*, Mar. 11, 1900.

44. "When Sheldon Published the Capital the Way He Thought Jesus Would."

45. "Editor Sheldon at Work," 1.

46. "No! Says Sheldon," *Kansas City World*, Mar. 10, 1900.

47. "Editor Sheldon at Work," 1.

48. "Jesus Is His Model."

49. "No! Says Sheldon."

50. Willets, "Pastor Sheldon's Editorial Experiences."
51. Herbert S. Houston, "Truth Drive Began in Early Days," *TDC*, July 5, 1936.
52. Ripley, "Another Look," 21.
53. "What the Papers Said," *TSJ*, Mar. 19, 1900, 2.
54. Quoted in *TSJ* Weekly, Mar. 22, 1900.
55. Houston, "Truth Drive." John Ripley, quoting the regional Episcopal journal, *The Church Standard* (Mar. 10, 1900), puts the figure at one-third of a cent per agate line per thousand copies. See Ripley, "Another Look," 31–32.
56. "Next Week," *TSJ*, Mar. 10, 1900.
57. Ripley, "Another Look," 28.
58. "When Sheldon Published the Capital."
59. Ripley, "Another Look," 26.
60. "A Big Row Is On," TSJ, Mar. 17, 1900, 1.
61. Ibid., 4.
62. "Row Is Growing," *Kansas City World*, Mar. 18, 1900, 1.
63. "Capital Compromise," *TSJ*, Mar. 19, 1900, 1.
64. Untitled article, *TSJ*, May 29, 1900.
65. Ripley, "Another Look," 36.
66. Edna Margaret Long, "It Is Good to Remember a Great Man," *Advance*, June 28, 1957, 19.
67. CMS, "A Preacher Edits the News," *CH* 69:3, (Mar. 1946), 21.
68. Nino Lo Bello, "When Christ Was City Editor," *Kiwanis Magazine* 39 (December 1954), 20.
69. Houston, "Truth Drive."
70. Ripley, "Another Look," 32.
71. Finley Peter Dunne, "Mr. Dooley XXIII—On Mr. Sheldon's Newspaper," *Harper's Weekly* 44:2262 (Apr. 28, 1900), 400.
72. Washington Gladden, "Mr. Sheldon's Newspaper," *Independent* 52:2679, Apr. 5, 1900, 807–9.
73. CMS, "The Experiment of a Christian Daily," *Atlantic Monthly* 134 (Nov. 1924), 632.
74. CMS, "Here, Boy! Give Me a Paper!" *CC* 41 (Apr. 24, 1924), 534–35.
75. "Dr. Charles M. Sheldon Is Dead; Author of 'In His Steps' Was 88," *New York Herald Tribune*, Feb. 25, 1946.
76. "Nation Wide Interest in Dr. Chas. M. Sheldon Criticism of the News," *TSJ*, Feb. 24, 1934.

6. The Social Reformer

1. For a discussion of Sheldon's vagueness on such matters, see Carl J. Swenson, Jr., "Charles Monroe Sheldon: A Critical Analysis" (M.A. thesis, Kansas State College of Pittsburg, 1966).

2. CMS, *A Charles M. Sheldon Year Book* (Topeka: Crane and Co., 1909), 155.

3. David Spencer Reynolds, "Shifting Interpretation of Protestantism," *Journal of Popular Culture* 9:3 (Winter 1975), 598.

4. CMS, "Is Life Worth Living?" 852.

5. CMS, "How to Know What Jesus Would Do," *Christian Endeavor World* 14:40 (July 5, 1900), 789.

6. CMS, "What Would Jesus Do?" *CH* 60:9 (Sept. 1937), 60.

7. CMS, "How to Know What Jesus Would Do," 789.

8. L.D. Whittemore, "Charles M. Sheldon."

9. Report on the Eighteenth International Christian Endeavor Convention, Detroit, July, 1899; pp. 113–18 have Sheldon's speech and questions and answers. Excerpts from report in John Ripley files, KSHS.

10. CMS, "The Law of Christian Discipleship," in *The First Christian Daily Paper and Other Sketches*, 85–88.

11. "Rev. Charles M. Sheldon: His Life, Labors and Aims," in ibid., 149–50.

12. CMS, *He Is Here* (New York: Harper and Brothers, 1931).

13. CMS, "The Choice of a Profession," *Youth's Companion* 68:3511 (Sept. 6, 1894), III.

14. See Johnson, "A Study of the Ideas of Charles M. Sheldon," 21 and 43, for a further discussion of this side of Sheldon's thinking.

15. CMS, "Opportunities Before the Church of To-Day," in Alfred Williams Anthony, ed., *New Wine Skins* (Boston: Morning Star Publishing House, 1901), 290.

16. A.B. MacDonald, "Walking 'In His Steps' No More Difficult Than Ever, Dr. Sheldon Asserts," *KCS*, Oct. 19, 1930.

17. CMS, "Life Is My Teacher," part 4, 60.

18. CMS, "What Would Jesus Do?" *Independent* 97:3664 (Mar. 1, 1919), 294.

19. See, for example, George A. Herron, *The New Redemption* (New York: Thomas Y. Crowell, 1893); George A. Herron, *The Christian Society* (Chicago: Fleming H. Revell, 1894).

20. CMS, *A Charles M. Sheldon Year Book*, 11.

21. CMS, letter to members of Central Church from Clifton Springs, New York, July 15, 1895; at KSHS.

22. Ronald C. White, Jr., "Social Religion and Popular Culture—Two Case Studies: (1) Charles M. Sheldon," ms., 1982, 18.

23. CMS, "Tho and Nevertheless—A Thanksgiving Sermon," *TDC*, Nov. 25, 1920, 4.

24. CMS, "Life Is My Teacher," part 4, 63.

25. Sheldon elaborated on this theme on several occasions. See especially CMS, "Are We Nearer the Master's Footsteps?" *Congregationalist* 111 (Jan. 7, 1926), 6–7.

26. CMS, *Life's Treasure Book* (Elgin, Ill.: David C. Cook Publishing Co., n.d.), 23.

27. "Ancient Flappers Scandalized Jerusalem," *TDC*, Feb. 26, 1928, 13B.

28. CMS, "The Common Task," *CH* 44:22 (May 28, 1921), 387.

29. CMS, "Summer Workers," *Youth's Companion* 69:3553 (June 27, 1895), II.

30. CMS, "The Great Catastrophe of 1913," *Independent* 74:3348 (Jan. 30, 1913), 233–36.

31. CMS, "A Vignette from the Great Iron-Miners' Strike," *Outlook* 52 (Sept. 21, 1895), 461–62.

32. CMS, "What Will You Do With Him?" *Kingdom* 9:43 (Feb. 5, 1897), 687.

33. CMS, "Short Talks with a Workingman," *Kingdom* 8:5 (May 17, 1895).

34. CMS, "Of Such Is the Kingdom," in *Heart Stories* (New York: The Christian Herald, 1920), 89–124.

35. CMS, "The Labor Situation in Colorado," *Independent* 57:2907 (Aug. 18, 1904), 361–62.

36. CMS, *In His Steps*, ch. 28.

37. CMS, *Malcolm Kirk* (Chicago: The Church Press, 1898), chs. 14–20.

38. CMS, *John King's Question Class*, 131–32.

39. CMS, *Born to Serve* (Chicago: Advance Publishing Co., 1900).

40. Ripley interview.

41. CMS, "The Servant in the House," *CH* 53:21 (May 24, 1930), 10.

42. CMS, "Some Servants in the House," *CH* 51:30 (July 28, 1928), 780.

43. CMS, "Servant and Mistress," *Independent* 52:2716 (Dec. 20, 1900), 3021.

44. CMS, "Short Talks with a Workingman—2," *Kingdom* 8:3 (May 3, 1895).

45. CMS, "Short Talks with a Workingman—3," *Kingdom* 8:4 (May 10, 1895).

46. Quoted in Hopkins, *The Rise of the Social Gospel in American Protes-*

tantism, 197, footnote. The editor of the *Social Forum* was reacting to the Sheldon edition of the *Topeka Daily Capital*.

47. "A Talk with Mr. Sheldon," *KCS*, Mar. 14, 1900, 1. Sheldon used a formulation much like this one on several occasions.
48. Autobiography, 182.
49. CMS, *The Heart of the World: A Story of Christian Socialism* (New York: Fleming H. Revell Co., 1905), 113–43.
50. See, for example, "To Better Cities," *Topeka Daily Herald*, Nov. 1, 1901.
51. CMS, *A Charles M. Sheldon Year Book*, 69.
52. Quoted in Johnson, "Study of the Ideas," 49.
53. See, for example, *In His Steps*, where small businessman Milton Wright and railroad superintendent Alexander Powers are made heroes for living up to their Sheldonesque ideals.
54. CMS, "Is Christianity Practical in Worldly Affairs?" *Ladies' Home Journal* 16 (Nov. 1899), 10.
55. CMS, "Kansans are Puritans—White Spendthrifts on Luxury—Sheldon," *TDC*, Apr. 23, 1922.
56. CMS, "Poverty Doesn't Frighten Me," *Rotarian* 49:5 (Nov. 1936), 16.
57. CMS, "The Statesmanship of Christ," sermon, Jan. 19, 1890; ms. in Sheldon Room.
58. CMS, *What Did Jesus Really Teach?* (Topeka: Capper Publications, 1930), 77.
59. CMS, *How to Succeed* (Chicago: Advance Publishing Co., 1902), 22. See also CMS, "How Greed for Money Is Undermining Our Life," *TDC*, Aug. 12, 1900, 4.
60. "To Better Cities," *Topeka Daily Herald*, Nov. 1, 1901.
61. CMS, "The Missionary Policeman," *Independent* 76 (Nov. 6, 1913), 259–60. This article was widely acclaimed and soon afterwards was reprinted, together with another Sheldon story from the same periodical, in booklet form.
62. CMS, "The New Police," *Colliers* 51 (July 5, 1913), 22–23.
63. CMS, "The Student and Humanity," *University Review* 13:2 (Sept. 1891), 5.
64. Letter from Emma Crabb, Topeka, to R.L. McNatt, Dukedom, Tenn., Jan. 15, 1966; in Sheldon Room.
65. CMS, "God's Fingerprints," *CH* 64:8 (Aug. 1941), 25.
66. "Dr. Sheldon Secretly 'in Prison' 40 Years Ago," undated clipping from a Topeka newspaper, in Sheldon Room.
67. Harvey R. Hougen, "Kate Barnard and the Kansas Penitentiary Scandal, 1908–1909," *Journal of the West* 17:1 (Jan. 1978), 9–18.
68. CMS, *Of One Blood* (Boston: Small, Maynard and Co., 1916).

69. See, for example, CMS, "The Editor's Mail," *CH* 46 (Apr. 14, 1923), 296.
70. Quoted in Cox, *Blacks in Topeka*, 144.
71. Charles Yrigoyen, Jr., "Charles M. Sheldon: Christian Social Novelist," *Bulletin of the Congregational Library* 33:2 (Winter 1982), 16.
72. Jack Wayne Traylor, "William Allen White's 1924 Gubernatorial Campaign," *Kansas Historical Quarterly* 42 (Summer 1976), 185.
73. CMS, "What Would Jesus Do About Anti-Semitism?" *Liberty* 16 (Apr. 29, 1939).
74. Swan, *The Ethnic Heritage of Topeka*, 75.
75. Stuenkel interview.
76. CMS, "Some Servants in the House," 780.
77. CMS, *A Charles M. Sheldon Year Book*, 247.
78. CMS, *John King's Question Class*, 137–38.
79. CMS, "The Statesmanship of Christ," sermon.
80. CMS, "Is Our Civilization Christian?" *Seminary Notes* 2:1 (October 1892), 56.
81. CMS, *A Charles M. Sheldon Year Book*, 50.
82. Ibid., 82.
83. CMS, *Some Facts Regarding City Government, Together with a Catechism on Good Citizenship* (Topeka: Crane and Co., 1902).
84. "Tribute to Sheldon," *TDC*, Apr. 22, 1899.
85. See, for example, CMS, "The Man Who Would Be Mayor," *CH* 65:10 (Oct. 1942), 46–8; CMS, "Why Not?" *Christian Century* 49:29 (July 20, 1932), 908–9.
86. CMS, *A Charles M. Sheldon Year Book*, 138.
87. See, e.g., CMS, *The High Calling* (New York: Hodder and Stoughton, George H. Doran Co., 1911). This sermon story praises a young man who eschews the party and runs for office as an independent. A straight-down-the-line party man is also important to the plot as a detestable character.
88. CMS, *In His Steps*, 66.
89. CMS, "The Editor's Mail," 296.
90. Letter from Alf Landon to Hector Leroy Cordova, Feb. 14, 1967; cited in Cordova, "Formation," 89.
91. CMS, "A Plea for a Christian Daily Newspaper—2," *Kingdom*, July 5, 1895, 182.
92. CMS, "Horizons Seen and Unseen," *CH* 61:10, (Oct. 1938), 40.
93. Davis, "Charles M. Sheldon, Novelist," 75–76.
94. CMS, "The Use and Abuse of Fiction," *Independent* 54:2786 (Apr. 24, 1902), 965–67.

95. CMS, "Is a Christian Theater Possible?" *Independent* 53:2728 (Mar. 14, 1901), 616.

96. CMS, "And I Said to Him, *CH* 47:6 (Feb. 9, 1924), 123.

97. CMS, "Reforming the Theater," *Independent* 68:3201 (Apr. 7, 1910), 756.

98. "Would Boycott Movies until Industry Learns to Film Cleaner Plots," *TDSJ*, Apr. 28, 1930.

99. CMS, "'Jazz' Morals," *CH* 43:19 (Feb. 28, 1920), 252.

100. "The Christian Life the Life That God Commands," sermon, Dec. 12, 1887, at Waterbury, Vt.; in Sheldon Room.

101. "Noted Religious Writer Scores Liquor Drinkers in Strangers Club Talk," *Arizona Republic*, Feb. 18, 1929, section 2, 1.

102. Quoted in "The Administration of John P. St. John," *Transactions of the Kansas State Historical Society* (Topeka) 9 (1905–6), 383.

103. CMS, "What Prohibition Has Done for Kansas," *Independent* 60:2996 (May 3, 1906), 1034.

104. CMS, *In His Steps*, 87.

105. CMS, *Who Killed Joe's Baby?* (Chicago: Advance Publishing Co., 1901).

106. CMS, *The Narrow Gate* (Chicago: Advance Publishing Co., 1903).

107. William D.P. Bliss, *The New Encyclopedia of Social Reform* (New York: Funk and Wagnalls, 1908), 716.

108. CMS, *Prohibition in Kansas*, pamphlet (Manchester, England: n.p., 1907), 5.

109. See, for example, untitled excerpts from a Sheldon address delivered in February, 1906; reprinted in *Transactions of the Kansas State Historical Society* (Topeka) 9 (1905–1906), 383.

110. A discussion of this theme can be found in Cordova, "Formation," 74–75.

111. "Dr. Sheldon Talks to Big Audience," *Chicago Daily Inter Ocean*, July 15, 1901.

112. Kansas Prohibition Clippings, vol. 6, 35–82, KSHS. See also CMS, "Opportunities Before the Church of To-Day," 294. The Kansas Prohibition Clippings volume contains the original clippings used by Sheldon and certifies that the roll was twenty-eight feet, nine inches long. When Sheldon recalled the gesture thirty-four years later, his memory, characteristically, failed him; he recalled that the roll had been six hundred feet long—more than twenty times the actual figure. See CMS, "Murder Will Out," *CH* 53:10 (Mar. 8, 1930), 10.

113. "Is Getting Tired," *TDSJ*, Feb. 2, 1929, 6.

114. Letter from CMS to Ernest H. Cherrington, n.d. (late 1928 or early 1929); in Cherrington papers, Ohio Historical Society.

115. Clinton N. Howard, "In Memoriam: Dr. Charles M. Sheldon, Kansas," *Progress* 46:3 (Mar. 1946), 3.

116. Autobiography, ch. 6.

117. CMS, "For a Better World," in J. Frank Hanly and Oliver Wayne Stewart, eds., *Speeches of the Flying Squadron* (Indianapolis: Hanly and Stewart, n.d. [ca. 1915]), 273.

118. CMS, "Why National Prohibition?" in ibid., 269.

119. "Heredity of Charles M. Sheldon," *Eugenical News* 11:4 (Apr. 1926), 49.

120. CMS, "When Carrie Nation Came to Kansas," *CH* 53:1 (Jan. 4, 1930), 18. (Nation preferred the spelling "Carry," but Sheldon followed the orthography commonly used by others.) The other two articles in this series, "Carrie Nation's Hatchet . . . Becomes a Crusade" and "If Carrie Nation Returned to Kansas," were published in the following two issues, on January 11 and 18, respectively. Actually, however, during Nation's principal Topeka crusade, early in 1901, Sheldon had been more cautious. Emotions were running at a fever pitch at the time, with "hatchitation" and mass meetings attended by thousands. On February 10, the date of one of the biggest anti-joint rallies, Sheldon preached moderation from his pulpit. As the *Topeka Capital* reported his sermon that day, Sheldon "did not favor the idea of the citizens of Topeka taking enforcement of the law into their own hands. . . . The better way would be to force the officers to enforce the law, and if they would not do it well enough, elect others who would." ("Begins at Home," *TDC*, Feb. 11, 1901, 2.) Thus Sheldon's support for Nation's confrontational methods seems to have been greater in retrospect than it was at the time. His support for her goals, however, was unwavering.

121. "A Message from Sheldon," *TDC*, Aug. 12, 1900, 4.

122. CMS, "Great Britain and the Liquor Business," *Independent* 65:3120 (Sept. 17, 1908), 643–44.

123. Ibid., 645, 648.

124. "England Makes No Effort to Protect American Soldiers," *TDC*, Jan. 28, 1918.

125. CMS, "The Biggest British Blunder," *Independent* 93:3613 (Mar. 2, 1918), 387.

126. See Autobiography, ch. 8.

127. "Liner with 'Lid On' Is Sheldon's Scheme," *St. Louis Globe-Democrat*, undated clipping in Sheldon Room.

128. Letter from Charles Merriam Sheldon to Timothy Miller, Dec. 11, 1982.

129. CMS, "Short Talks About Vocations," 30–31.

130. CMS, *For Love of Country* (Topeka: n.p., 1915).

131. CMS, "If I Were a Teacher," *Household* 36:4 (Apr. 1936), 36.

132. CMS, "Compulsory Pagan Education," *Kansas Woman's Journal* 3:7 (June 1924), 6.

133. Ibid., 1.

134. CMS, "If I Were a Teacher," 36.

135. CMS, "Horizons Seen and Unseen," 72.

136. CMS, "The Bible's Place in the Schools," *Dr. Sheldon's Scrap Book* (New York: Christian Herald Association, 1942), 161.

137. CMS, *The Everyday Bible* (New York: Thomas Y. Crowell, 1924).

138. Letter from CMS to Arthur J. Carruth, Jr., Feb. 18, 1939; property of the Carruth family.

139. CMS, "Can Religion Be Taught?" *Atlantic Monthly* 136:4 (Oct. 1925), 472.

140. CMS, *Edward Blake: College Student* (Chicago: Advance Publishing Co., 1900), 244–50. A sermon story.

141. Ripley interview.

142. Menninger interview.

143. Quoted in L.H. Robbins, "Militant Pacifist," *New York Times Magazine*, Dec. 3, 1939.

144. Quoted in "World Peace Is the Goal of a Famous Kansas Minister," *KCS*, Dec. 9, 1934.

145. CMS, "If Jesus Came Back Today," *CC* 51:26 (June 27, 1934), 863.

146. CMS, "$100,000 for Peace," *CH*, July 28, 1923.

147. CMS, "What Would Happen?" *CC* 41, May 22, 1924, 662.

148. "Sheldon Attacks Navy War 'Game,'" *Cleveland Plain Dealer*, Apr. 30, 1935.

149. Letter from CMS to James Wise, Episcopal Bishop of Kansas, June 9, 1926.

150. CMS, "Military Pomp," *CH* 55:5, May, 1932, 26.

151. CMS, *A Charles M. Sheldon Year Book*, 168.

152. "Dr. Sheldon at Eighty-Six Has New Ideas on Religion."

153. Chase, "Charles M. Sheldon, Author, Preacher, Editor," 13.

154. For one such optimistic assessment see "Dr. Sheldon Through Snow to Speak Here," *Colby Free Press-Tribune*, Apr. 8, 1936.

155. CMS, "Christmas Sermon," *CH* 60:12 (Dec. 1937), 39.

156. CMS, "The Forward Sweep of the Peace Poster Idea," *CH* 56 (Jan. 1933), 7.

157. "Interest in Peace Posters," Topeka newspaper, n.d.; clipping in Sheldon Room.

158. Emma Crabb, "World War I," ms. in Sheldon Room.

159. Ibid.

160. CMS, "A Sermon for War Time," *CH* 40:19 (May 9, 1917), 536.

161. CMS, "Isaiah's League of Nations," *CH* 42:18 (May 3, 1919), 511.

162. Undated (1941) clipping from Waterbury newspaper; supplied by G.W. Ayers, Waterbury Historical Society.

163. CMS, "The Adventure of Peace," *CH* 65:12 (Dec. 1942), 18.

164. Helsley, "St. Charles of Topeka," in Henrichs, ed., *St. Charles of Topeka*, 67.

165. CMS, "Blessed Are the Peacemakers," *CH* 65:4 (Apr. 1942), 39.

7. The Religious Reformer

1. Quoted in Robbins, "Militant Pacifist."

2. Aaron I. Abell, *The Urban Impact on American Protestantism* (Cambridge: Harvard Univ. Press, 1943; rpt., London: Archon, 1962), 89, 98.

3. CMS, "Is Our Civilization Christian?" *Seminary Notes* (a Univ. of Kansas publication) 2:1 (Oct. 1892).

4. CMS, "A Plea for the Unity of Christendom," sermon preached Mar. 5, 1893; at KSHS and Sheldon Room.

5. CMS, "If Jesus Came Back Today," 863.

6. CMS, "Fewer Churches, More Religion," *CH* 53:9 (Mar. 1, 1930), 4.

7. Ibid., 4–5.

8. CMS, "All One Body We," *CH* 53:18 (May 3, 1930), 10.

9. CMS, "Fewer Churches, More Religion," 5. See also CMS, "A Plea for the Unity of Christendom."

10. Quoted in Arthur J. Carruth, "Under the Whispering Willow," *TDSJ*, Apr. 11, 1942, 8.

11. Quoted in Jennie Small Owen, "Kansas Folks Worth Knowing: Dr. Charles M. Sheldon," *Kansas Teacher* 46:2 (Dec. 1937), 32.

12. CMS, "A Plea for the Unity of Christendom."

13. Ripley, "Strange Story," 3–4.

14. CMS, "Opportunities Before the Church of To-Day," 291–92.

15. CMS, "The Adventure of Peace," 55.

16. CMS, *The Miracle at Markham: How Twelve Churches Became One* (Chicago: The Church Press, 1899).

17. CMS, "Untheological Christianity," *Christian Century* 43 (July 1, 1926), 836–38.

18. CMS, "Can Religion Be Taught?" 467–68.

19. Quoted in Clark, *Man Who Walked In His Steps*, 39.

20. Interview with Lena Schenck, July 14, 1981.

21. CMS, "Human or Superhuman?" *Atlantic Monthly* 119:1, (Jan. 1917), 80–85.

22. CMS, "The Ministers' Strike at Westport, Kansas," TDSJ, May 28 and June 4, 1938. (Sheldon invited his readers to submit alternate endings to the story, and on June 11 the paper printed the one Sheldon liked best.)

23. Letter from CMS to Arthur J. Carruth, Jr., June 6, 1931; property of the Carruth family.

24. CMS, "Hindrances and Helps in the Ministry," *Independent* 52:2709 (Nov. 1, 1900), 2616–17.

25. Letter from CMS to Charles F. Scott, Iola, Kans., Apr. 13, 1929; at KSHS.

26. CMS, "Turn It Around!" *CC* 46:32 (Aug. 7, 1929), 987–88.

27. CMS, "As to the Preliminaries," *Independent* 58:2951 (June 22, 1905), 1418. See also CMS, "Down with the Deadly Preliminaries," *Rotarian* 61:3 (Sept. 1942), 33–35.

28. "Dr. Sheldon at Eighty-Six."

29. CMS, "Prayer Meeting at Eleven A.M.," *CC* 47:8 (Feb. 19, 1930), 241–42.

30. "Dr. Sheldon at 86." See also CMS, "If I Were Back Again," *CH* 63:5 (May 1940), 19, 68.

31. CMS, *Howard Chase, Red Hill, Kansas* (New York: George H. Doran, 1918), ch. two.

32. "Author of 'In His Steps,'" *TDC*, Apr. 22, 1899.

33. CMS, "Try the New Thing!" 60.

34. CMS, *The Revival, or the Spirit's Power* (Cleveland: F. M. Barton, 1906).

35. CMS, quoted in "Dr. C. M. Sheldon," obituary editorial, *Coffeyville* [Kansas] *Leader*, Feb. 28, 1946.

36. CMS, "Christianity and Mr. Sunday," ms. ca. 1916, KSHS.

37. CMS, "Our Pagan Funerals," 58.

38. Ibid.

39. Sheldon provided what he described as a typical case of death and funeral expenses, showing how it cost a man making $1800 per year some $1700 to die, in "The High Cost of Dying," *CH* 43 (May 15, 1920), 603. The article is not entirely original; it very much resembles another Sheldon article published a decade earlier: "The Cost of Dying," *Independent* 68:3193 (Feb. 10, 1910), 306–7. The details, including the amounts of money listed, differ in the two articles, however.

40. CMS, "From Grave to Gay: Funerals and Weddings," *CH* 51:3 (Jan. 21, 1928), 59–60.

41. "Dr. Charles M. Sheldon Dies," *KCT*, Feb. 25, 1946.
42. "How to Help Mankind," *TSJ*, Nov. 9, 1891.
43. Quoted in Margaret Whittemore, "Humor and Playfulness of Dr. Sheldon Revealed in Prized Letters to Friends," *KCS*, Mar. 29, 1946.
44. CMS, "What Is a Sermon?" *Outlook* 49 (Feb. 24, 1894), 362.
45. "Protestant Churches Need a Confessional, Contends Dr. Sheldon," *TDSJ*, Jan. 8, 1940.
46. CMS, "A Protestant Confessional," *Atlantic Monthly* 129 (Jan. 1922), 21.
47. "For a Protestant Confessional," *Literary Digest* 47:7 (Aug. 16, 1913), 251.
48. "Dr. Sheldon's Confessional," *Literary Digest* 47:20 (Nov. 14, 1913), 950.
49. CMS, "Protestant Confessional," *CH* 63:9 (Sept. 1940), 26, 48.
50. CMS, "Practical Eugenics," *Independent* 73:3323 (Aug. 8, 1912), 321.
51. CMS, "What Would Jesus Teach about Social Hygiene?" *Liberty* 14:19 (May 8, 1937), 9.
52. CMS, *Life's Treasure Book*, 87.
53. CMS, "My First Sermon," *CH* 51:1 (Jan. 7, 1928), 26.
54. CMS, *A Charles M. Sheldon Year Book*, 39.
55. News item in *Columbus* [Ohio] *Dispatch*, Jan. 22, 1900; in John Ripley notes, KSHS.
56. Fred Barton, "The Parson's Sensational Book," *CH* 82 (Mar. 1959), 50–51.
57. CMS, *A Charles M. Sheldon Year Book*, 125.
58. CMS, "How to Keep Sunday?" *CH* 46:24 (June 16, 1923), 476.
59. CMS, *A Builder of Ships* (New York: George H. Doran Co., 1912), 217.
60. CMS and W.D.P. Bliss, "The Church and Social Service," *Independent* 60:2991 (Mar. 29, 1906), 737–38.
61. Quoted in "In His Steps Fifty-Six Years," undated clipping from a Kansas City newspaper, ca. late 1928 or early 1929; in Sheldon Room.
62. CMS, *Richard Bruce*, 179, 183.
63. CMS, *His Brother's Keeper* (Boston: Congregational Sunday-School and Publishing Society, 1896), 145–6.
64. Ibid., 152.
65. CMS, "The Program of the Kingdom of God," sermon delivered at the annual meeting of the American Missionary Association, Worcester, Mass., Oct. 17, 1905; in Sheldon Room.
66. Clark, *The Man Who Walked In His Steps*, 7.
67. CMS, *A Charles M. Sheldon Year Book*, 104–5.

68. CMS, "The Confessions of a Vegetarian," *Independent* 60:3003 (June 21, 1906), 1457–58.
69. CMS, "If Jesus Were Here Today," 61.
70. CMS, "What Is the Matter with Kansas?" 6–7.
71. CMS, *In His Steps To-day* (New York: Fleming H. Revell Co., 1921), ch. 9.
72. See CMS, "The Great Revival at Westville," *Christian Century* 54:34 (Aug. 25, 1937), 1045–48, for Sheldon's program for church revitalization through promoting family values and eschewing frivolous amusements. In the story the church members at Westville, Kansas, decide that each will give up a single "luxury or amusement he could get along without" for year and donate the money saved to the church. Soon the church's mortgage is paid off and a big local religious revival is under way.

8. St. Charles of Topeka

1. Taylor, "Twentieth Century Utopia—Topeka," 6.
2. Fritts, "Author of 'In His Steps,'" 540.
3. "Read by Two Continents," *KCS*, May 28, 1899, 11. This article deals at some length with Sheldon's refusal to be interviewed and finally draws a sketch of his life and work based on materials gathered elsewhere. A line drawing of Sheldon illustrates the article; Sheldon, it is noted, refused even to be photographed for publication.
4. Bruce Barton, "Nobody is Interested in Religion," *American Magazine* 60:3 (Sept. 1930), 158.
5. CMS, *He Is Here*; CMS, *In His Steps To-day*.
6. CMS, "What Would Jesus Do?" *CH* 69:1, 24.
7. "Contrast Shows Vividly Growth of the Central Congregational Church," *TDC*, Jan. 14, 1926.
8. CMS, quoted in *Seventy-Five Years of Central Congregational Church*.
9. Sheldon wrote three very similar articles outlining what he called a typical day in his life: "A Sixteen-Hour Day," *Independent* 66:3148 (Apr. 1, 1909), 690–92; "An Eighteen-Hour Day," *CH* 51:16 (Apr. 21, 1928), 431–32; "Sixteen Hours in the Life of Dr. Charles M. Sheldon," *CH* 60:2 (Feb. 1937), 16. The first two articles are very similar hour-by-hour reports; although the second was published after Sheldon's retirement, it purports to be taken from earlier years. The third article is a Sheldon rarity: a self-plagiarism. Twenty-eight years after the publication of the original article in the *Independent*,

Sheldon slightly rewrote part of it (much of it is verbatim), shortened it somewhat, and published it in another periodical. Nowhere else, to my knowledge, did Sheldon use his material more than once, except in the case of articles which became parts of books. On the other hand, he always said that if a sermon was good it was perfectly acceptable to use it more than once.

10. "Dr. Charles M. Sheldon Decries Shipping of Scrap Iron and Oil to Be Used in Killing Chinese," *TSJ*, Dec. 8, 1938.

11. Central Church records, church office.

12. Willets, "Pastor Sheldon's Editorial Experiences."

13. Gilson Willets, "Pastor Sheldon Is Now an Editor," *CH* 23 (Mar. 14, 1900), 212.

14. Telephone interview with Louise Adkins, Aug. 21, 1981.

15. Cordova, "Formation of the Social Gospel," 65. Cordova's account of the Merriam inheritance is based on an interview with Charles Helsley, one of Sheldon's successors at Central Church.

16. See, for example, L. Cady Hodge, "Recollections of Dr. Chas. M. Sheldon," undated ms. in Sheldon Room.

17. Quoted in Greene, "'In His Steps' Author."

18. Tape of interview with John Ripley, in Jeff Chaney and Craig Templeton, "Charles M. Sheldon and the Kindergarten in Tennesseetown," oral history project at Topeka West High School, 1977.

19. CMS, "Hindrances and Helps in the Ministry," 2616–17.

20. Interview with C. Benjamin Franklin, Aug. 13, 1981.

21. Letter from L.C. Barnett, Topeka, to Tim Miller, Oct. 3, 1981. Barnett lived across the street from Central Church.

22. CMS, "700 B.C., 1928 A.D.," *CH* 51:1 (Jan. 7, 1928), 8.

23. CMS, "The Religious Hunger of Youth," *Good Housekeeping* 82:2 (Feb. 1926), 187–88.

24. The Rev. J.D. Countermine, "How Sheldon's City Endeavors," *Christian Endeavor World* 14:47 (Aug. 23, 1900), 911.

25. Emma Crabb, "Tenth Anniversary of the Dr. Charles M. Sheldon Study-Museum at Gage Park," 1975, ms. in Sheldon Room.

26. Among the sources providing the numbers of missionaries and their destinations are *Seventy-Five Years of Central Congregational Church* and a manuscript list of twenty-seven missionaries in the Sheldon Room.

27. Clark, *The Man Who Walked In His Steps*, 7.

28. CMS, "Life Is My Teacher," part 4, 61. An interesting account of Sheldon's visit to the Hopi is CMS, "The Hopi Snake Dance," *Independent* 57:2918 (Nov. 3, 1904), 1026–31.

29. Guy P. Cross, "Our 75th Anniversary Year: Remembering," flyer, 1963.
30. "Heard 70 Miles," *Kansas City Journal*, Mar. 8, 1901. John Ripley has reported (personal communication, Dec. 1982) that "ATT has no record of any earlier address or sermon via long distance."
31. Autobiography, 195.
32. Philip Eastman, "In His Steps," *Nickell Magazine*, Nov. 1899, 275.
33. Willets, "Pastor Sheldon Is Now an Editor," 212.
34. Robbins, "Militant Pacifist."
35. Letter from CMS to Arthur J. Carruth, May 6, 1935; in possession of the Carruth family.
36. "What the Preacher Was Like," *Chicago Journal*, Mar. 13, 1900, 5.
37. Charles Merriam Sheldon to Timothy Miller.
38. Interview with Charles Sheldon Graves and Betty Graves, July 10, 1981.
39. Letter from CMS to O.H. White, July 4, 1927.
40. Letter from CMS to Lida R. Hardy, Topeka, July 11, 1935.
41. "Random Thoughts," *KCS*, Mar. 10, 1946.
42. CMS, *A Charles M. Sheldon Year Book*, 148.
43. Quoted in Barton, "Nobody Is Interested in Religion," 158.
44. Zula Bennington Greene, "Amusing Errors," *TCJ*, Dec. 16, 1981.
45. CMS, "Why Ministers Enjoy Life," in *Dr. Sheldon's Scrap Book* 207–8.
46. Hodge, "Recollections."
47. Ripley interview.
48. Charles Merriam Sheldon to Timothy Miller.
49. "Two Are Hurt in Collision," TDC, Mar. 14, 1945. Despite the title of this article, the story clearly relates that three persons were injured, one of them only slightly.
50. Letter from CMS to Jennie Small Owen, Dec. 12, 1936; at KSHS.
51. CMS, "Too Busy for Friends," *CH* 53:25 (June 21, 1930), 10.
52. Helsley, "St. Charles of Topeka," in Henrichs, ed., *St. Charles of Topeka*, 54.
53. Menninger interview.
54. Interview with Ralph Glenn, Aug. 12, 1981.
55. Interview with Peggy Greene, Aug. 10, 1981.
56. Mrs. Charles M. Sheldon, article in the *Christian Herald*, n.d. This article has been preserved without title or date at KSHS.
57. Undated article from Topeka newspaper, ca. Feb. 1941, in Sheldon Room.
58. Stratton interview.
59. Anonymous interviewee, 1981.

60. Interview with Vivian Rutter, July 23, 1981.
61. Stanley J. Kunitz and Howard Haycraft, eds., *Twentieth Century Authors* (New York: H.W. Wilson Co., 1942), 1273.
62. Ripley interview.
63. Interview with Edna Burkhardt, July 20, 1981.
64. Sheldon's grandson believed that the cottage was built "about 1905" (Charles Merriam Sheldon to Timothy Miller), but Congregationalist George Bohman says that the cottages there were built between 1911 and 1920 (letter from Paul A. Miller to Timothy Miller, Nov. 11, 1981). Since the Sheldons were summering there regularly by the latter part of the decade, their cabin must have been built by sometime before 1920.
65. Charles Merriam Sheldon to Timothy Miller.
66. Margaret Whittemore, "Tough on Teeth," *Nature Magazine*, Mar., 1940, 152.
67. Letter from CMS to Charles F. Scott (Iola, Kansas, Apr. 13, 1929); at KSHS.
68. Charles Merriam Sheldon to Timothy Miller.
69. Clark, *The Man Who Walked In His Steps*, 47–48.
70. Autobiography, 167.
71. Central Church minutes, church office.
72. "Sheldon to Lecture Now," *KCS*, May 29, 1912.
73. *Fiftieth Aniversary of Central Congregational Church 1888–1938*, pamphlet published by Central Church.
74. Johnson, "Ideas of Charles M. Sheldon," 84.
75. "Off for England," *TDSJ*, Oct. 6, 1917.
76. "Kansas Message Pleases England," *TDC*, Dec. 29, 1917.
77. "Dr. C.M. Sheldon Is Made Editor of Christian Herald," *TDC*, Dec. 23, 1919.
78. "Central Congregational Is Fifty-Four Years Old Today," *TDC*, Apr. 7, 1943, 10. (In fact Central Church's fifty-fourth birthday occurred in December 1942).
79. Margaret Hazard, "Dr. Sheldon as I Knew Him," ms. in Sheldon Room.
80. Mrs. C.B. Van Horn, "First Fruits," undated ms. in Sheldon Room.
81. "Dr. Sheldon Is Our Editor-in-Chief," *CH* 43:1 (Jan. 3, 1920), 1–2.
82. Ripley interview.
83. CMS, "The Editor's Mail," 296.
84. Autobiography, 176–78.
85. CMS, "I Wish I Might Go Again," *CH* 59:9 (Sept. 1936), 66.
86. Ibid., 39, 66. See also Carmie Wolfe, "Charles M. Sheldon—World Citizen," 45.

87. CMS, "Big Business," *CH* 69:5 (May 1946), 20.
88. Wolfe, "Charles M. Sheldon—World Citizen," 44.
89. Ibid.
90. "Name in Stone," *TSJ*, Jan. 30, 1936.
91. Cecil Howes, "New Honors for the Topeka Author of 'In His Steps,'" *KCS*, Apr. 12, 1936, C1.
92. "In His Steps 56 Years," undated clipping (ca. late 1928-early 1929), from Kansas City paper, in Sheldon Room.
93. Clark, *The Man Who Walked In His Steps*, 47–51.
94. CMS, *Two Old Friends* (Cincinnati: Christian Home Magazine, 1925), 30.
95. CMS, *A Charles M. Sheldon Year Book*, 319.
96. Menninger interview.
97. Clark, *The Man Who Walked In His Steps*, 59–60.
98. Ibid., 60.
99. CMS, "Cheerful Funerals," 332.
100. CMS, "Public Funerals," *CH* 56:2 (Feb. 1933), 24.
101. Helsley's account was contained in an interview recounted by Cordova, "Formation," 102.
102. Interview with Mae Fisk, Nov. 9, 1982.
103. Charles W. Helsley, funeral service for CMS, ms. in Sheldon Room.
104. Helsley, "Charles Monroe Sheldon." See also "Topeka Flags at Half Staff in Tribute to Dr. Sheldon," *TSJ*, Feb. 25, 1946, 1–2.

Appendix

1. Emma Crabb, "Publishers of *In His Steps*: United States and Great Britain," *Shawnee County Historical Society Bulletin* 44 (Winter 1967), 28; Gene DeGruson, *Kansas Authors of Best Sellers* (Pittsburg, Kansas: Kansas State College of Pittsburg, 1970), 20–21. I have made no comprehensive effort to verify the listings of Crabb and DeGruson. Two of the publishers listing editions at the time of my compilation (mid-1986) published two editions each, one of the extra editions a large-print version. Also in print were Sheldon's *Bible Stories* (Putnam Publishing Group) and *Jesus Is Here!* (Capper's Books).
2. Crabb lists "Dodson Donohue, 1900," but DeGruson, confirming Crabb's entries independently, apparently could not find any evidence other than Crabb's list for "Dodson."
3. Technically Crabb doesn't list this edition, but her list appears as one of several supporting articles in the same volume.

Bibliography

I. Works by Sheldon:
Books, Pamphlets, Selected Articles*

The Adventure of Peace." *CH* 65 (Dec. 1942), 18, 55.
"All One Body We." *CH* 53 (May 3, 1930), 10.
"All Over Forty." *CC* 50 (Aug. 30, 1933), 1081–85.
All the World. New York: George H. Doran, 1918.
"And I Said to Him." *CH* 47 (Feb. 9, 1924), 123.
"Are We Nearer the Master's Footsteps?" *Congregationalist* 111 (Jan. 7, 1926), 6–7.
"As to the Preliminaries." *Independent* 58 (June 22, 1905), 1417–18.
"Attack on American Traditions." *CH* 62 (July 1939), 37, 48.
"Big Business." *CH* 69 (May 1946), 20.
"The Biggest British Blunder." *Independent* 93 (Mar. 2, 1918), 343, 384–87.
"Blessed Are the Peacemakers." *CH* 65 (Apr. 1942), 38–39.
Born to Serve. Chicago: Advance Publishing Co., 1900.
A Builder of Ships. New York: George H. Doran, 1912.
"Can Religion Be Taught?" *Atlantic Monthly* 136 (Oct. 1925), 467–72.
"Carrie Nation's Hatchet . . . Becomes a Crusade." *CH* 53 (Jan. 11, 1930), 8.
Charles M. Sheldon: His Life Story. New York: George H. Doran, 1925.
A Charles M. Sheldon Year Book. Topeka: Crane and Co., 1909.
"Cheerful Funerals." *CH* 42 (Mar. 22, 1919), 332.
"The Choice of a Profession." *Youth's Companion* 68 (Sept. 6, 1894), III.
"A Christian Daily." *TDC*, Apr. 23, 1895, 4.
"Christmas Sermon." *CH* 60 (Dec. 1937), 39, 63.
"The Church and Social Service." *Independent* 60 (Mar. 29, 1906), 737–39. With W.D.P. Bliss.
"The Common Task." *CH* 44 (May 28, 1921), 387.

*Certain clippings in the Sheldon Room at Central Church and at the Kansas State Historical Society are not clearly attributed. Although some of these items were used in the text and cited in the endnotes, they are not cited in the bibliography.

"Compulsory Pagan Education." *Kansas Woman's Journal* 3 (June 1924), 1, 5.

"Confessions of a Vegetarian." *Independent* 60 (June 21, 1906), 1457–58.

"The Cost of Dying." *Independent* 68 (Feb. 10, 1910), 306–7.

"The Craigstone Meteorite," part 1. *Youth's Companion* 65 (June 16, 1892), 305–6.

"The Craigstone Meteorite," part 2. *Youth's Companion* 65 (June 23, 1892), 317–18.

The Crucifixion of Phillip Strong. Chicago: A.C. McClurg and Co., 1894.

"The Daily Papers and the Truth." *Outlook* 65 (May 12, 1900), 117–18.

The Day That Changed the World. London: Hodder and Stoughton, n.d. This title is listed in the National Union Catalogue as being the work of our Charles M. Sheldon. My examination of the book, however, leads me to believe that the author was probably a different C.M. Sheldon.

"The Demand for Thrills." *CH* 45 (Jan. 14, 1922), 22.

"The Devil's Elbow." *Christian Endeavor World* (Nov. 20, 1902), 147.

"The Divine Dignity of Labor." *CH* 51 (Feb. 18, 1928), 178, 186. Reprinted in pamphlet form, Baltimore: Norman T.A. Munder and Co., 1928.

"Dr. Charles M. Sheldon Saw Custer's Cavalry on Last Ride to Indian War." *TDC*, June 25, 1922.

"Dr. Sheldon Has Found What's Matter with State." *TSJ*, Nov. 11, 1939.

Dr. Sheldon's Scrap Book. New York: Christian Herald Association, 1942.

"Down with the Deadly Preliminaries." *Rotarian* 61 (Sept. 1942), 33–35.

"The Editor's Mail." *CH* 46 (Apr. 14, 1923), 296.

Edward Blake: College Student. Chicago: Advance Publishing Co., 1900.

"An Eighteen-Hour Day." *CH* 51 (Apr. 21, 1928), 431–32.

"The Ethics of Some Publishers." *CC* 50 (Sept. 27, 1933), 1206–8.

The Everyday Bible. New York: Thomas Y. Crowell, 1924.

"The Experiment of a Christian Daily." *Atlantic Monthly* 134 (Nov. 1924), 624–33.

"Extra, Extra: A New Way to Promote Peace!" *CH* 55 (Feb. 1932), 10–11, 53.

"Fewer Churches, More Religion." *CH* 53 (Mar. 1, 1930), 4–5, 25.

The First Christian Daily Paper and Other Sketches. New York: Street and Smith, [1900].

First Sermon Preached in the Chapel of the Central Congregational Church, Topeka, Kansas, June 23, 1889. No imprint. Pamphlet.

"For a Better World." In *Speeches of the Flying Squadron*, edited by J. Frank Hanly and Oliver Wayne Stewart. Indianapolis: Hanly and Stewart, n.d. [ca. 1915], 271–80.

For Christ and the Church. New York: Fleming H. Revell, 1899.

For Love of Country. Topeka: n.p., 1915. Pamphlet.

"The Forward Sweep of the Peace Poster Idea." *CH* 56 (Jan., 1933), 7.

"Four People I Knew." *CH* 59 (Oct. 1936), 30–32, 82.

"From Grave to Gay: Funerals and Weddings." *CH* 51 (Jan. 21, 1928), 59–60, 78.

"God's Fingerprints." *CH* 64 (Aug. 1941), 25, 54.

God's Promises. New York: Rae D. Henkle Co., 1927.

The Golden Book of Bible Stories. New York: Grosset and Dunlap, 1941.

"Great Britain and the Liquor Business." *Independent* 65 (Sept. 17, 1908), 643–48.

"The Great Catastrophe of 1913." *Independent* 74 (Jan. 30, 1913), 233–36. Reprinted as pamphlet, together with "The Missionary Policeman," no imprint, ca. 1913.

"The Great Revival at Westville." *CC* 54 (Aug. 25, 1937), 1045–48.

"The Greatest World Problem?" *CH* 64 (Apr. 1941), 37, 59.

"Guests of Honor." *Youth's Companion* 85 (Dec. 14, 1911), 677.

The Happiest Day of My Life. Cincinnati: The Church and Community Press, n. d. Booklet.

He Is Here. New York: Harper and Brothers, 1931.

He Is Here: An Episode from the Story of the Same Name. Dramatic rendering by Mary Bennett Harrison. Boston: Walter H. Baker, 1937. Booklet.

The Heart of the World: A Story of Christian Socialism. New York: Fleming H. Revell, 1905.

Heart Stories. New York: The Christian Herald, 1920.

"Here, Boy! Give Me a Paper!" *CC* 41 (Apr. 24, 1924), 534–35.

The High Calling. New York: Hodder and Stoughton, George H. Doran Co., 1911.

"The High Cost of Dying." *CH* 43 (May 15, 1920), 603.

"A Hilarious Giver." *CH* 53 (Feb. 15, 1930), 9.

"Hindrances and Helps in the Ministry." *Independent* 52 (Nov. 1, 1900), 2616–17.

His Brother's Keeper. Boston: Congregational Sunday-School and Publishing Society, 1896.

His Mother's Prayers. Chicago: Advance Publishing Co., 1903.

The History of "In His Steps." Topeka: privately printed, 1938.

"The Hopi Snake Dance." *Independent* 57 (Nov. 3, 1904), 1026–31.

"Horizons Seen and Unseen." *CH* 61 (Oct. 1938), 40–41, 71–72.

"How to Keep Sunday?" *CH* 46 (June 16, 1923), 476.

"How to Know What Jesus Would Do." *Christian Endeavor World* 14 (July 5, 1900), 789.

How to Succeed. Chicago: Advance Publishing Co., 1902. Pamphlet.
Howard Chase, Red Hill, Kansas. New York: George H. Doran, 1918.
"Human or Superhuman?" *Atlantic Monthly* 119 (Jan. 1917), 80–85.
"I Wish I Might Go Again." *CH* 59 (Sept., 1936), 38–39, 66, 71.
An Ideal Town. Waterbury, Vt.: n.p., 1888. Pamphlet.
"If Any Man Can Show Just Cause." *CH* 53 (June 7, 1930), 8.
"If Carrie Nation Returned to Kansas." *CH* 53 (Jan. 18, 1930), 8.
"If Christ Came to New York." *Liberty* 14 (June 12, 1937), ll–13.
"If I Could Take My College Course Over Again." *CH* 55 (Oct. 1932), 11.
"If I Were a Teacher." *Household* 36 (Apr. 1936), 36.
"If I Were Back Again." *CH* 63 (May 1940), 19, 68.
"If I Were President." *CH* 59 (May 1936), 10–11, 37.
"If Jesus Came Back Today." *CC* 51 (June 27, 1934), 863–64.
"If Jesus Were Here Today." *CH* 68 (Dec. 1945), 18, 61.
"Immortality." *CH* 63 (July 1940), 19.
In His Steps. Chicago: Advance Publishing Co., 1897.
In His Steps To-Day. New York: Fleming H. Revell, 1921.
In His Steps Today. Elgin, Ill.: David C. Cook, 1928.
"Is a Christian Theater Possible?" *Independent* 53 (Mar. 14, 1901),
    616–18.
"Is Christianity Practical in Worldly Affairs?" *Ladies' Home Journal* 16
    (Nov. 1899), 10.
"Is Life Worth Living?" *CC* 45 (July 5, 1928), 852–53.
"Is Our Civilization Christian?" *Seminary Notes* [Univ. of Kansas] 2 (Oct.
    1892), 56.
"Isaiah's League of Nations." *CH* 42 (May 3, 1919), 511.
"'Jazz' Morals." *CH* 43 (Feb. 28, 1920), 252.
Jesus Is Here! New York: Hodder and Stoughton, George H. Doran Co.,
    1914.
John King's Question Class. Chicago: Advance Publishing Co., 1899.
"Kansans are Puritans—White Spendthrifts on Luxury—Sheldon." *TDC*,
    Apr. 23, 1922.
"The Labor Situation in Colorado." *Independent* 57 (Aug. 18, 1904),
    361–62.
Lend a Hand. Chicago: Fleming H. Revell, 1899.
"Let Us Open the Meeting." *CH* 50 (Sept. 17, 1927), 795–96, 812.
Let's Talk It Over. Elgin, Ill.: David C. Cook, 1929.
"Life Is My Teacher." In four parts. *Household Magazine* 36 (Nov. and Dec.
    1936) and 37 (Jan. and Feb. 1937), 5, 42–43; 5, 37–39; 7, 29,
    34–35; and 17, 60–63, respectively.
The Life of Jesus. New York: Thomas Y. Crowell, 1926.
Life's Treasure Book. Elgin, Ill.: David C. Cook, 1929.
A Little Book for Every Day. Boston: Pilgrim Press, 1914.

"The Little Sins of Good People." *TDC*, June 1, 1908, 4.

"A Local Negro Problem." *Kingdom* 8 (Apr. 10, 1896), 828.

"Making Your Words Count." *Rotarian* 55 (Nov. 1939), 20–22.

Malcolm Kirk. Chicago: The Church Press, 1898.

"The Man Who Would Be Mayor." *CH* 65 (Oct. 1942), 46–48.

The Mere Man and His Problems. New York: Fleming H. Revell, 1924.

"Military Pomp." *CH* 55 (May 1932), 26.

"The Minister and His Young People." *Independent* 57 (Dec. 29, 1904), 1501–4.

"Ministers Strike." *CH* 64 (June 1941), 22–23, 46.

"The Ministers' Strike at Westport, Kansas." *TSJ*, May 28, 1938; June 4, 1938; June 11, 1938.

The Miracle at Markham: How Twelve Churches Became One. Chicago: The Church Press, 1899.

"The Missionary Policeman." *Independent* 76 (Nov. 6, 1913), 259–60. Reprinted as pamphlet, together with "The Great Catastrophe of 1913," no imprint, ca. 1913.

"The Modern Newspaper." *Independent* 73 (July 25, 1912), 196–201.

Modern Pagans. New York: Methodist Book Concern, 1917. A reissue of *The Revival, or The Spirit's Power*.

"The Morning Shudder." *CC* 51 (Jan. 31, 1934), 149–50.

"Murder Will Out." *CH* 53 (Mar. 8, 1930), 10.

"My Damascus Road." *CH* 69 (Apr. 1946), 20, 74.

"My First Sermon." *CH* 51 (Jan. 7, 1928), 26.

"My Most Unusual Layman." *CH* 64 (Dec. 1941), 42.

The Narrow Gate. Chicago: Advance Publishing Co., 1903.

New Opportunities in Old Professions. Chicago: John A. Ulrich, 1899. Pamphlet.

"The New Police." *Colliers* 51 (July 5, 1913), 22–23.

"A New Way to Advertise Peace." *CH* 56 (Nov. 1933), 7, 29.

"News from Mars." *TDC*, Dec. 25, 1920.

"A Note from Mr. Sheldon." *Christian Endeavor World* 14 (Apr. 5, 1900), 559.

Of One Blood. Boston: Small, Maynard and Co., 1916.

"On a Diet." *CH* 51 (Aug. 18, 1928), 859.

One Hundred and One Poems of the Day. Andover, Mass.: n.p., 1886.

"$100,000 for Peace." *CH* 46 (July 28, 1923), 588.

One of the Two. Chicago: Fleming H. Revell, 1898.

"Opportunities Before the Church of To-Day." In *New Wine Skins*, edited by Alfred Williams Anthony. Boston: Morning Star Publishing House, 1901.

"The Origin of the First Christian Daily Newspaper." *Advance* (June 27, 1895), 1396–97.

"Our Pagan Funerals." *CH* 69 (Feb. 1946), 58.

Paul Douglas—Journalist. Chicago: Advance Publishing Co., 1909.

Peace Be to This House: A Dramatic Adaptation from the Story "He Is Here." Dramatic rendering by Mary Bennett Harrison. Boston: Walter H. Baker, 1937. Booklet.

"Personal Politics." *CH* 53 (Aug. 2, 1930), 10.

"Personalities of Topeka." *TSJ*, Oct. 30, 1935.

"A Plea for a Christian Daily Newspaper." In two parts. *Kingdom* (June 28 and July 5, 1895), 164–65 and 181–82.

A Plea for the Unity of Christendom. Topeka: n.p., 1893. Pamphlet.

"Poverty Doesn't Frighten Me." *Rotarian* 49 (Nov. 1936), 15–17.

"Practical Eugenics." *Independent* 73 (Aug. 8, 1912), 319–21.

"Practical Sociological Studies." *Andover Review* 14 (Oct., 1890), 369–77.

"Prayer." *CH* 62 (Nov. 1939), 37, 63.

"Prayer Meeting at Eleven A.M." *CC* 47 (Feb. 19, 1930), 241–42.

"A Preacher Edits the News." *CH* 69 (Mar. 1946), 21, 64.

"A Preacher: Old Style." *CH* 53 (Apr. 19, 1930), 10.

"The Problem of the Country Church." *Andover Review* 10 (Oct. 1888), 382–87.

The Program of the Kingdom of God. No imprint, ca. 1905. Pamphlet.

Prohibition in Kansas. Manchester, Eng.: n.p., 1907. Pamphlet.

"A Protestant Confessional." *Atlantic Monthly* 129 (Jan. 1922), 14–22.

"Protestant Confessional." *CH* 63 (Sept. 1940), 26, 48.

"Public Funerals." *CH* 56 (Feb. 1933), 24.

"The Real Issue." *CH* 46 (Nov. 10, 1923), 894.

"The Real Sacrilege." *Christian Endeavor World* 14 (Apr. 12, 1900), 576.

The Redemption of Freetown. Boston and Chicago: United Society of Christian Endeavor, 1898.

"Reforming the Theater." *Independent* 68 (Apr. 7, 1910), 756–58.

"The Religious Hunger of Youth." *Good Housekeeping* 82 (Feb. 1926), 24–25, 186–90, 193–94.

"Reporting Crime." *CH* 51 (Feb. 18, 1928), 176.

The Revival, or The Spirit's Power. Cleveland: F.M. Barton, 1906.

Richard Bruce, or The Life That Now Is. Boston and Chicago: Congregational Sunday-school and Publishing Society, 1892.

The Richest Man in Kansas. New York: Christian Herald, 1921.

Robert Hardy's Seven Days. Boston and Chicago: Congregational Sunday-school and Publishing Society, 1893.

"A Sermon for War Time." *CH* 40 (May 9, 1917), 536.

"Servant and Mistress." *Independent* 52 (Dec. 20, 1900), 3018–21.

"The Servant in the House." *CH* 53 (May 24, 1930), 10.

"700 B.C., 1928 A.D." *CH* 51 (Jan. 7, 1928), 8.

"Sheldon as a Crusader." *Progress* 46 (Mar. 1946), 5.

"Short Talks about Vocations." *Kansas Authors Club Yearbook*. Topeka: n.p., 1944, 30–31.

"Short Talks on the Kindergarten." Series of five articles. TDC, Jan. 24–28, 1893.

"Short Talks with a Workingman." Series of four articles. *Kingdom* 8 (Apr. 26–May 17, 1895).

"Six of Him." *The Club Member* 1 (May 1905), 6–8.

"A Sixteen-Hour Day." *Independent* 66 (Apr. 1, 1909), 690–92.

"Sixteen Hours in the Life of Dr. Charles M. Sheldon." *CH* 60 (Feb. 1937), 16.

"Sociology from the Preacher's Standpoint." *Seminary Notes* [Univ. of Kansas] 1 (Dec., 1891), 78–82.

"Some Experiments Worth Trying in the Ministry." *Andover Review* 16 (Sept. 1891), 265–72.

Some Facts Regarding City Government, Together with a Catechism on Good Citizenship. Topeka: Crane and Co., 1902. Pamphlet.

"Some Servants in the House." *CH* 51 (July 28, 1928), 779–80, 794.

"Some Slaves of Civilization." *Independent* 53 (Aug. 29, 1901), 2029–32.

The Statesmanship of Christ. Topeka: n.p., 1890. Series of eight pamphlets; only three are known to survive.

"The Story of 'In His Steps.'" *CH* 68 (Nov. 1945), 89–94.

"The Student and Humanity." *University Review* 13 (Sept. 1891), 1–7.

"The Student Waiters." *Youth's Companion* 64 (July 9, 1891), 385–86.

"Summer Workers." *Youth's Companion* 69 (June 27, 1895), 11.

Thine Shall Be the Glory: A Dramatic Adaptation from the Story "He Is Here." Dramatic rendering by Mary Bennett Harrison. Boston: Walter H. Baker, 1937. Booklet.

"Think It Over." *CH* 46 (July 21, 1923), 574.

The Thirteenth Resolution. Elgin, Ill.: David C. Cook, 1928.

"Tho and Nevertheless—A Thanksgiving Sermon." *TDC*, Nov. 25, 1920, 4.

"Too Busy for Friends." *CH* 53 (June 21, 1930), 10.

"Try the New Thing!" *CH* 68 (Oct. 1945), 32, 60.

"Turn It Around!" *CC* 46 (Aug. 7, 1929), 987–88.

The Twentieth Door. Boston and Chicago: Congregational Sunday-school and Publishing Society, 1893.

Two Films. No imprint; ca. 1915. Pamphlet.

Two Old Friends. Cincinnati: Christian Home Magazine, 1925. Pamphlet.

"Untheological Christianity." *CC* 43 (July 1, 1926), 836–38.

"The Use and Abuse of Fiction." *Independent* 54 (Apr. 24, 1902), 965–70.

"A Vignette from the Great Iron-Miners' Strike." *Outlook* 52 (Sept. 21, 1895), 461–62.

What Did Jesus Really Teach? Topeka: Capper Publications, 1930.

"What I Would Do If I Were a Farmer." *Report of the Kansas State Board of Agriculture.* Vol. 24. Topeka: State Board of Agriculture, 1905, 210–15.

"What Is a Sermon?" *Outlook* 49 (Feb. 24, 1894), 362–63.

"What Is the Matter with Kansas?" *Magic Mirror* 1 (Nov. 1939), 5–7.

"What Prohibition Has Done for Kansas." *Independent* 60 (May 3, 1906), 1033–35.

"What Prohibition Has Done for Kansas." *Independent* 75 (July 3, 1913), 25–26.

"What Will You Do with Him?" *Kingdom* 9 (Feb. 5, 1897), 687.

"What Would Happen?" *CC* 41 (May 22, 1924), 662.

"What Would Jesus Do?" *CH* 60 (Sept. 1937), 33, 60.

"What Would Jesus Do?" *CH* 69 (Jan. 1946), 24.

"What Would Jesus Do?" *Independent* 97 (Mar. 1, 1919), 294.

"What Would Jesus Do about Anti-Semitism?" *Liberty* 16 (Apr. 29, 1939), 55–56.

"What Would Jesus Teach about Social Hygiene?" *Liberty* 14 (May 8, 1937), 8–9.

"When Carrie Nation Came to Kansas." *CH* 53 (Jan. 4, 1930), 4, 16, 18.

Who Killed Joe's Baby? Chicago: Advance Publishing Co., 1901.

"Why National Prohibition?" In *Speeches of the Flying Squadron,* edited by J. Frank Hanly and Oliver Wayne Stewart. Indianapolis: Hanly and Stewart, n.d. [ca. 1915], 267–70.

"Why Not?" *CC* 49 (July 20, 1932), 908–9.

"Work with Humanity at First Hand." *Commons* 53 (Dec. 1900), 6–7.

The Young People's Book of Bible Stories. New York: Grosset and Dunlap, 1963. Reprinted as *Bible Stories.* New York: Putnam Publishing Group, 1978.

Many of Sheldon's sermons at Waterbury, Vermont, were published as untitled pamphlets. Three are known to survive, from January 8, March 11, and July 22, 1888. Gene DeGruson, in *Kansas Authors of Best Sellers* (Pittsburg: Kansas State College of Pittsburg, 1970), lists several additional pamphlets that I have not been able to verify. Many of Sheldon's articles were republished as pamphlets, and some of them have probably escaped the notice of all of his bibliographers.

Other important Sheldon material exists in manuscript and in published ephemeral materials. Most material of that type is located in Topeka at Central Church and the Kansas State Historical Society, and in Lawrence at Spencer Research Library at the University of Kansas.

II. Secondary Works*

Abell, Aaron I. *The Urban Impact on American Protestantism, 1865–1900.*
  Cambridge: Harvard Univ. Press, 1943. Rpt., Hamden, Conn.:
  Archon, 1962.

"Author of 'In His Steps.'" *TDC*, Apr. 22, 1899.

Barton, Bruce. "Nobody Is Interested in Religion." *American Magazine* 60
  (Sept. 1930), 69, 158.

Barton, Fred. "The Parson's Sensational Book." *CH* 82 (Mar., 1959),
  33–34, 40–41, 50–52.

Barton, William E. "What Would Jesus Do?" *Christian Endeavor World* 14
  (May 17, 1900), 674–75.

Blackmar, Frank W. "Charles M. Sheldon: a Man with a Mission." *Harper's
  Weekly* 43 (Aug. 5, 1899), 769, 772.

Bliss, William D.P., ed. *The New Encyclopedia of Social Reform.* New York:
  Funk and Wagnalls, 1908.

Bos, William, and Clyde Faries, "The Social Gospel: Preaching Reform,
  1875–1915." In *Preaching in American History*, edited by DeWitte
  Holland. Nashville: Abingdon, 1969.

Boyer, Paul S. "*In His Steps*: A Reappraisal." *American Quarterly* 23 (Spring
  1971), 60–78.

Chamberlin, James A. "If Jesus Were an Editor." *Kingdom* 9 (Apr. 2, 1897),
  820–21.

Chase, Frank M. "Charles M. Sheldon, Author, Preacher, Editor." *Dearborn Independent* 22 (Feb. 4, 1922), 13.

Chase, Harold T. "Mr. Sheldon in the Editor's Chair." *Christian Endeavor
  World* 14 (Apr. 5, 1900), 567.

Chevrin, Henri Georges. "Socialisme Chrétian ou Christianisme Social,
  Étude Comparative Entre Herron et Sheldon." Thesis, Univ. of Paris,
  1901.

"A Christian Daily." *TDC*, Apr. 23, 1985, 4.

Clark, Glenn. *The Man Who Walked In His Steps.* St. Paul, Minn.: Macalester Park Publishing Co., 1946.

Cordova, Hector Leroy. "The Formation of the Social Gospel of Charles
  Monroe Sheldon, 1886–1919." M.A. thesis, San Jose State College,
  1967.

Countermine, J.D. "How Sheldon's City Endeavors." *Christian Endeavor
  World* 14 (Aug. 23, 1900), 911.

*Only a few of the most important of the newspaper articles cited in the text are
listed here.

Cox, Thomas C. *Blacks in Topeka, Kansas, 1865–1915.* Baton Rouge: Louisiana State Univ. Press, 1982.

Crabb, Emma. "Publishers of *In His Steps*: United States and Great Britain." *Shawnee County Historical Society Bulletin* 44 (Winter 1967), 28.

Cutts, Richard. *Index to The Youth's Companion: 1871–1929.* Metuchen, N.J.: The Scarecrow Press, 1972.

Davis, George T.B. "Charles M. Sheldon, Novelist." *Our Day* 18 (Mar. 1899), 74–77.

DeGruson, Gene. *Kansas Authors of Best Sellers.* Pittsburg: Kansas State College of Pittsburg, 1970.

"Dr. Sheldon Is Our Editor-in-Chief." *CH* 43 (Jan. 3, 1920), 1–2.

"Dr. Sheldon's Confessional." *Literary Digest* 47 (Nov. 15, 1913), 950.

"Dr. Sheldon's Work." *TDC,* Oct. 14, 1899.

Doran, George H. *Chronicles of Barabbas.* New York: Harcourt, Brace, 1935.

Dunne, Finley Peter. "Mr. Dooley XXIII—On Mr. Sheldon's Newspaper." *Harper's Weekly* 44 (Apr. 28, 1900), 400.

Durand, George Harrison. *Joseph Ward of Dakota.* Boston: Pilgrim, 1913.

Eastman, Philip. "In His Steps." *Nickell Magazine* (Nov. 1899), 270–75.

Ek, Richard A. "The Irony of Sheldon's Newspaper." *Journalism Quarterly* 51 (Spring 1974), 22–27.

Elzey, Wayne. "'What Would Jesus Do?': *In His Steps* and the Moral Codes of the Middle Class." *Soundings* 58 (Winter 1975), 463–89.

Everett, Betty Steele. "St. Charles of Topeka." *Sunshine Magazine* 45 (Apr. 1968), 7.

"Fashion in Fiction." *Blackwood's Edinburgh Magazine* 166 (Oct. 1899), 531–42.

Fiftieth Anniversary of Central Congregational Church 1888–1938. Pamphlet.

Fletcher, Joseph. *Situation Ethics.* Philadelphia: Westminster Press, 1966.

"For a Protestant Confessional." *Literary Digest* 47 (Aug. 16, 1913), 251–52.

Fritts, John Pond. "The Author of 'In His Steps.'" *Critic* 34 (June 1899), 540–42. Rpt., *Current Literature* 27 (Jan. 1900), 18–19.

Giles, Frye W. *Thirty Years in Topeka: A Historical Sketch.* Topeka: Capper Special Services, 1886; rpt., 1960.

Gladden, Washington. *The Christian League of Connecticut.* New York: The Century Co., 1883.

———. "Mr. Sheldon's Newspaper." *Independent* 52 (Apr. 5, 1900), 807–9.

Gohdes, Clarence. "In His Steps." *Georgia Review* 8 (Fall 1954), 354–56.

Goldman, Eric F. "Books that Changed America." *Saturday Review* 36 (July 4, 1953), 9, 38.

Greene, Peggy. "Dr. Sheldon and Tennesseetown." *Shawnee County Histori-cal Society Bulletin* 58 (Nov. 1981), 117–20.

Halbert, Leroy. *Across the Way: A History of the Work of Central Church, Topeka, Kansas, in Tennesseetown.* Topeka: Privately printed, 1900. Booklet.

Handy, Robert T. *The Social Gospel in America, 1870–1920.* New York: Ox-ford Univ. Press, 1966.

Hayes, Rutherford B. "When Topeka Was the Focal Point of All Christen-dom." *TDC*, Mar. 10, 1940.

Henrichs, Henry F., ed. *St. Charles of Topeka.* Litchfield, Ill.: Sunshine Press, 1948.

"Heredity of Charles M. Sheldon." *Eugenical News* 11 (Apr. 1926), 49.

Herron, George D. *The Christian Society.* Chicago: Fleming H. Revell, 1894.

———. *The New Redemption.* New York: Thomas Y. Crowell, 1893.

Hickman, Russell K. "First Congregational Church of Topeka, 1854–1869." *Shawnee County Historical Society Bulletin* 3 (Mar., 1949), 3–4.

Hodge, L.C. "Problem of Self-Help." *Civic Pride* 1 (May 1904), 74–75.

Hopkins, Charles Howard. *The Rise of the Social Gospel in American Protes-tantism 1865–1915.* New Haven: Yale Univ. Press, 1940.

Hougen, Harvey R. "Kate Barnard and the Kansas Penitentiary Scandal, 1908–1909." *Journal of the West* 17 (Jan. 1978), 9–18.

Howard, Clinton N. "In Memoriam: Dr. Charles M. Sheldon, Kansas." *Progress* 46 (Mar. 1946), 3.

Howe, Ed. Series of "Lay Sermons." Six-part series. *TSJ*, Mar. 13–17, 1900.

Hutchins, John K. "People Who Read and Write." *New York Times Book Review*, Mar. 10, 1946, 27.

"The Interest Is Increasing." *Christian Endeavor World* 14 (Feb. 22, 1900), 450.

Jensen, Billie Barnes. "A Social Gospel Experiment in Newspaper Reform: Charles M. Sheldon and the *Topeka Daily Capital.*" *Church History* 33 (Mar. 1964), 74–82.

Johnson, David G. "A Study of the Ideas of Charles M. Sheldon.' M.A. thesis, Univ. of Kansas, 1965.

The Kansas Congregational Conference, Fifty-Ninth Annual Session, 1913. KSHS.

Kittell, A.G. "Early Day Incidents in 'Sheldon's Church.'" *TDC*, Nov. 27, 1938.

Kunitz, Stanley J., and Howard Haycraft, eds. *Twentieth Century Authors.* New York: H.W. Wilson Co., 1942.

Lee, James Melvin. *History of American Journalism*. Boston and New York: Houghton Mifflin, 1923.

Lewis, Theodore Graham, ed. *History of Waterbury, Vermont, 1763–1915*. Waterbury, Vt.: Harry C. Whitehill, 1915.

Lo Bello, Nino. "When Christ Was City Editor." *Kiwanis Magazine* 39 (Dec. 1954), 19–21.

Long, Edna Margaret. "It Is Good to Remember a Great Man." *Advance*, June 28, 1957, 19.

McDonald, Gerald D. "*In His Steps*—All-Time Best Seller on Nobody's Best Seller List." *Shawnee County Historical Society Bulletin* 44 (Winter 1967), 1–6.

Marty, Martin E. "Martin Luther's Reckless Grasp of Grace." *CC* 100 (Oct. 26, 1983), 963–64.

Martyn, Charles. *The William Ward Genealogy*. New York: Artemus Ward, 1925.

Marvin, James C. "A Lively Septuagenarian." *Shawnee County Historical Society Bulletin* 44 (Winter, 1967), 2.

May, Henry F. *Protestant Churches and Industrial America*. New York: Harper, 1949. Rpt., New York: Octagon Books, 1963.

Miller, Timothy. "Charles M. Sheldon and the Uplift of Tennesseetown." *Kansas History* 9:3 (Autumn 1986), 125–37.

———. "Charles M. Sheldon's *In His Steps*: Kansas's Great Accidental Bestseller." *Religion: Journal of the Kansas School of Religion* 21 (Feb. 1984), 1–6.

"Mr. Sheldon's Sermon Stories." *Spectator* 82 (June 3, 1899), 789.

"Mr. Sheldon's Symposium." *TDC*, July 3, 1896.

Mott, Frank Luther. *Golden Multitudes: The Story of Best Sellers in the United States*. New York: Macmillan, 1947.

———. *A History of American Magazines*. Vol. 4. Cambridge: Harvard Univ. Press, 1957.

National Cyclopaedia of American Biography. New York: James T. White Co., 1927.

"Necrology." *Congregational Year-Book* (1913), 31–32.

Owen, Jennie Small. "Kansas Folks Worth Knowing: Dr. Charles M. Sheldon." *Kansas Teacher* 46 (Dec. 1937), 31–32.

Parrington, Vernon Louis. *American Dreams: A Study of American Utopias*. New York: Russell and Russell, 1964.

Pickering, Isaac O. "The Administration of John P. St. John." *Transactions of the Kansas State Historical Society* 9 (1905–6), 378–94.

"Rev. C. M. Sheldon." *TDC*, July 4, 1898.

Reynolds, David Spencer. "Shifting Interpretation of Protestantism." *Journal of Popular Culture* 9 (Winter 1975), 593–603.

Ripley, John W. "Another Look at the Rev. Mr. Charles M. Sheldon's Christian Daily Newspaper." *Kansas Historical Quarterly* 31 (Spring 1965), 1–40.

————. "'In His Steps' on Stage and Screen." *Shawnee County Historical Society Bulletin* 43 (Dec. 1966), 66–69.

————. "Last Rites for a Few Myths." *Shawnee County Historical Society Bulletin* 44 (Winter 1967), 14–26.

————. "The Strange Story of Charles M. Sheldon's *In His Steps.*" *Kansas Historical Quarterly* 34 (Autumn 1968), 1–25.

Robbins, L.H. "Militant Pacifist." *New York Times Magazine*, Dec. 3, 1939, 14, 26.

Rowe, Henry K. *History of Andover Theological Seminary.* Newton, Mass.: n.p., 1933.

Seventy-Five Years of Central Congregational Church, Topeka, Kansas, 1888–1963. Pamphlet.

Sheldon Congress of Mothers, 1906–7: Parents Meeting at Sheldon Kindergarten. Pamphlet.

Sheldon, Stewart. *Gleanings by the Way.* Topeka: Crane and Co., 1889.

"The Sheldon Uplift of the Old and Young." *TDC*, Sept. 9, 1906.

Smith, H. Shelton, Robert T. Handy, and Lefferts A. Loetscher, eds. *American Christianity.* Vol. 1. New York: Charles Scribner's Sons, 1963.

Smith, William T., Jr. "Sheldon Capital." *Seventy-Fifth Anniversary Souvenir, Topeka Typographical Union No. 121,* 1957.

Smylie, James H. "Sheldon's *In His Steps*: Conscience and Discipleship." *Theology Today* 32 (Apr. 1975), 33–45.

Socolofsky, Homer E. *Arthur Capper.* Lawrence: Univ. of Kansas Press, 1962.

Stead, W.T. *If Christ Came to Chicago.* Chicago: Laird and Lee, 1894.

Stidger, William L. "'In His Steps' Brought No Wealth." *Dearborn Independent* 26 (June 12, 1926), 2, 30.

Suderman, Elmer F. "Religion in the American Novel: 1870–1900." Ph.D. diss., Univ. of Kansas, 1961.

Swan, Robert A., Jr. *The Ethnic Heritage of Topeka, Kansas: Immigrant Beginnings.* N.p.: Institute of Comparative Ethnic Studies, 1974.

Swenson, Carl J., Jr. "Charles Monroe Sheldon: A Critical Analysis." M.A. thesis, Kansas State College of Pittsburg, 1966.

Taylor, Blanche M. "Twentieth Century Utopia—Topeka." *Shawnee County Historical Society Bulletin* 44 (Winter 1967), 6–9, 28.

Traylor, Jack Wayne. "William Allen White's 1924 Gubernatorial Campaign," *Kansas Historical Quarterly* 42 (Summer 1976), 180–91.

Ward, Mrs. Humphrey (Mary Augusta Ward). *Robert Elsmere.* New York and London: Macmillan, 1888.

Weeks, Edward A. "The Best Sellers Since 1875." *Publisher's Weekly* 125 (Apr. 21, 1934), 1503–7.

White, Ronald C., Jr., and C. Howard Hopkins. *The Social Gospel: Religion and Reform in Changing America.* Philadelphia: Temple Univ. Press, 1976.

Whittemore, Margaret. "Charles M. Sheldon: 'Funning and Punning.'" *Topeka,* Nov. 1976, 21–27, 37.

———. "Tough on Teeth." *Nature Magazine,* Mar., 1940, 152.

Willets, Gilson. "A Day with Sheldon." *TDC,* Mar. 9, 1900.

———. "Pastor Sheldon Is Now an Editor." *CH* 23 (Mar. 14, 1900), 212.

———. "Pastor Sheldon's Editorial Experiences." *CH* 23 (Mar. 21, 1900), 230–31.

———. "Pastor Sheldon's Week of Trial." *CH* 23 (Mar. 28, 1900), 255.

———. "A Sunday With Pastor Sheldon." *CH* 23 (Mar. 7, 1900), 187.

Williams, Peter W. *Popular Religion in America.* Englewood Cliffs, N.J.: Prentice-Hall, 1980.

Wolfe, Carmie S. "Charles M. Sheldon—World Citizen." *Shawnee County Historical Society Bulletin* 38 (Dec. 1962), 43–46.

Yrigoyen, Charles, Jr. "Charles M. Sheldon: Christian Social Novelist." *Bulletin of the Congregational Library* 33 (Winter 1982), 4–16.

Index

Following In His Steps was designed by Dariel Mayer,
composed by G&S Typesetters, Inc., printed by Thomson-Shore,
Inc., and bound by John H. Dekker & Sons. The book was set in
ITC Berkeley Old Style and printed on 60-lb. Glatfelter.